T0271243

THE KNOW NOTHINGS
IN LOUISIANA

THE
KNOW
NOTHINGS
IN LOUISIANA

Marius M. Carriere Jr.

University Press of Mississippi / Jackson

www.upress.state.ms.us

The University Press of Mississippi is a member of
the Association of American University Presses.

Copyright © 2018 by University Press of Mississippi
Manufactured in the United States of America

First printing 2018

∞

Library of Congress Cataloging-in-Publication Data

Names: Carriere, Marius M., Jr., 1942– author.
Title: The Know Nothings in Louisiana / Marius M. Carriere Jr.
Description: Jackson: University Press of Mississippi, [2018] | Includes
bibliographical references and index. |
Identifiers: LCCN 2017054856 (print) | LCCN 2018002939 (ebook) | ISBN
9781496816856 (epub single) | ISBN 9781496816863 (epub institutional) |
ISBN 9781496816870 (pdf single) | ISBN 9781496816887 (pdf institutional)
| ISBN 9781496816849 (cloth: alk. paper)
Subjects: LCSH: American Party—Louisiana. | Louisiana—Politics and
government—1803–1865.
Classification: LCC JK2341.A8 (ebook) | LCC JK2341.A8 L684 2018 (print) | DDC
324.2732—dc23
LC record available at https://lccn.loc.gov/2017054856

British Library Cataloging-in-Publication Data available

To Mimi, Noelle, Beaux, and Charlotte

CONTENTS

Contents

ACKNOWLEDGMENTS

At times I thought finishing this manuscript project would never occur, but there are so many friends, colleagues, and archivists who encouraged me to keep going. My interest in Louisiana politics was always there since I grew up hearing fascinating stories about Louisiana icons such as Huey and Earl Long, and deLesseps S. Morrison. Interest in nineteenth-century politics would come later as a student at the University of Louisiana-Lafayette and a graduate student at LSU.

My work on the Know Nothing Party grew out of an interest in how Louisiana, with its large Catholic population, could have had a rather successful anti-Catholic and anti-foreign political party during the 1850s. Many of my colleagues encouraged me to pursue this research interest and they all deserve many thanks for their helpful suggestions and careful reading of my work. In particular, Bill Cooper, professor emeritus at LSU, has continued to encourage me to see this project through to completion.

There are numerous individuals at many libraries and historical collections who helped in many different ways. Of course, the staff at the Louisiana and Lower Mississippi Valley Collections at Louisiana State University was instrumental in making my work less onerous. Staff members at the State Library of Louisiana, Tulane University, the New Orleans Public Library, the Historic New Orleans Collection, the Mississippi Department of Archives and History, and Christian Brothers University were all very helpful to me in my research. Charles Crawford's first reading was most helpful, too.

I also need to thank a number of friends and former fellow LSU graduate students for keeping me focused, suggesting better sentence structure, and telling me the project was worth all of the work. To Chip, George, and Larry, you were invaluable throughout all of the time I put into this work. To Frank, Terry, Tom, and Roger, you were great listeners and always ready with words of encouragement. And Charles's continuing warm interest in my work and well-being is greatly appreciated.

The support of the staff at the University Press of Mississippi was also invaluable.

Finally, to my family, Mimi, Noelle, and Beaux, I am thankful for you putting up with me during discouraging times and cheering me on at times of more optimism. In particular, most of the technical aspects of the work would not have been possible without the expertise of my artist and philosopher son, Beaux Michael Carriere.

While so many critiqued, suggested, and encouraged, the final product is mine and I accept responsibility for whatever value it has.

The Know Nothings
in Louisiana

INTRODUCTION

Anti-foreign hatred in Louisiana, particularly in New Orleans, grew so prevalent that violence and election fraud became commonplace in the 1830s and 1840s. Nativists directed their anti-foreign venom at immigrants, but several of them refused to passively accept the persistent attacks. As the number of Irish immigrants increased during the 1830s, the nativists' hostility and aggression multiplied. Publishing heated rhetoric, anti-immigrant newspapers sold widely. In 1839, the one Irish immigrant who opened his own newspaper to respond to the anti-foreign criticisms became bold enough to trade editorial attacks with the nativist press. Not unexpectedly, violence exploded when nativist William Christy and his two sons wielded axes to smash the Irishman's press. The Irishman shot the nativist and one of his sons, but the Irishman had to shut-down his press.

The 1840s and 1850s' continuing anti-foreignism and allegations of Election Day frauds intensified the mayhem, and instances of violence at the polls became common. For example, Louisiana's Democratic candidate for governor in 1849 allegedly called his Whig opponent "a damned Irishman" while the Democrats reminded Irish citizens that a Whig had murdered an Irishman at an event sponsored by the Whig Party. Meanwhile, aggravating the Whigs, Democrat John Slidell became infamous among nativists for his 1840s Election Day frauds where he flaunted votes of hundreds of Irish immigrants to ensure his party's victories. Perhaps the most bizarre event, however, occurred in New Orleans during the city's municipal elections in 1858. Nativists and so-called Independents armed themselves and held strategic barricaded positions in different sections of the city. Despite these tensions, the city narrowly averted a civil war.

Outside of Greater New Orleans, Louisianians worried that the growing number of immigrants coming into the state would change the culture and politics of the state. While most of the arriving immigrants remained in New Orleans, the rest of the state's Anglo inhabitants, nonetheless, realized they could not escape the increasing nativistic conflicts. These conflicts would, indeed, reach a crescendo in the 1850s with the demise of the Whig Party and the attempt of party leaders to address the changing political conditions with which they now faced.

During the 1850s, a startling major third party appeared on the American scene. Its members and its critics called the new party by various names but usually people referred to it as the American or the Know Nothing Party. The new party tried to address itself to the new political landscape of the 1850s but embraced old political issues, foremost among them nativism. At a time of political uncertainty, with the Whig Party seemingly on the verge of collapse, the Know Nothing or American Party seemed destined to become a permanent fixture.

The upstart party prospered in the North, and historians have largely focused attention there and produced several studies on that section. This book turns attention toward the South, especially to Louisiana. While there is a decent body of work on the Know Nothings in the North, there is much about the party in Louisiana that needs further elaboration. This study reveals perspectives about the party by focusing on Louisiana. For example, who joined the Know Nothings in Louisiana? Why did the party gain traction in that state? What was their program, and did the Louisiana program square with that of the party elsewhere? And probably most important, how would the party be able to survive the sectional turmoil of the times?

Naturally, historians disagree about the origin of the American Party in the South. Some contend that southerners welcomed the American Party, not so much because of antagonism to foreigners and Roman Catholics, but because of a hesitation to join the Democrats who agitated the sectional question.[1] Or, more specifically, many former Whigs saw the new party as a useful political vehicle to oppose the Democracy.[2] Thus, one scholarly approach postulates that the American Party in the South appeared to be an attractive alternative to either political stagnancy or an uncomfortable alliance with the Democrats. However, there were a few areas of the South that had a significant foreign population, a population in the minds of many contemporary observers that exacerbated the existing problems of pauperism, intemperance, and demagogy.[3] Maryland, Missouri, and Louisiana all had sizable foreign-born populations and all had a history of Native American activity. Louisiana, especially New

Orleans, not only had a large foreign-born population, but it had a sizable Catholic population, as well. Scholars have disagreed about the role that nativism played in Know Nothing success in the South and Louisiana. Because many foreigners found a home in Louisiana, a central issue is to answer the question of how the state could be a hotbed of nativism, as some contend.[4]

It is also worth examining what role anti-Catholicism played in the state. There is no question that anti-Catholicism was important to the American or Know Nothing Party in the North, but Louisiana stood in contrast to much of the South by providing a home to a large Roman Catholic population in the 1850s. Historian W. Darrell Overdyke recognizes a fanatical anti-Roman Catholic faction of Know Nothingism in Louisiana. But Overdyke downplays the anti-Catholicism and considers it was unimportant. He develops the idea that despite its nativist sentiment, Louisiana was an exception to the anti-Roman Catholicism of the American Party elsewhere.[5] But there are those who take exception with Overdyke's thesis that Louisiana Know Nothingism demonstrated a "tolerance" for Roman Catholics. According to Robert Reinders's study of the Know Nothings in the state, a significant anti-Catholic sentiment existed. But Reinders contends those Roman Catholics who belonged to the American Party were mainly anti-clerical, that is, they were concerned about the status of the clergy rather than being opposed outright to the church itself, something the Roman Catholic Church recognized quite clearly.[6] Therefore, while anti-Catholicism looms as an important issue to Know Nothings in the state and could have proved embarrassing to the nativists, the Know Nothing Party was a national party, and its impact went beyond the South and Louisiana. To better understand Louisiana Know Nothingism and how it functioned within the national picture, it is also necessary to understand more about the party across the country.

Previous scholarship explained the American Party's meteoric rise as a result of a socioeconomic upheaval in the 1850s. From this view, the demise of the Whig Party and the success of Know Nothingism can be partially attributed to what historian Michael Holt argues was "a general malaise and a sense of dislocation caused by rapid social and economic change."[7] Some scholars also contend that a disdain for politicians and partial rejection of traditional party politics best explains the rise of the American Party. One account, for example, argues that in three urban southern cities, the Know Nothings captured control of government in these cities by meeting the demands for reform. Due to this disdain, historian William Evitts contends that Know Nothings purportedly attracted "most of its local leaders from new men, men who were younger and poorer than most politicians."[8]

Subsequently, historians presented fresh research that altered views about 1850s politics and Know Nothingism. Those who identified the rise of the American Party with a sudden social and economic upheaval have adjusted that view to include political distresses, in addition to social pressures. These historians have also widened their scope of causation to include anti-party, temperance, antislavery, anti-southernism, Sabbatarianism, and nativism.[9] In particular, more emphasis can be placed on the role of antislavery sentiment in the rise of the Know Nothings. Clearly, antislavery and anti-southernism had no role for Louisiana Know Nothings, but the looming sectional conflict intensified, a result of the Kansas-Nebraska Act that Congress had passed in 1854, complicating politics nationally and in Louisiana. In response, some Louisianians joined the Know Nothings, it seemed, looking for an anti-Democracy movement or, as one scholar calls it, "an anti-party front."[10]

Historians who put antislavery sentiment in the mix for the Know Nothings' rise also place almost equal focus on other issues. By contrast, others stress that antislavery was primary in the Americans' success. "Slavery, not nativism destroyed the second American party system," writes historian Tyler Anbinder. In one of the most comprehensive studies of Know Nothingism, Anbinder sees Kansas-Nebraska as having caused the political crisis of the mid-1850s, giving the northern members of the American Party an antislavery reputation.[11] Naturally, this was problematic for Southern and Louisiana Know Nothings. Louisiana Know Nothings, as well as other members of the party throughout the South, would probably have agreed in what Anbinder also finds for the party by 1856. To him, the party became dominated by "conservative ex-Whigs who are more interested in preserving the Union and maintaining friendly relations between North and South than the threat posed by immigrants."[12]

These debates highlight how historians differ fundamentally over what constituted the Know Nothing movement in the nation, the South, and Louisiana. As far as Louisiana (and the South), no recent, significant study of this movement exists.[13] Louisiana was unique in 1850s politics. A state with a relatively large Catholic population and with few foreign-born residents, outside of Greater New Orleans, witnessed an anti-Catholic and anti-foreign-born party gaining a large political following; this appeared to be an incredible turn of events. Previous studies of Louisiana's Know Nothing movement do not address these issues or, for that matter, other questions about why Know Nothingism flourished in the state in the 1850s.

Identifying significant members of the Know Nothings in Louisiana, beyond basic census information, is difficult because of the scarcity of personal papers. There is limited human material to explain what motivated many Louisianians to join a political party that seemed so incongruous for southerners in general and, in particular, for Louisianians to have joined.[14] There were few foreign-born in the South and few in much of Louisiana. Interestingly, for heavily Catholic south Louisiana, the Know Nothings offered what appears to be a strange attraction. It jolted many traditional politicians to see that Louisiana nativists mounted a serious challenge to the Democrats and achieved so much success during a four-year run. Some former Whigs took comfort to know that a party existed to allow them to continue their political life in opposition to the Democrats. Drawing their leaders from diverse elements of Louisiana's society, did the leaders of the Know Nothings conform to traditional views of Louisiana politics in the 1850s? Most of the Louisiana Know Nothings were old Whigs who found comfort in continuing their opposition to the Democrats.

Other questions lingered about what parts of Louisiana Know Nothing leaders represented and what sorts of backgrounds they had. They came from various parts of the state, but their strength, for the most part, would be in south Louisiana, the north Louisiana cotton parishes, and in Greater New Orleans. Were they part of an older, large, slave-holding commercial class found in the traditional studies of 1850s politics? In what did these Know Nothings believe? Nativism was crucial to many former Whigs, as well as some Democrats, who brought the old 1830s and 1840s nativism to the Americans of the 1850s. Louisiana was something of a hotbed of nativism, and these Know Nothings did not seem to resemble the traditional view of older, slaveholding, business-oriented men that differentiated them from the Democrats of that decade.

There was a history of Native Americanism in Louisiana for over two decades, beginning even before the 1830s, but the twin elements of preserving the Union and maintaining a conservative outlook was also important to Know Nothings. A number of Louisianians labeled immigrants as opponents of slavery. The Know Nothings would use the foreign-born issue to skirt the nation's sectional controversy by branding the immigrants as a danger to the South because of their alleged antislavery agenda.

Perhaps looming above other controversies, many remained puzzled about why south Louisiana Catholics belonged to a party that many saw as anti-popish. One approach to analyzing that puzzle is that many Louisiana Catholics saw papal authority differently from Catholics elsewhere. Many

Louisiana Catholics not only saw papal authority differently, they also distinguished themselves from Catholics elsewhere. Many allied themselves with what they called Gallican Catholicism. Of course, for some Louisiana Catholics, the anti-Catholicism of the national party was a deal-breaker, but for many—possibly even most Louisiana Catholics—that was not enough to dampen their support of this American Party.

Finally, and most important, this study addresses how Know Nothings in Louisiana managed the intensifying sectional stress tearing the fabric of the Union during the 1850s. Clearly, the Americans in the state did not handle the sectional controversy effectively—which meant that Know Nothings, like many other United States politicians of the 1850s, found the sectional controversy impossible to resolve. Often, the Know Nothings appeared to be, as one American editor wrote, "directionless." In the end, the slavery question for the Louisiana Know Nothings was the same poison pill that led to the fall of the Whigs.

To address these analytical issues and questions, this book examines the interaction of politics, nativism, slavery, and the sectional tensions of the 1850s through the lens of the Know Nothing movement. Who and what the Know Nothings were, and in what they believed and why, can aid in a better understanding of why nativism was overshadowed and how Union and conservatism finally failed.

ONE

Early Political Nativism in Louisiana: 1832–49

Geography, ethnic differences, and immigration greatly influenced Louisiana's politics between 1830 and 1861. The geographical features determined what kind of agriculture was feasible and profitable. The native population, descendants of the French and Acadians, gave direction to early territorial politics and resented the large number of Americans who immigrated to Louisiana. Another wave of immigration added color and often violence to Louisiana politics as foreign immigrants came in increasing numbers after 1840, with most coming from Ireland and Germany.

Geographically, Louisiana can be divided into two general areas; the hill country and the level country. The hill country consists of piney woods parishes which make up the Florida parishes north of Lake Pontchartrain; the north Louisiana Uplands, consisting of Morehouse, Union, Claiborne, Bossier, Bienville, and Jackson parishes; and the west Louisiana Uplands, west of the Calcasieu and Red rivers. The level country consists of pine flats, prairies, alluvial lands, wooded swamps, and coastal marshes. In the southern half of the Florida parishes are the pine flats; the prairie country is located in the south central parishes of St. Landry, parts of St. Martin and Lafayette, St. Mary, Vermilion, and Calcasieu parishes. The alluvial lands are located in those parishes adjacent to the Mississippi River and the other major rivers of the state, such as the Red. The wooded swamps and coastal marshes are generally found in the extreme southern part of the state along the Gulf Coast.[1]

During the antebellum period, the state's wealthy planters lived in the alluvial parishes. The plantation economy dominated, with either cotton or sugar as the primary staple. In the parishes of northwest Louisiana and in the northern half of the Florida parishes, less successful farmers worked small farms. Remoteness from markets and inadequate soil prevented staple crop agriculture from succeeding in this area. Poor whites barely subsisted in the pine barrens of extreme southeast and southwest Louisiana along the Pearl and Sabine rivers, respectively.[2] Most of the inhabitants of the prairie country in southwest Louisiana were descendants of the Acadians or French who grew a little cotton, sugar cane, and rice, and also grazed cattle. Except for a few fishermen and trappers, descendants of the Acadians, the Gulf Coastal marshes were largely uninhabited.[3]

Despite the immigration of Americans into what is present-day Louisiana, before the United States acquired the state and during the territorial period, the Creole[4] population outnumbered the Americans, particularly in south Louisiana, where most of the French resided. A continuing influx of Americans gradually eroded this majority, but even as late as 1810 Creoles still outnumbered the Americans by at least two-to-one.[5] American immigrants found New Orleans, the northern parishes, and the Florida parishes more congenial, while the Creole population lived mainly in the lower river parishes or in New Orleans. In 1840, "the French were preponderant in fifteen parishes to the North and East."[6]

In addition to Americans immigrating to Louisiana, a significant influx of foreign immigrants added to the population. Although many remained in the South's largest commercial city, many others continued up the Mississippi River to St. Louis and the great Midwest. New Orleans' attraction for these immigrants is evident in the 1850 census. Their numbers grew until by 1850 the foreign-born accounted for 42 percent of the total population, or 51,227 persons out of 119,460.[7] This substantial and growing minority played an important part in Louisiana's political history with both major parties seeking its votes.

The ethnic differences of Louisiana, along with the results of immigration, led to religious controversy. The Americans brought their Protestant religion with them to north Louisiana. In fourteen south Louisiana parishes, only one Protestant church is listed in the census of 1860. American immigration eventually turned New Orleans into a strong Protestant city, but Protestant strength was in north Louisiana, where most Protestants were Baptists or Methodists. There were no Roman Catholic churches in fourteen north Louisiana parishes by 1850. In the southern part of the state, the "French" Catholics dominated that denomination, and New Orleans, the Catholic diocesan seat, remained an important Roman Catholic area.[8]

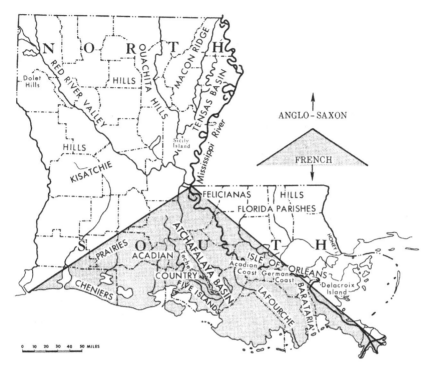

Map of Louisiana; Courtesy LSU Press

Prior to 1850, the French descendants outnumbered the Americans and this numerical strength permitted the Creoles to remain influential in state politics. Creoles and Americans resented each other, and with the admission of Louisiana to the Union, politics in the state became inextricably involved with a Creole-American rivalry. However, a tacit agreement to rotate the governorship between a Creole and an American prevented the rivalry from becoming extreme and too violent. The Americans violated the agreement in 1824 when the American candidate Henry Johnson succeeded American Thomas Robertson as governor. Provoked by the cupidity of the Americans, the Creoles succeeded in electing Pierre Derbigny as governor in 1828 and they then elected A. B. Roman in 1831.[9] The Creoles, or a candidate of their choosing, won succeeding gubernatorial elections until 1842.[10]

During this period, particularly in the 1820s and 1830s, Creole political leaders concerned themselves with state and local affairs more than with national politics. Jacksonian and anti-Jacksonian politics moved them little. Andrew Jackson's popularity helped him carry Louisiana in 1828 and

1832, but Creole lethargy in national campaigns played an important role. Despite the success of the Jacksonians in Louisiana in national elections, they did not win a state election until 1842.[11]

Following Jackson's victory in 1832, the Democrats and the Whigs adjusted to the ethnic rivalry in Louisiana. Both the gubernatorial election of 1835 and the presidential election of 1836 appear to belie this adjustment, for both campaigns were reminiscent of the past with the Creole or Whig faction succeeding in the state election and the American Democrats in the national race.[12] However, both parties by this time made appeals to the Creole population and to the increasing number of Irish immigrants in New Orleans. John Slidell, a new Democratic leader in Louisiana, wooed Creole politicians in order to strengthen his party. Then, too, the Democrats shrewdly ran a Creole for governor in the 1838 gubernatorial campaign. The Whig nominee and Creole, André B. Roman, won the election, but in 1842 another Creole and Democrat, Alexandre Mouton, defeated an American who had received the Whig nomination.[13]

The Democrats' initial victory for a state office came in this 1842 guber-natorial race and indicated growing support for that party. American immigration to north Louisiana, southwestern Louisiana, and the Florida parishes continued and most of the new residents voted Democratic. New Orleans became more Americanized and Democratic as well. Most of these Americans obviously brought their Jacksonian politics from their native states because they continually supported Jacksonian candidates. After arriving in Louisiana, they chafed under the restrictive and aristo-cratic Louisiana Constitution, which had been written in 1812. They called constantly, but futilely, for a constitutional convention. They wanted par-ticularly to change property requirements for holding office, and taxpaying requirements for voting.[14]

Proponents of constitutional revision finally passed a resolution in Louisiana's General Assembly calling for a convention to modify the 1812 document, and Governor Roman signed it in 1841. Originally planned to meet in Jackson, the convention found that site inadequate and recon-vened in New Orleans on August 24, 1844. The convention completed the new organic law on May 16, 1845, and the people of the state ratified it on November 5, 1845.[15]

The old constitution was a reflection of Louisiana in 1812. It required candidates for the lower house to own property valued at $500, those for the senate to own property worth $1,000, and a gubernatorial candidate to own property valued at $5,000. To vote, one had to be a male citizen of the United States, free, white, and twenty-one years old, but a voter also had to be a tax payer or purchaser of land from the United States. The 1812 Constitution required a periodic adjustment of the representation in the lower house according to the population of the electorate, but the senate had fixed election districts and that body possessed veto power over all legislation. Few elective offices existed, and the governor appointed, with senatorial advice and consent, most officials, including judges and sheriffs.[16]

The Constitution of 1845 mirrored the temper of the times and gave Louisiana a much more democratic form of government than its predecessor. The new document curtailed legislative power, abolished property requirements for seeking office and taxpaying requirements for voting, and increased the number of elective offices. Article 10, Title II of the new organic law increased the residency requirement for electors from one to two years. Wary of the increasing number of foreigners coming to New Orleans, both Democrats and Whigs supported this measure. However, the Democrats from north Louisiana fought this provision since it would temporarily disfranchise American farmers immigrating to Louisiana. Whether an immigrant was a foreigner or from another state, the Whigs favored this provision since both usually became Democrats.[17]

Representation in the General Assembly came about by a compromise between New Orleans and "black belt" delegates. Representation in the lower house of the General Assembly continued to be based on the total population of the adult white male electorate. The "black belt" planter class again received favored treatment in apportioning the senate, the basis of representation being total population including blacks. The constitution limited New Orleans to one-eighth of the membership in the senate. Even though New Orleans and the southern parishes lost seats in the General Assembly to north Louisiana parishes, the city held the balance of power in the lower house while the "black belt" retained a majority in the senate.[18]

Nativistic attacks on foreigners, particularly Roman Catholic foreigners from Ireland, were not absent from the South and Louisiana during the 1830s and 1840s. Part of this is explained by an irrational fear of papal power in the United States that continued to grow with the ever-increasing flood of foreign immigrants to the United States, particularly the influx of Catholic immigrants from Ireland. Few of these immigrants landed in the South, but the rhetoric of the nativists and anti-Roman Catholic propagandists found its way below Mason and Dixon's line. In fact, the Roman Catholic Bishop John England established the first Catholic journal in the United States at Charleston, South Carolina, in 1822. England founded this journal, the *United States Catholic Miscellany,* as a rebuttal to the anti-Roman Catholic propaganda. Bishop England also felt obligated to participate in a newspaper debate between Catholics and Protestants in the *Charleston Courier* in the late 1830s. Such debates, concerning whether or not Roman Catholicism was a threat to America, were quite commonplace during the decade.[19]

During the propaganda campaign against Roman Catholics, Protestants established newspapers in Bardstown, Kentucky, and Baltimore, Maryland. The Reverend Nathan L. Rice published the *Western Protestant* in Bardstown beginning in 1836, and the Reverend Robert Breckinridge and the Reverend Andrew Cross started the *Literary and Religious Magazine* in 1835 in Baltimore. Typical of the nativistic press of this time, these journals often maligned Roman Catholics, charging them with immorality. When libel suits did reach the courts, convictions were never obtained.[20]

Because of the South's peculiar institution of slavery, the anti-Roman Catholic propaganda acquired a peculiar slant. Fear of slave insurrections became part of a possible Catholic-black alliance.[21] Such a menace, along with problems of foreign immigration, made it difficult for any region of the United States to escape the nativist mania.

A major commercial city like New Orleans, which attracted foreign immigrants, did not escape the nativist and anti-Roman Catholic propaganda of the 1830s. By the fall of 1835, a nascent nativist spirit culminated in the formation of the Louisiana Native American Association. The principles of the association echoed those of nativist groups throughout the United States. In an address to the people of Louisiana, it deplored "the outcast and offal of society, the vagrant and the convict—transported in myriads to our shores, reeking with the accumulated crimes of the whole civilized world."[22] Strong language, to be sure, but the Native Americans in Louisiana feared the growing number of immigrants and the possibility of the Creoles, because of the common Roman Catholic faith, forming a political alliance with them.

Louisiana's problems with nativism did not escape the notice of an editorial writer for the *New Orleans Bee.* In a lengthy article, the writer accused Native Americans from states other than Louisiana of trying to exclude foreigners "from the fruits of America." This writer felt that the underdeveloped condition of the United States called for more workers and, therefore, immigrants should be encouraged to immigrate. To him, America's resources were plentiful and educated Europeans brought their knowledge to help develop this country. "May not," asked the author, "a naturalized foreigner be as competent and eligible a citizen of Louisiana as a citizen of another state?" Admirable as this defense appears, the writer left the door open to future discrimination because he believed foreigners "should be admitted freely until the United States came of age."[23]

Nativists, meanwhile, lost no time attacking their enemies. For example, the race for governor in 1834 resulted in various ethnic slurs. The Whig candidate, Edward Douglass White, had to contend not only with his Democratic challenger but also his own Irish ancestry. Correspondents to the New Orleans Bee accused White, the protégé of another Irishman, Judge Alexander Porter, of using his Irish background by appealing to Irish voters to win the election.[24] Both political parties were guilty of demagoguery in their appeal to both French and Irish voters. However, the frustration of the nativists can be imagined since White won 70 percent of the vote.[25]

The 1834 gubernatorial campaign and White's lopsided triumph did not augur well for the adherents of nativism. Neither did the continued immigration of Irish into the state, particularly New Orleans. The number of Irish qualified to vote after 1835 should have assured that ethnic group control of Louisiana's largest city, but they failed to vote thus obviating any chance to achieve political hegemony in New Orleans. This failure to vote can perhaps be attributable to political naiveté, but whatever the reason, the possibility of Irish political control always remained in the minds of the nativists. The possibility of political control by the foreign-born, plus White's victory, contributed to the creation of the secretive Louisiana Native American Association.[26]

White had hardly begun his term when his detractors accused him of favoring the foreign-born for political office over Native Americans. According to these patriots, political appointments should go to American natives. In the spring of 1835, a Native American meeting passed a resolution stating "that it is politic, natural and just that native born Americans should be appointed to office in preference to foreigners."[27]

In response to such a resolution, an editorial in the Bee defended foreign immigrants. Obviously becoming well-seasoned in such matters, the writer pointed out that foreigners fought in the American Revolution and added to the United States by bringing their "arts and skills." Even Governor White's alleged appointments of foreign-born to political office did not withstand close scrutiny. For example, in New Orleans, White made thirty-eight appointments with just seven non-Native Americans being appointed to office. Of these seven positions, only two could be considered positions which brought financial remuneration.[28]

Following this editorial support of foreign immigrants, those opposed to the increased nativistic sentiment held a unity meeting in April 1835 and deprecated this rise in bigotry. Those who attended the meeting at the office of the *Bee* had as their goal harmony and fellowship among all Americans. These "friends of union and of peace" listened to a speech by the publisher of the *Bee* who endorsed the unity theme of the meeting.[29]

However, it was difficult to promote mutual trust in Louisiana, and particularly in New Orleans, during the 1830s. Those seeking to exclude foreign immigrants from the American political scene were equally as determined to assert their control over the Creoles. Antipathy toward the foreign-born and Creoles became indistinguishable as the latter sought to retain their political dominance in Louisiana by wooing foreign immigrants. Jacksonian supporters attacked the Whigs as enemies of naturalized citizens and asserted that the Democrats had always supported naturalized citizens.[30] But in the 1830s the Creoles generally belonged to the Whig Party; yet the Creoles' desperate political situation forced them to seek aid from foreign immigrants. To confuse the situation even more, one of the founders of the Louisiana Native American Association, William Christy, was a Democrat.[31]

Like most secret, nativist organizations of that time, nonmembers knew little about the workings or membership of the association. Nullification of the naturalization laws and restoration of the Alien and Sedition laws figured prominently on the list of priorities of the association. The association also called for a twenty-five year residency requirement before granting citizenship and resolved to vote only for a Native American.[32] While generally secretive about itself, the leaders saw to it that their propaganda reached the people. For example, one of the leading organizers of the association, John Gibson, edited the *True American*.[33] This nativistic newspaper operated throughout the mid-to late 1830s. Then, in 1839, Dr. James McFarlane, a native of South Carolina, founded another pro-nativist organ the *Native American*.[34]

Agitation of anti-foreignism by the nativist press continued in the late summer of 1835. Incensed, because the governor appointed a naturalized citizen to the position of Sheriff of Orleans Parish, the editor of the *True American* incited the American section of the city against the Creoles. The *Bee* accused him of making disparaging remarks about the city police and the Roman Catholic clergy, and denounced the paper's attempt to divide the city.[35]

A divisive spirit certainly pervaded New Orleans and soon after this incident the state legislature partitioned the city into three municipalities. Americans had long clamored for this action and as early as 1832 the cry for an American mayor of New Orleans had also been heard.[36] Creole politicians whose districts crossed ethnic boundary lines found it expedient to be aware of these American sensibilities.[37] Each municipality was a separate corporation and possessed a council and recorder elected by the people. A mayor presided over a general council legislating in matters of common interest. The old town, where most of the Creoles resided, made up the First Municipality. The Faubourg St. Mary and uptown New Orleans, above present-day Canal Street, composed the Second Municipality, where the Americans and some immigrants resided. The Third Municipality, Faubourg Marigny, which many of the foreign immigrants called home, lay below present-day Esplanade Avenue.[38]

Nativism became so widespread in Louisiana and New Orleans, especially in the 1830s, that opponents felt obliged to organize in opposition to the Louisiana Native American Association. A notice in the *Bee* on February 10, 1836, called for a meeting to form an association of "Loyal Americans." This group sought legislative incorporation in reaction to a similar move taken by the Louisiana Native American Association. Not all opponents of nativist groups approved of this proposed organization. An editorial comment in the *Bee* stated that an opposition group would only harden prejudices of nativists. Nevertheless, the meeting took place on February 11, 1836, and the attendees elected Gilbert Leonard of Plaquemines Parish president of the "Louisiana Loyal American Association." Vice presidents elected were J. H. Holland, president of the New Orleans Navigation Company, and the former governor of Louisiana Jacques Dupre of Opelousas. The Louisiana Loyal Americans denounced the Louisiana Native American Association for continuing to make distinctions among Louisianians and not setting forth as its goal the bringing together, in a feeling of "union and benevolence," all citizens of Louisiana.[39]

The names of some of those attending the organizational meeting indicate that the Loyal Americans made an effort to include all ethnic groups as well as both Democrats and Whigs. Not only were French names evident, but numerous American and Irish names stood out. Interestingly enough, one name in particular deserves mention. Christian Roselius, a New Orleans attorney, attended this anti-nativist meeting; his appearance demonstrates that his prejudices developed slowly, because by the 1850s he became a leading member of the Know Nothing movement.[40]

Nativism and anti-Roman Catholicism continued in the 1838 state election campaign. André Roman, a former governor and the Whig candidate, received a scathing attack because of his alleged opposition to naturalized citizens. At the same time, the Creole Roman's accusers also pointed to his disapproval of Americans. They claimed he would never appoint an American to office if a Creole could be found. The supporters of Roman's Democratic opponent, Denis Prieur, mayor of New Orleans, indirectly attacked Roman's Catholicism. Since Roman had attended a Catholic school in Baltimore, his detractors felt that the priests had "smothered that love of country and admiration for liberty" necessary in an elected official.[41]

Violence closed out the 1830s. To combat the nativists and their press, an Irishman cranked up an anti-nativist paper in 1839. Appropriately named, the *Anti-Native American*[42] (a friendly paper called it the "*Anti-Humbug*") pulled no punches. The *Bee* reported that the publisher of the *Anti-Native American* had made discourteous remarks about Colonel William Christy of the Louisiana Native American Association. Thereupon the colonel and his two sons attacked the Irishman's headquarters with axes. The publisher shot Christy and one son, but they achieved their goal; the paper ceased publication.[43]

The advent of the 1840s witnessed no respite in the continuing hostilities between nativists and anti-nativists. The first outbreak occurred during the election for mayor of New Orleans in the spring of 1840. Party lines became more tightly drawn than in the 1830s. Additionally, the Whig Party frequently echoed Native American rhetoric and at times supported avowed nativists for election to public office. In this New Orleans election, the Whigs re-nominated Charles Genois. A Native American party (referred to at times as the Native American Repeal Party) organized for the election and nominated William Freret, owner of one of the largest cotton presses in New Orleans and a resident of the American section of the city. The *Bee* referred to a Mr. Kennedy as the regular administration candidate, a Van Buren man. He received the anti-Native American label, and the *Bee* predicted Irish and German naturalized citizens would vote for Kennedy. Although some considered Freret exclusively as a Native American, others thought of him as a Whig. The Whigs realized Freret's Native American Party nomination and his stand on repealing the naturalization laws would cost him the vote of many naturalized Whigs.[44]

Freret won the election with 1,051 votes to Genois's 942. Kennedy and lesser candidates received no more than 200 votes among them.[45] One newspaper's analysis of the election estimated that Freret lost at least 300

Whig votes in the First Municipality. But despite the presence of a large number of naturalized Whigs in the First and Third Municipalities, he managed to win. These naturalized Whigs received assurances of Freret's good intentions and the promise that his position on "an abstract question" (repeal of the naturalization laws) would not prevent him from fulfilling the duties of mayor. Those naturalized Whigs, who could not vote for Freret because of his nativist views, were urged to "rejoin" the party since, according to one political observer; Freret's victory had assured the ascendancy of the Whig Party in New Orleans.[46]

Following this election, the Native American Repeal Party sought to extend its newfound strength beyond New Orleans. The nativists "drafted" Judge George Guion, a Whig from Lafourche Parish, as the Native American candidate for Congress from the First Congressional District. Although he felt drawn to the Repeal Party because of sympathy with their stand on repeal of the naturalization laws, he declined the nomination because of the lateness of the offer and because the Whig Party had already nominated him. Instead, he urged the people to support the Whigs in their fight against the Democrats.[47] Nativists recognized the need to protect the franchise and to repeal the naturalization laws, but most, like Judge Guion, apparently were not ready for a political party based exclusively on nativistic principles. Such was true particularly outside New Orleans, where the foreign immigrant had not yet made much of an impact.

However, a Native American Convention held in New Orleans in 1841 attracted delegates from across the state. Judge Guion, who had recently declined the nomination of the Native American Repeal Party, figured quite prominently as the president of this convention. Guion's active participation confirmed his attraction to nativist principles. The delegates from across Louisiana who came to this convention urged the United States Congress to restrain itself from passing laws naturalizing foreigners and to prohibit state legislatures from doing the same.[48] With Judge Guion presiding, the convention turned down a resolution offered by Thomas Green Davidson[49] calling for a third party. Apparently the success of the Repeal Party in New Orleans did not impress the delegates from other sections of the state. Yet, they did recommend a national convention of like-minded persons to meet in Washington, DC, on July 4, 1842.[50]

A year after this convention, the Native Americans lost their hold on the mayoralty of New Orleans. The Native American Association had queried the mayoralty candidates about their views of the naturalization laws. The Democratic nominee and former mayor of New Orleans, Denis Prieur, did not favor repeal or the exclusion of the foreign-born from office. The incumbent, William Freret, a Whig and nativist, received the nomination of the Native American Party. He stood four-square behind the Native American Association's demand for the repeal of the "defective" naturalization laws. Although the Whig Party made no official nomination, it supported Freret's candidacy.[51]

Following Prieur's victory over Freret by a count of 1,334 votes to 1,069 votes, the editor of the Whig paper, the *Bee*, mourned Freret's defeat. In a lengthy election postmortem, the newspaper's political writer explained Freret's defeat. He believed that Freret's failure to receive the regular Whig endorsement and the irreparable harm done by the nativist newspaper the *Louisiana American*[52] played important roles in the loss. An Election Day article in the *Louisiana American* disputed that the issue at hand was between Democrats and Whigs. Instead, the issue was "Native American versus anti-Native American, and the ballot box must decide whether we are to govern ourselves or to be governed by imported patriots." The article also intimated that Creoles bullied voters at the polls, and to cap off this scathing polemic, the *American* printed the article in an Irish dialect. The *Bee* claimed that many naturalized citizens, including naturalized Whigs, resented these insults and deserted Freret on Election Day.[53] Native Americans also suffered a defeat outside New Orleans when their candidate for mayor of Baton Rouge lost his election bid in 1842.[54]

The 1842 gubernatorial campaign gained momentum immediately after the New Orleans mayoralty election. New Orleans Whigs warned country Whigs not to be hoodwinked by the Democrats into believing the New Orleans election had been a test of Whig Party strength. The Whigs believed Freret's defeat came, not because of Whig weakness, but from mixing in "extraneous questions" in the election.[55] Obviously, these "extraneous questions" meant the issue of nativism versus anti-nativism which the Whigs hoped would not become part of this state campaign. One Whig editor feared that if his party would "permit themselves to be led astray by irrelevant or collateral issues (as upon a recent occasion), they will be beaten."[56]

Nevertheless, nativism did surface during the 1842 state campaign. The Democrats accused the Whig candidate, Henry Johnson, of being a nativist, and his identification with the Native American Party did not bring any denials. One Johnson supporter denied the candidate's association with the Native American Party, saying that Johnson stood "uncommitted on the question of Native Americanism." But this same Johnson proponent wondered how the Democratic candidate, Alexandre Mouton, stood on this question since a Louisiana newspaper had reported that Mouton warmly supported the Native American Party.[57] Late in the campaign, according to the *Bee,* the Democratic *Louisiana Courier* tried to impugn Johnson's character. The *Courier* reported that Johnson had stated that he "was sure of enough American (Anglo-Saxon) votes to elect him and cared little for what the Creoles or their French allies may do." The *Courier* wondered how the Creole population could trust him after this statement.[58] The *Bee* felt sure that the Creoles in the state would not believe Johnson felt so assured of American support, and thought that last-minute tactics which attempted to divide American and Creole Whigs would work against the Democratic Party.[59] Regardless, Mouton won and became the first Democratic governor in the history of the state.

Nativism continued unabated in Louisiana and appeared next in the race for United States Congress in 1843 in the First Congressional District. Nominated by the Whigs and Democrats were George K. Rogers and John Slidell, respectively. The Whigs attempted to convince naturalized citizens that Democrats gave naturalized citizens no credit for intelligence when they promised to assist immigrants in voting if they voted for Slidell. In contrast, the Whig Party felt it never appealed to immigrants' prejudice. Whiggery better represented the working class to which many naturalized citizens belonged. Whigs felt their party protected labor and industry in the United States from "the hostile legislation of European monarchies."[60]

Even though the Whigs felt it was politically necessary to appeal to the foreign-born, they remained alert to the possible attempt of the Democratic Party to illegally vote the foreigners. The concern about fraud led them to warn election judges to carefully check naturalization papers. When Slidell won the election, the Whigs accused him and the Democratic Party of the wholesale manufacture of illegal voters. One Whig partisan estimated that between 500 and 600 "naturalized citizens" voted illegally. The same source noted that the illegal naturalization of foreign immigrants occurred in the city of Lafayette (a New Orleans suburb). The Democrats chose Lafayette because the ten dollars per person fee for naturalization papers in New Orleans exhausted the Democratic treasury, and the price in Lafayette was lower. Additionally, the Whigs found that the vote in Plaquemines Parish exceeded that of any previous year. In fact, there were more votes cast in Plaquemines Parish than white males over twenty-one.[61]

The Whigs bemoaned their defeat and readily attacked the Democrats for this fraud. Considering that the total vote in Plaquemines exceeded the number eligible to vote and that Slidell received 270 votes out of a total of 340 votes, the Whigs appear justified in their allegation of fraud in Plaquemines Parish. However, the Democratic naturalization of immigrants prior to this election forced the Whigs into the realization of the need to naturalize foreigners as well. Soon after the election, the Whigs announced that party members could obtain legal information to assist immigrants in becoming naturalized. Ironically, the Whigs chose Colonel William Christy, the leading nativist, to disseminate the legal advice.[62]

The question of naturalized citizens fraudulently voting remained a significant problem in Louisiana. From the winter of 1843 to the spring of 1844, this topic concerned both Democrats and Whigs. Following a special election which sent the New Orleans Whig James Freret to the state legislature, the Democrats cried fraud. The Democrats' complaints were understandable since the Whigs had guarded against voters with fraudulent naturalization papers and excluded from voting those in particular who possessed naturalization papers issued by Judge Benjamin Elliott of the City Court of Lafayette.[63]

In another New Orleans special election to fill an unexpired term in the state senate, Thomas Slidell, a Democrat and brother of John Slidell, defeated Christian Roselius, a Whig. The Whigs believed that Judge Elliott's "naturalized citizens" contributed to Roselius's defeat. To prove their charge of fraud, the Whigs noted that the number of votes cast nearly doubled from the recent election of James Freret. They accused Elliott of issuing approximately 1,800 naturalization certificates, some to people not even present in court.[64]

The controversy over Judge Elliott's citizens emerged next in the New Orleans mayoralty election of April 1, 1844. The city had become so imbued with nativism that both parties either nominated or unofficially supported a candidate allegedly tainted with that prejudice. The Whigs renominated William Freret and challenged the voters of the city not to tolerate the voters created by Judge Elliott. The Democrats supported Edgar Montegut, who, the Whigs reminded the public, had been the Native American candidate for mayor of New Orleans back in 1840. Montegut won, whereupon the Whig press bitterly attacked the Democrats calling the election a prostitution of the ballot box. The Whigs reported that election judges accepted some seventy-five Elliott votes in the 4th Ward, First Municipality where the total votes cast was over 300. Usually this ward polled only 200 votes. In the more heavily immigrant Third Municipality, 2nd Ward, election judges accepted over 100 Elliott votes. It was no wonder the Whigs fumed over these incidents of what they called illegal voting by foreigners.[65]

Election-weary Louisianians received no respite in 1844. Two crucial elections held on July 1, 1844, decided representation in the state legislature and the constitutional convention. The importance of both elections, particularly the election for delegates to the convention, prompted both parties to conduct their campaigns vigorously. Having generally disapproved the calling of a constitutional convention, the Whigs threw themselves into the contest in order to control the proceedings. Because of election fraud in recent elections, primarily in the New Orleans area, the Whigs seemed determined to deny illegally naturalized citizens the franchise.

Once the election had been completed, complaints and accusations from both sides flowed freely. The Whigs charged the Democrats with denying well-known citizens the right to vote. The Democrats did so, according to the Whigs, in anticipation that Judge Elliott's "citizens" would be turned away from the polls. The charges continued for a month after the election by which time it became clear that the Whigs had generally succeeded in both elections.[66]

The Whigs improved their legislative position and did well in the convention election. In the lower house, the Whigs gained two seats over 1843, leaving them with a slight majority. Although the Democrats maintained their majority in the senate, the Whigs gained one seat over 1843 and reduced the Democratic majority to one. In the important convention race, the Whigs captured the majority by one. However, one Whig paper noted that allied with conservative Democrats or nonpartisan conservative delegates, the Whigs would forestall any loco-foco attempts to "radicalize" the organic law of Louisiana.[67]

The 1845 Constitution was certainly more democratic than the 1812 document. As discussed above, the convention overturned property requirements and taxpaying prerequisites for holding office and voting, respectively. Besides reflecting Jacksonian tendencies, the convention mirrored the rising alarm over foreign immigration. Whigs particularly distrusted foreign immigrants. The Whigs claimed that foreign immigrants, along with immigrants from other American states, were not capable of comprehending Louisiana's local laws and institutions.

The Whigs wanted to include nativist principles in the new constitution to protect what they considered their vested interests. One successful candidate to the convention, Judah P. Benjamin, felt immigration to Louisiana dangerous for the state. Shortly after the election of delegates, Benjamin called for the formation of a "nativist" party. He obviously thought the existing parties incapable of dealing with the immigrant problem. Benjamin, a

Whig, along with other leading Whigs, such as former Governor W. C. C. Claiborne and Glendy Burke of New Orleans, favored strict rules governing residency requirements. They hoped to prevent anyone other than a native form becoming the chief executive. When this move failed, they succeeded in having the convention adopt a fifteen-year residency requirement for the governor and lieutenant governor.[68]

While the Whigs did well in the 1845 convention, it was the 1844 presidential election that became a particular challenge for the Whigs. Yet the Whigs were confident they would carry Louisiana. However, the Democrats were equally as determined as the Whigs were to win the election. Fearful that the Democrats would use foreigners illegally in the contest, the Whigs formed a committee armed with a list of every foreign male who had entered Louisiana from a foreign port since 1840. Everyone on this list would be ineligible to vote according to Louisiana's Constitution.[69] This committee obviously did not count on John Slidell shipping boatloads of "voters" to Plaquemines Parish, a virtual Democratic Party fiefdom, to vote for James K. Polk, a maneuver which put Louisiana in Polk's column and elicited bitter denunciations from the Whigs.[70]

Becoming more visceral in its editorials, the *New Orleans Bee* referred to the immigrants who allowed themselves to be used by Slidell as vagabonds and loafers. The *Bee* felt that the Plaquemines frauds would surely bring about the formation of a Native American Party.[71] The Plaquemines frauds also sparked a renewed agitation for the repeal of the naturalization laws. In December 1844, United States Senator Henry Johnson of Louisiana formally requested that the Senate Judiciary Committee:

> inquire into the expediency of modifying the naturalization of [*sic*] laws of the United States, so as to extend the time allowed to enable foreigners to become citizens; to require greater guard against fraud in the steps to be taken in procuring naturalization papers; and to prevent, as practicable, fraud and violence at elections.[72]

However, one observer commented that changing the naturalization laws would have no effect on suffrage. Nativists should emulate Louisiana's constitutional requirement which prevented anyone from voting who had not been a citizen of the United States for two years.[73]

Nativists in Louisiana apparently thought this constitutional provision insufficient. They organized a Native American Party for the 1846 gubernatorial election and nominated Charles Derbigny of Jefferson Parish for governor and L. Deshields for lieutenant governor. The Whig press generally supported the need for protecting the franchise, but, as before, opposed a third-party movement based on nativist principles. Whigs would have preferred to keep nativism at a low level since they hoped to gain votes from naturalized citizens. They also believed the Native Americans could not survive as an independent, third-party movement. The Whigs, therefore, argued that their party represented the greatest protection for the franchise.[74]

Of course, the Whigs had to contend with the Democrats as well. The Democratic Party had labeled William DeBuys of New Orleans, the Whig candidate for governor, a Creole. Referring to him as a Creole, contended the *Bee,* lessened DeBuys's appeal to the Anglo-Saxons. At the same time, Whigs defended DeBuys from charges that he was a nativist. One Democratic paper, the *Louisiana Courier,* charged that DeBuys, while a representative in the legislature, had opposed Governor White's alleged favoritism of foreigners over natives for public office. The *Bee* denied that DeBuys opposed naturalized citizens and sought to disprove the Democratic charge that DeBuys participated in the Louisiana Native American Association.[75] The *Bee* must not have researched its files well because on March 2, 1841, General William DeBuys's name appeared in the *Bee* as a vice president at the Native American Convention in New Orleans.

The Democrat Isaac Johnson won the election, and the Whigs blamed their defeat on the bad weather and the competition of Derbigny's candidacy. However, Derbigny ran poorly throughout the state receiving only 588 votes out of some 23,000 cast.[76] Even if all of Derbigny's votes had gone to DeBuys, the Whig nominee would not have won. For the second time in the 1840s, nativists in the state were unsuccessful in consolidating their position beyond New Orleans. As a political movement, Native Americanism succeeded periodically in the city, but was not a durable threat to either the Whigs or the Democrats. Most politicians who adhered to the nativist ideology felt more secure in one of the major parties and eschewed these early nativist parties. Apparently, influence and rewards that party brought were too attractive at this time for politicians to break away from one of the major parties.

Although anti-foreign sentiment never ceased, it did wane in the late 1840s and early 1850s. Derbigny's miserable showing in 1846 indicated that nativism as an issue was being pushed into the political background. David Wilmot's proviso, the Mexican War, and the Compromise of 1850 absorbed the attention of most Americans and Louisianians during this period. However, continued foreign immigration and fraudulent voting permitted nativism to remain a visible if not a viable issue.

Consequently, the Whigs continued to criticize the Democrats' alleged use of what one writer called "the immense floating and alien vote" to defeat Whig candidates.[77] Even naturalized citizens were suspect. During the congressional campaign in 1847, Whigs reminded election inspectors that recently naturalized citizens had a two-year residency requirement before being eligible to vote. But nativism lost out to a national issue—the Democratic charge that the Whigs wanted to negotiate a dishonorable peace with Mexico took precedence.[78]

Hostility to foreigners did not play a significant role in the 1848 presidential election in Louisiana. Foreshadowing the mid-1850s, most of the electioneering centered on the issue of slavery, particularly slavery in the territories and the Wilmot Proviso. Democrats and Whigs had different views over how to best protect slavery in the territories and both deprecated the Wilmot Proviso. Louisiana's Democrats wanted to guarantee slave property in any territory acquired from Mexico while Whigs looked to Zachary Taylor to protect their slave interests. Because the Whig party's "no territory" position had failed them and slavery remained paramount in this campaign, Louisiana Whigs made a minimal effort to defend themselves from nativist charges. A typical allegation of nativism, according to a pro-Zachary Taylor newspaper, was seen in the Democrats' portrayal of the Whig nominee as antipathetic to Germans and Irish. Taylor also favored, according to the Democrats, a twenty-one year waiting period before giving the franchise to naturalized citizens.[79]

Unfortunately for Louisiana Whigs, Zachary Taylor's success in 1848 did not help the Whig state ticket in 1849. When the gubernatorial campaign began in the summer of 1849, as in the recent presidential election, national issues continued to dominate.[80] However, nativism did appear, with the Whigs as usual accusing the Democratic Party of appealing to foreigners only at election time. Hoping not to antagonize foreign-born voters, the Whigs thought that the Germans and Irish were particularly susceptible to this kind of electioneering, not because of dishonesty, but because of a misguided belief of what the Democrats could do for them. The Whig press reminded the foreign-born that their nominee for governor, Alexander Declouet, had voted against a legislative resolution to Louisiana's congressional delegation calling for the repeal or modification of the naturalization laws. Declouet's position took on added significance, according to his supporters, since his anti-nativism stance occurred when the Native American Party and its ideology received it greatest support.[81]

Whigs took the allegation of anti-foreignism directly to the Democratic camp. They charged Joseph Walker, the Democratic candidate for governor, with anti-foreign prejudice. Apparently, Walker had called Alexander Porter a "damned Irishman" after Porter defeated Walker for United States senator in 1834. To prove the charge, the Whig press printed letters from those who attested to Walker's feelings. One correspondent stated that Walker did not approve of appointing naturalized citizens to high positions such as United States senator.[82] Therefore, Whigs asked: who could be called the friend of naturalized citizens and foreigners? And they answered: not Joseph Walker. If their accusation concerning Walker's statement about Porter did not convince the voters, the Whigs had additional proof of Walker's antipathy to foreigners. As a state legislator, Walker had voted against an appropriation for the Catholic Male Orphan Asylum of New Orleans which aided many immigrant children.[83] The *Louisiana Courier* denied that Walker had ever called Judge Porter any such thing as "a damned Irishman," and that paper asked the Irish Democrats if they intended to permit the Whigs to cajole them "out of a single vote."[84] The Democratic paper also reminded the Irish voters that the recent murder of an Irishman had been committed by a participant in a Whig outing, in full view of numerous Whigs, and they took no action against the assailant.[85]

Despite all the charges of Democratic insincerity toward foreigners, the Whigs remained convinced of the corruptibility of the foreign-born. Alarmed by the number of foreigners making declarations to become citizens, the Whigs reminded them of the two-year residency requirement for voting. Whigs felt that this warning would go unheeded and they knew many foreigners planned to commit "fraud and perjury" in this election.[86] This conviction undoubtedly made it difficult for the Whigs to accept the result of the election in which Walker received 17,673 votes while Declouet garnered 16,601 votes. Declouet received a majority in the Second Congressional District, which included the strong Whig sugar parishes, while Walker won majorities in the other three districts.[87]

Nativism in Louisiana received a tremendous impetus from continued foreign immigration. In this sense, Louisiana differed little from the rest of the country. At times, the nativist rhetoric became anti-Roman Catholic. But, in the 1830s and 1840s, Louisiana did not experience a rabid anti-papal sentiment. Nativists, at times, did include Catholic Creoles in their denunciation because Creoles had attempted to form a political alliance with the immigrants, but Creoles soon identified with the Whig party, which exhibited a clear anti-foreign feeling.

However, formal nativist organizations competed with the Whig Party in Louisiana during this period of the state's history and launched two third-party movements in New Orleans and in the state. Obviously, with most of the immigrants residing in New Orleans, these organizations and party movements had most of their success in the city. But even in New Orleans, the Native American Repeal Party and the Native American Party received mostly ideological support and generally failed to acquire political acceptance. That acceptance would have to wait until the 1850s.

⁘T̃WO

Resurgence of Nativism: 1850–55

Nativism, ethnic prejudice, and anti-foreignism received little attention in Louisiana during the early 1850s. The Compromise of 1850, Cuba, and a new state constitution occupied the attention of the politicians and the press to a large extent, with the Whig Party affirming the Compromise, opposing intervention in Cuba, and supporting the call for a new constitution. The Democrats reluctantly accepted a new constitution.[1] When nativism did appear, it usually occurred within the framework of a broader issue. By 1853 and during 1854, however, nativistic and anti-Roman Catholic sentiment assumed more importance as foreign immigration increased and the United States Roman Catholic hierarchy became more assertive because of the large-scale immigration of foreign Catholics to the United States. This continuing foreign immigration and assertiveness of the Catholic hierarchy, along with the demise of the Whig Party, coincided with the formation of a nationwide political nativist party which made its first appearance in Louisiana during an 1854 New Orleans election.

An early manifestation of nativism in the 1850s in Louisiana occurred during the national debates over the Compromise of 1850. The Whig Party heartily supported the Compromise measures and used every opportunity to commit itself to that measure.[2] Although the Democrats accepted the finality of the Compromise, they did so in a more subdued manner.[3] The Democrats objected to what the *Louisiana Courier* referred to as "the bigoted nativism of the Whig press."[4] The Whig press had roughly handled the United States senator from Louisiana, Pierre Soulé, for his vote against the Compromise, with much of the criticism centering on Soulé's foreign birth. One Whig paper stated that a foreigner like Soulé could not grasp the essence of the United States government.[5] Another journal pointed out that Senator Soulé's supporters were "not native and to the manor born."[6] Wondering about this Whig logic, the *New Orleans Daily Delta* queried if a non-Englishman could not grasp American laws, how could an Englishman understand Louisiana codes?[7]

In addition to national affairs, local and state issues also furnished a forum for nativistic rhetoric. The consolidation of the three municipalities of New Orleans and the writing of a new state constitution were controversial issues in 1851 and 1852. These two issues contributed to the ethnic rivalries and appeals to naturalized citizens. Whig newspapers opposed consolidating New Orleans because they believed it would revive pre-1836 ethnic hostilities.[8] Not until 1852, when the predominately American suburb of Lafayette had been included in the consolidation package, did consolidation succeed. Whigs were more positive when it came to rewriting the organic law of Louisiana, seeking the inclusion of an elective judiciary, state aid to public works, and a system of free banks.[9] Democrats were not opposed to these features but felt that either constitutional amendments or legislative acts would be better than a new constitution. However, in late 1852, to demonstrate that Whigs and Democrats were not too far apart on business issues, John Slidell assured Whig James Robb that the Democratic candidate for the state senate from New Orleans would support "pro-business measures."[10] Still, there was not a complete agreement since the Democrats refused to be censured by the Whigs for the illiberal features of the 1845 Constitution which prohibited naturalized citizens from voting for two years after becoming a United States citizen. In fact, the residence requirement had been extended to two years for all new residents. The Democratic *Louisiana Courier* laid the blame for this clause on the Whig Party and a few conservative Democrats.[11]

These incidents of nativism were minor, but events throughout the country, and in Louisiana, precipitated more virulent forms of bigotry and ultimately led to organized political nativism. The continued influx of immigrants into the United States, many of whom were Roman Catholics, augured ill for toleration. Louisiana received 52,011 immigrants in 1851, or more than one-eighth of the total number of immigrants that arrived in the country that year.[12] In contrast, only 22,148 immigrants had arrived in Louisiana during 1846, just five years before.[13]

Most of the support for the principles of nativism in Louisiana came from the Whig Party and its political press. One reason for the Whig stand was the success that the Democrats had in courting immigrants. At election time, the Democrats reminded the immigrant population of the past Whig association with Native Americanism. For example, the Democratic Party tied Whiggery to nativism during the election for Orleans Parish sheriff in 1851. The Whig candidate James Freret had been associated with the Louisiana Native American Convention back in the 1840s, and that convention had approved the repeal of all laws naturalizing foreigners and favored excluding naturalized citizens from the franchise. The Democrats naturally brought before the foreign-born population Freret's involvement with the Native American Convention.[14] The Whigs opposed this Democratic appeal to a particular class of people,[15] but the Democrats won the election, inaugurating a string of Democratic victories in the state.

Several elections in 1852 furnished additional forums for appeals to the foreign-born population of Louisiana. The presidential campaign, a New Orleans municipal race, the votes on a new state constitution, and the state elections all witnessed partisan appeals to the foreign-born. Of course, the issues of slavery, abolitionism, internal improvements, foreign policy, and filibustering each played roles[16] in the presidential campaign, but both parties effectively used bigotry as a weapon. While the Democrats criticized Winfield Scott for his past flirtations with nativism,[17] the Whigs attacked Franklin Pierce as anti-Catholic and, in a foreshadowing of things to come, alleged that Pierce was also opposed to slavery.[18] The Whigs also made good use of Thomas Green Davidson's, a Democratic elector, Native American background. He had been prominent in the 1840s nativist Louisiana Native American Association.[19] Partisan presses continually inflamed national prejudices with appeals to adopted citizens. The *Daily True Delta* of New Orleans urged naturalized citizens to vote against the Whig mayor of that city because he had "permitted thugs to menace the lives of adopted citizens."[20] Whigs and Democrats also blamed each other for the distinctions between foreign-born and native citizens in the 1845 state constitution, and both parties reminded the voters when they went to the polls to decide on a new constitution[21] that they opposed such distinctions.[22] Finally, the Whigs characterized the Democratic candidate for governor, Paul O. Hébert, as a pro-foreigner or an ambitious Creole, depending on the section of New Orleans or the state in which they campaigned.[23]

Whigs claimed that they had always been liberal toward naturalized citizens, but Democrats and the foreign-born scoffed at such a claim.[24] Even when the Whigs ran a naturalized citizen for public office, the candidate had little affinity for the recent immigrants of Louisiana. For example, the Whig candidate for chief justice of the Louisiana Supreme Court in 1853,

Christian Roselius, was a naturalized citizen. However, Roselius's former association with the Louisiana Native American Association probably cost him the election because his Democratic opponent, Thomas Slidell, made Roselius's association with nativism an important issue.[25] A large percentage of the immigrants of the state lived primarily in the Third (Municipal) District of New Orleans. That district gave Slidell a 305 vote majority out of 1,351 cast.[26] The success of the Democrats in attracting immigrants to their party, the Democratic disregard for the naturalization law, and the growing lawlessness on Election Day alarmed nativists. They feared what they saw as the increased influence of foreigners in both the country and the state.

The state and congressional elections of 1853 furnished the Whigs with a perfect example of how they believed the Democrats abused the naturalization law, perpetrated Election Day frauds, and used the immigrant and foreign-born citizen as unsuspecting tools to further their ends. In the midst of the campaign, the Whig Party asserted that the Democrats of New Orleans "manufactured citizens"[27] by naturalizing foreigners who had not passed the required five years of residency and who could not even speak English. To ensure friendly surroundings, the Democratic Judge Donatien Augustin, who issued these naturalization papers, chose the Sixth District Court Building of New Orleans. This was not even the bench over which Judge Augustin presided. However, it was in the same building as police headquarters, and the Democrats at that time controlled the police of the city. Therefore, the Democratic judge could proceed without fear of interruption. To make sure that these "naturalized" citizens voted for the straight Democratic ticket, a Democratic officer of the state collected the naturalization papers. Compounding the fraud, the Democrats held the papers until Election Day to assure a correct vote.[28] Outraged at these tactics, the Whigs predicted that the only thing left for the Democrats to do was to use these debased "citizens" to commit outrages at the polls.[29] And the Democrats did use these "citizens." One Democratic stronghold, in the First District of New Orleans, part of what became known as the "Irish Channel,"[30] returned a vote of 1,098 where previously the vote had never exceeded 950. This particular vote and a similar increase throughout the city occurred despite the recent yellow fever epidemic which had taken its toll on the population of New Orleans.[31] The Democratic victory in this 1853 election[32] brought charges of fraud from the Whigs and a former Democrat, Charles Gayarré, the unsuccessful Independent candidate for Congress in the First Congressional District. Gayarré's charges mainly concerned the internal problems of the Democratic Party which focused on Gayarré's allegations of fraud by John Slidell. Gayarré charged that one-fourth of the entire vote in New Orleans was spurious. The Democrats, predictably, claimed he was nothing but a disappointed office-seeker and they demanded the charges of fraud be proved. However, sympathetic with Gayarré over his defeat, Democrat James Aburton confirmed Gayarré's allegations. He wrote Gayarré that his loss had come at the hands of a too controlling and less-than-honest Democratic Party. Both Gayarré and the Whigs agreed on the illegal use Democrats made of "the debased of foreign lands."[33] They also agreed that a complete board of Democratic inspectors at the polls and the Democratic police force resulted in many Whig votes not being counted. Throughout the state, there were those citizens like Henry Marston of the Florida parishes who wrote friends that wherever the Democrats rule, "there is room for reform."[34]

Related to the anti-foreign prejudice was anti-Catholicism because many of the newly arrived immigrants were adherents of that faith. Similar to anti-foreignism, anti-Roman Catholicism received more attention as immigration increased. With increased immigration, membership in the Roman Catholic Church in the United States increased, too. This increased membership, according to many nativists, made the Roman Church uncompromising. It must have appeared to nativists that the church sought to be as dominant in America as it had been in Europe. Nativists seized upon what they thought was a sometimes arrogant posture of the Roman Catholic hierarchy of the country to prove how aggressive that faith was. Roman Catholic editors exacerbated the situation by heaping abuse on Protestants and encouraging their fellow Roman Catholics to profess openly their religion. One bold Roman Catholic editor wrote the following:

> Our object is to show, once more, that Protestantism is effete, powerless, dying out though disturbed only by its proper gangrenes, and conscious that its last moment is come when it is fairly set, face to face, with Catholic truth.[35]

According to the nativists, other examples of the arrogance of Roman Catholicism was the attempt of the church to remedy the problems of sectarian instruction in the schools, to divide the public school fund, and to settle the ownership of church property, the last referred to as the trustee problem.[36] Nativists in the United States and Louisiana looked unfavorably upon the steps taken by the Catholic hierarchy in the eastern United States to gain title to church property and to divide the public school fund.[37] Louisiana had had an experience with the trustee problem in 1842 when the

St. Louis Cathedral hierarchy asserted their control over church property.[38] At that time, nativists condemned what they considered the anti-republican feature of the hierarchy's ownership of property. Although this trustee problem in Louisiana had occurred earlier, events during the 1850s in the northeastern states furnished local nativists with sufficient current news on this sensitive issue. The Vatican increased the tension when it sent a papal nuncio, Monsignor Gaetano Bedini, to the United States in 1853 to solve the trustee problem.[39] Violence followed the travels of Monsignor Bedini, and when Louisiana nativists learned that the papal nuncio would possibly visit New Orleans, inflammatory placards inciting violence against Bedini appeared around the city. These placards stated:

> BEDINI, THE TIGER, who is Guilty of the Murder of Hundreds of Patriots, their wives and Children in Italia, who Ordered that Ugo Bassi, the Patriotic Catholic Priest be Scalped before he was Executed; will this Abominable Servant of Despoty [sic] Receive the same Honors as the Heroes of Freedom, or will we Follow the Action of the Brewers of London against Haynau.[40]

Most of the newspapers in New Orleans, and some of the country presses, opposed the outbreak of invective against Bedini, and hoped that New Orleans would demonstrate that "all sects are free to come and go as they please in this country."[41]

However, there were those in Louisiana who obviously did not share this tolerant stance and who hoped mob violence would rule. These radical Louisiana nativists invited the ex-priest and liberal-thinking Italian evangelical Alessandro Gavazzi to lecture in the state.[42] The nativists undoubtedly knew that Gavazzi's rhetoric usually led to turbulence. Gavazzi's logic, however, did not appeal to all nativists in the state. The editor of the *Baton Rouge Weekly Comet,* George A. Pike, could not understand Gavazi's attraction for so many Protestants in America. Pike denied that America's success was due to its Protestantism and that Roman Catholicism and republicanism were inimical. Pike, nevertheless, was unrelenting in his brand of anti-Catholicism when he asserted that Gavazzi really intended to advance Roman Catholicism in the United States and that the ex-priest Gavazzi was a Jesuit in disguise.[43]

Nativists also opposed Catholics meddling in the education of the children of the state, particularly when that meddling involved the public schools. It mattered little to the nativists that public education in the state affected very few children. In 1852, the enrollment in public schools throughout Louisiana was only 17,000 and the total budget was a paltry $250,000.[44] At times, this controversy became involved with party politics, as in the New Orleans municipal election of 1851. A Democratic paper charged the Second Municipal (public) School Board with requiring sectarian prayers and the reading of a Protestant Bible. The municipal council repealed the requirement, thus removing it as a campaign issue.[45]

Anti-Roman Catholic sentiment became more prevalent whenever a division of the public school fund seemed possible. Editor Pike appeared to be the self-appointed protector of public education and the public school fund. His suspicions about Roman Catholicism prompted him to question the real intentions of the "Catholic Free Schools" in Baton Rouge; he hoped they would teach "good and whole-some doctrines."[46] Pike also wrote about the failure of the state legislature to provide adequately for public education, and he made it a campaign issue in the 1853 state elections. The Baton Rouge editor lectured the electorate to show concern for whom they voted, charging that poor public education had resulted in the Jesuits assuming a greater influence in educating the children of Louisiana.[47] Protestants received Pike's assurance that any Catholic agitation of the public school fund question and legislation to implement such a division of the fund would meet defeat.[48]

However, nativists wanted a substantive solution to the immigrant and Catholic problem rather than a barrage of prejudicial newspaper editorials and articles. Nativist appeals continued in the newspapers of Louisiana, but by the spring of 1854 these appeals supported the American or Know Nothing Party. The failure of the Whig Party, nationally and locally,[49] left numerous Louisiana Whigs without an effective political vehicle to oppose the Democrats, and the past affinity of the Whigs for political nativism permitted many to join the anti-foreign and anti-Catholic Know Nothings.

One historian has written that the Know Nothing movement in Louisiana began in the late fall of 1853 and early 1854,[50] but there is no mention of its existence in Louisiana until late winter and early spring of 1854. The first notice of this secretive political party appeared during the 1854 New Orleans Municipal election, and its notoriety quickly spread throughout the state. The origins of the party in Louisiana are not clear, but some of the local opponents credited a New Yorker, E. Z. C. Judson, also known as Ned Buntline,[51] with founding the national party and having a hand in establishing local wigwams (lodges) in New Orleans, which were subordinate to Judson's lodge in New York City.[52] It is certainly plausible that Judson played a role in the formation of the party in Louisiana. Edward

Zane Carroll Judson Jr., an American publicist, journalist, and writer of the overstated biography of Wyatt Earp, did come to New Orleans in the early 1850s as an ardent follower of the filibustering expeditions of the late 1840s and early 1850s. He hoped to annex Cuba to the United States and to extend the influence of slavery as a result. He was also an ardent anti-papist and opponent of the Jesuits. While living in St. Louis, Judson (Buntline) became involved in a nativist riot in the 1840s.[53]

The Know Nothing Party was not like the Democratic or Whig parties. As one observer noted, its objectives were part religious and part political. Its end was the disfranchisement of adopted citizens and their exclusion from political office. Because of Louisiana's large Catholic population, it comes as no surprise that Louisiana Know Nothings denied that they were anti-Roman Catholic; opponents, however, claimed that the American Party intended a perpetual war on Catholics.[54]

Admission to national Know Nothing ranks was restrictive. The applicant for admission had to be a native-born citizen, of native-born parents, and could not belong to the Roman Catholic religion. In Louisiana, Know Nothings, understandably, waived the latter requirement. The applicant had to renounce his previous political affiliation and had to cooperate exclusively with the new order. The National American principle requiring a member to hold no "political, civil, or religious intercourse with any person who is a Catholic," and "to use all available means to abolish the political and religious privileges he (meaning any Roman Catholic) may at present enjoy," caused the Louisiana branch of the party continuing problems, particularly in south Louisiana.[55] Know Nothings also had to pledge that they would not vote for anyone for political office who was not a native-born citizen of the United States, nor could Know Nothings vote for someone who might be disposed, if elected, to appoint foreigners or Roman Catholics to any position of "emolument or trust."[56]

Americans organized their party along the lines of a secret fraternal order. Lodges, passwords, signs of recognition, a grip, and challenges were all part of the party. Members, as noted previously, called their lodges "wigwams." Secrecy was so important that members were warned not to divulge the name of the party or any of its proceedings to nonmembers. When questioned about the party, members were instructed to reply, "I know nothing"; therefore, the term "Know Nothing" became a more commonly accepted name for the party. Also used regularly in campaigns was the symbol "Sam." This was readily applied to the American Party and was part of the secrecy surrounding the order.[57]

When seeking admission to a meeting of a local wigwam, the applicant knocked at an outer door a specific number of times. After knocking, he whispered, "What meets here, today, (or night)?" The interrogator behind the door then responded, "I don't know," to which the applicant replied, "I am one," and was then admitted to a second door. At the second door, the applicant rapped four times. While the door was being opened, he whispered to its guard, "Thirteen," and then finally he entered the meeting. Similar signs had to be given upon retiring from a meeting before adjournment, and the members used other signs, warnings, and the grip in public to identify and assist each other.[58] The Americans never published notices of meetings. In fact, in the early days of the party no records of anything concerning the party were kept. Members called emergency meetings by scattering small squares of white paper over the public streets or nailing them to posts.[59]

There were three degrees of membership in the American Party. Between each degree, three weeks had to pass. The First Degree of initiation simply required that the candidate meet the requirements of membership of the party and support its candidates and objectives. The Second Degree permitted those who became eligible to seek public office. The Third Degree, or Union Degree, authored by North Carolina Know Nothing Kenneth Rayner, specifically pledged Know Nothings to "discourage and denounce any and every attempt . . . designed or calculated to subvert [the Union] or weaken its bonds." Clearly, by this time, the sectional controversy had become a threat to the Union. The Third Degree meant to nationalize the party and it pledged the members to support "the Union of these States."[60] That this secret organization with all its ritual made an appearance in New Orleans surprised no one because the city ranked second only to New York City in the number of yearly immigrants. Also, the city had a history of turbulent elections. At first, this nativist movement had an innocuous beginning with a call for a mass meeting to organize an Independent Reform movement. The notice for the meeting, to be held at Lafayette Square in the American section of New Orleans, appeared in the local Whig papers, and announced that the purpose of the meeting was to nominate, irrespective of party, efficient and independent candidates.[61]

The Democrats thought very little of this Independent Reform movement and noted that the organizers of the mass meeting did not specifically mention any reforms they intended to carry out. The Democrats called the movement a "grand burlesque" generated by former Whigs, Native Americans, and the refuse of the Democratic Party to secure the re-election

of Whig office-holders.[62] One anti-Reform Party paper compared the movement to a "hybrid, guerilla [sic] force, free to act according to the views and
interests of each little petty leader who can obtain certain advantages for
himself or his friends."[63]

To prove that the Reform Party had no intention to reform anything,
the *Daily True Delta* and the *Louisiana Courier* brought out some interesting facts about the movement and its candidates. The Independent Reform
Party candidate for city surveyor had the support of nearly every contrac-
tor in the city, and its candidate for mayor, the former Democrat, Colonel
J. W. Breedlove, had been accused by the Whigs of misappropriating public funds when he last held public office.[64] But the most newsworthy accusation against the Reform Party pointed to the involvement of the board
of directors of the New Orleans, Jackson, and Great Northern Railroad
Company in the movement. The *Daily True Delta* reported that some of
the leading reformers were connected with that railroad corporation, one
as director, and that these men had "packed the Know Nothings with [their]
own advantages." Specifically, the paper mentioned Charles Pride and Jesse
Gilmore, Reform candidates for alderman, and Colonel W. S. Campbell,
Reform candidate for assistant alderman.[65]

Throughout the campaign and after the election, the *Daily True Delta*
continued to expose the connection between the railroad directors and
the Know Nothings. The paper believed it had uncovered a vast conspiracy[66] that involved the president and former president of the railroad,
Colonel W. S. Campbell and James Robb, respectively. Campbell had
been a member of the state legislature which approved state aid for that
road, while Robb, who had purchased the bonds for the New Orleans,
Jackson, and Great Northern Railroad at a sizable profit for himself,
was an originator of the Reform or Know Nothing movement. The *True
Delta* also reported that the bond sale had increased the bonded indebt-
edness of New Orleans by five million dollars.[67] To carry on the Reform
campaign, the *True Delta* alleged that Robb and the other Reform "con-
spirators" had assessed railroad companies, candidates, and contractors.
The unsuspecting citizens of the city, who had contributed to Robb's success at the election, thought they had done so in the name of reform.
After the election, the *True Delta* offered further proof that reform had
had no place among the goals of the leaders of the movement. The paper
published a letter from Reform candidate Colonel Campbell in which
he admitted that the movement had been "a mere affair of bribery and
corruption, in which a handful of speculators, unseen, arranged the plot
and directed its execution."[68]

As often happens in a political campaign, the Democratic *Daily True Delta* was guilty of oversimplification and the failure to completely inform the public. Although the *True Delta* alleged that all the Reformers wanted was "to obtain possession of power,"[69] that paper failed to note that before any party can implement a program, political power must first be obtained. The connection between the Reformers and the railroads was not denied by the Reform party, nor were the financial contributions made to that party made by railroad companies and contractors. It was a matter of public record that Colonel Campbell was president and that James Robb had been president of the New Orleans, Jackson, and Great Northern Railroad, and that both were leading members in the Reform Party. In addition, the conspiracy claimed by the *True Delta* lost its credibility when the paper reported that "these plunderers first began to lay the foundation of their nefarious schemes when they were successful in re-writing the constitution."[70] The *True Delta* was alluding to the 1852 constitutional convention at which James Robb and the Whig Party were primarily responsible for the constitutional article permitting the public subscription to railroad companies. However, the *True Delta* omitted any reference to its own 1852 newspaper account that many Democrats had followed the leadership of the Whigs and James Robb in securing this constitutional revision. The paper also failed to tell its Democratic readers that the state's leading Democrat, John Slidell, was very close to Whig and railroad executive James Robb.[71]

The Reform meeting at Lafayette Square may not have addressed itself to specific reforms, but the Reform press did agitate certain problems which it considered needed correcting. These Reform newspapers pointed out that faction and spoilsmen, who served federal politicians and not New Orleans, ruled the city. In addition, fraudulent voting had gotten out of hand, rowdyism controlled a prostituted ballot box, and Irish and German immigrants, ignorant of United States laws, caused the political corruption in the nation and the state.[72] Obviously the Reformers believed their success at the polls would help eliminate corruption, but they also called on the legislature to pass a registry law for the city in order to control the high incidence of fraudulent voting. The Whigs of the state had called for this reform ever since the 1852 Constitution mandated the legislature to pass such a law, but Whigs and now Reformers alleged that Democrats in the assembly and a Democratic governor opposed what they considered a tyrannical measure because New Orleans held the balance of power in state elections.[73]

To a large extent the Reform party remained on the defensive, trying to refute Democratic charges that the Reform ticket was a Whig trick and a prejudiced Know Nothing movement. However, the reformers claimed that most of their candidates belonged to the Democratic Party, and their party would renominate any Democrat who performed well in office. The Democrats denied that most of the Reform candidates were Democrats and that those who belonged to that party were "hackneyed politicians who have been thrown aside before."[74] The so-called reformers were nevertheless closely related to Louisiana businessmen and throughout their existence in Louisiana continued to promote their nonpartisanship even though they inherited many of its members and principles from the Whig Party. As historian Frank Towers writes in his study on urban history of the southern Know Nothings, "former Whigs ran the American party" in New Orleans and in St. Louis.[75]

The alleged bigotry of the Reform Party and its association with Know Nothingism proved to be a more serious allegation than the charge of its being a Whig trick. Democrats searched in vain for a naturalized citizen on the Independent Reform ticket,[76] and predicted proscription of the foreign-born citizen if this secret organization succeeded on Election Day. The *Daily True Delta* reiterated its assertion that the Know Nothings intended not to reform, "but to stigmatize as unworthy to share in the government of New Orleans everyone not born on the soil."[77] This same newspaper published some interesting statistics in refutation of the Reformers' charges that "foreigners ruled us." In 1854, Louisiana had one hundred and sixty-eight important federal, state, congressional, Orleans Parish, and city offices, and only thirty-two individuals of foreign origin or naturalized citizens filled those positions.[78]

When Know Nothingism made its first appearance in the city, Democrats put Roman Catholics on their guard.[79] Opponents of the Know Nothing Independent Reform ticket stressed that the organization had religious as well as political objectives. These religious objectives, according to the Democrats, included perpetual war on Catholics. The *Daily True Delta* printed what it termed the "cardinal principles" of the Know Nothings, which restricted membership in the organization to "native-born citizens, of native born parents, and not of the Catholic religion," and disallowed "political, civil, nor religious intercourse" with Catholics. Most important, a Know Nothing could not vote for a Catholic candidate.

The sizable Catholic population in New Orleans had to be considered by both parties in this New Orleans election. Many of these Catholics had been members of the Whig Party, the party which the Democrats now alleged had thrown its support behind the bigoted Reform ticket. The Reformers denied the anti-Catholic charges, as they had denied any anti-foreign animus, and their ticket, Reformers noted, did include Catholic candidates. The Reform ticket listed twelve Catholic candidates out of forty-two.[80] However, one explanation for Catholics joining a party hostile to their religion was that with the Whig Party virtually defunct, many Catholic Whigs, most of whom were Creoles who opposed the John Slidell Democracy, simply did not feel comfortable in the Democratic Party.[81] The major issues of the 1830s and 1840s may have become obsolete, but the animosity these ex-Whigs had for the Democrats had not.

The campaign created tremendous excitement, and as expected, Election Day brought violence at the polls. The charges of anti-foreignism, anti-Roman Catholicism, and personal attacks exacerbated the situation, and culminated in riots and murder. The Seventh Precinct witnessed two murders, the attempted murder of the police chief, and the destruction of the ballot box.[82] The Reformers accused the Irish of voting illegally and condemned the police for being in the forefront of the disturbances.[83] Once again, the Reformers demanded that the legislature follow the mandate of the new constitution and pass a registry law for the city.[84] Despite all their protests of fraud, the Reform Party won control of the municipal government. Even though their candidate for mayor lost, they captured the other key citywide positions and a majority of the alderman and assistant alderman seats.[85] This success in New Orleans led to a reduced police force, a reduction in funding for the police, and foreign-born Democrats on the force losing their jobs. The force went from 38 percent Native American to 78 percent native in 1855. The police force also became too small and ineffective and became a source of Know Nothing patronage.[86]

While the Democrats despaired over their defeat in the city,[87] events following the success of the Reformers in New Orleans must have given the Democracy additional cause for alarm. It soon became apparent that the Democratic Party could expect significant statewide Know Nothing opposition. Former Whig papers throughout the state applauded the Reformers' success in New Orleans and approved "the end of vote buying, voting the dead, and that rightful sovereigns of the country will be able to vote without intimidation."[88] These papers reported that members of the Know Nothing Party could be found in every section of Louisiana. New Orleans purportedly had several wigwams and between one and five thousand members.[89] A Know Nothing meeting in East Baton Rouge Parish condoned the violence in the New Orleans election if reform required that action.[90] Located in Iberville and St. Mary parishes, and the Red River region were lodges whose members were "good and respectable" gentlemen who conducted their meetings "with order and decorum."[91] From Catahoula Parish the *Harrisonburg Independent*, although it disdained the title of a Know Nothing organ, it was "disposed to give it (Know Nothingism) . . . aid and assistance."[92]

In addition to their election triumph in New Orleans, the Know Nothings also gained victories in other areas of the state. Despite Democratic attacks on the Know Nothings in Clinton[93] the party succeeded in electing E. T. Herrick as district judge for East and West Feliciana parishes,[94] a notable achievement since the Felicianas had previously supported the Democracy. In two separate special legislative elections, one in New Orleans and another in East Baton Rouge Parish, Know Nothing candidates won seats in the state assembly. These two victories were particularly noteworthy because in New Orleans the Know Nothing Party swept the election, which, ironically included a Catholic candidate, and they now showed strength in formerly solid Democratic East Baton Rouge.[95] Finally, from Thibodaux the senior editor of the *Thibodaux Minerva* felt no regrets over the rise of Know Nothingism and looked "upon the results of the late state elections as harbingers of the purity of the elective franchise."[96]

This rapidly growing Know Nothing order used every opportunity during the remainder of 1854 to express itself on various topics, but the rhetoric did not change drastically from that used in New Orleans. Anti-foreign, anti-Roman Catholic, and the spirit of '76 sentiment filled the speeches, editorials, and lecture halls whenever nativists wrote or spoke.[97] The adverse effects of a large-scale immigration policy received much attention from the Know Nothings. According to them, the "dregs of European life" arrived yearly in the United States in such large numbers that they subsequently contributed to the rising crime rate, a leveling tendency of democracy, the pauperism that the immigrant brought, the lawlessness at elections, and they even prospered at the expense of natives.[98] The Americans asserted that the tendency of the immigrants to band together upon arriving in the United States made them easy prey for demagogic politicians who contributed to foreigners' undue political influence.[99] Know Nothing newspapers carried excerpts from George Washington's "Farewell Address," warning natives of the evils of foreign influence, and printed patriotic poetry and sayings.[100] Patriotic literature would not remedy the problems of immigration. The panacea for nativists remained the extension of the naturalization period, and as soon as possible the repeal of all naturalization laws.[101]

Not only did the nativists want an extension of the naturalization law, or its total repeal, they were ever alert to any legislation that would encourage further immigration. The possibility of Congress passing a homestead bill received no support from the Louisiana Know Nothing Party. According to Know Nothings, a homestead bill would result in more decadent foreigners coming to the United States, and because of their large numbers they would soon control the government. The only purpose of such a bill, alleged the Know Nothing press, was "to swindle honest men for the benefit of rogues." Know Nothings noted that with increased immigration, pauperism had risen and American labor had been driven from employment as well.[102] The Democratic *Daily True Delta* refuted these nativists' arguments against a homestead bill, and argued that such a bill would advance the United States by peopling unproductive territory. The same paper did not believe that immigration had or would hurt American labor, stressing that the country needed more immigrant labor. Louisiana already had a labor shortage that resulted in wages on the levees of New Orleans as high as four and five dollars a day. If the labor scarcity continued, wages would continue to climb, hence the *True Delta* hoped the Know Nothings could find a substitute for the immigrant labor that they feared.[103]

During these discussions over a homestead bill, the *New Orleans Bee* raised a crucial point for the South and Louisiana. The *Bee* might have agreed with the *Daily True Delta* about a labor shortage, but to this Know Nothing Party, the stakes were higher. If Europeans, who knew little about or were opposed to slavery, primarily peopled the territories, the institution of slavery would be endangered.[104] The issue of slavery had destroyed the Whig Party, and the Know Nothings understood its divisive qualities. Many of the former Whigs now in the American Party tried to persuade their former northern colleagues not to adopt any issues that included agitating the slavery issue. So aware of the divisiveness of slavery were the Know Nothings that at the 1854 National Council meeting at Cincinnati, they adopted North Carolina Kenneth Rayner's Third Degree of membership, the Union Degree. The Union or Third Degree required from those who took a pledge of fidelity to the Union and "to seek an amicable adjustment of all political differences that threatened its continuance."[105] Louisiana Know Nothings demonstrated a determination to uphold the "Third Degree" in their opposition to Senator Douglas's Nebraska bill. The Know Nothing papers of the state called the bill "injudicious and unnecessary," arguing that the repeal of the Missouri Compromise Line would do nothing more than renew the agitation of the slavery question. Kansas-Nebraska would "give new life to the fanaticism of the North" while accomplishing nothing for the South. According to the Know Nothing press, slavery could not exist there,[106] and, indeed, they wondered why Missouri and Kentucky had remained slave states for so long.[107] It is interesting, however, that prior to the formal introduction of Know Nothingism into Louisiana, the opinions on the Nebraska bill differed. On March 13, 1854, Duncan Kenner, a Whig from Ascension Parish, submitted a joint resolution which stated:

> that the Nebraska territorial bill, now pending in Congress, so far as designed to carry into effect and perpetuate this principle of non-intervention as to the institution of slavery, meets our approval and we request our Senators and Representative to support the same.

Two days later, the resolution received unanimous approval.[108] Kenner and several other senators who would become members of the Know Nothing Party had at this time no objections to the Nebraska bill.

Whereas the Know Nothings thought the Nebraska bill was "injudicious," the Democrats believed Douglas's bill attempted to "carry out in good faith the Compromise of 1850."[109] The Democrats took issue with the Know Nothing Party that the Missouri Compromise was "irrepealable," arguing that the doctrine of nonintervention should apply to Kansas and Nebraska.[110] The Democrats discovered that slavery was a serious threat to the unity of the national Know Nothing Party, and Louisiana Democrats quickly took advantage of the weakness. Therefore, not only would the Louisiana Know Nothings have to defend themselves from the charges of anti-foreignism and anti-Catholicism, but now the local nativists had to deny the Democratic accusations that free-soil proclivities tinged their northern Know Nothings colleagues.[111]

Historians have recognized that a large number of northern Know Nothings were antislavery. The "slave power" rhetoric had played well in the North and often was an equal partner with the pope as subverting American liberty. Stephen Maizlish, for example, argues that in the North antislavery was responsible for the American party's strength and to some northern nativists, "Catholicism was itself a form of slavery." Historian William Gienapp agrees with Maizlish that along with temperance and nativism, an anti-southernism and antislavery caused party realignment in the mid-1850s. Gienapp also sees northern Know Nothing warring against an American proslavery platform because it would destroy the party in the North. Other recent studies on northern Americans similarly believe that an anti-southern bias, or the idea of the slaveocracy's unchecked political power, was strong within the northern American fold. Finally, for southern Americans, Michael Holt believes that the antislavery radicalism attached to the northern branch of the American Party was devastating for many Know Nothing candidates in the South.[112]

Clearly, the northern Americans' antislavery views were a problem for Louisiana Americans that continued to distress Know Nothings in the state. Yet, there were other issues that bedeviled the party in Louisiana. The anti-foreign stance of the Know Nothings provoked numerous attacks from unsympathetic Louisianans because of the anti-republican posture of the party. But the recently concluded New Orleans election demonstrated that the Know Nothing position on Catholicism could prove to be a greater liability. Nevertheless, the party continued to deny any anti-Catholic sentiment or any intention to interfere with any religion or sect. One sympathetic paper reported that "it [Know Nothingism] is no more hostile to Catholicism than any other religion if it keeps within its sphere."[113] Of course, the sphere Know Nothings wanted Roman Catholics to eschew was the temporal or secular. Then, too, nativists continued their opposition to the accumulation of power and wealth of the Catholic Church as typified by New York Archbishop Hughes's attempts to vest control of New York church property in the hierarchy of the church. Although Louisiana had no religious leader comparable to Archbishop Hughes to excite the nativists, the Irish Catholic attempt to divide the public school fund created considerable agitation in the state. Finally, and ironically, there was nothing more frightening to the secretive Know Nothings than the secretive Jesuits, described by the Know Nothing Party as "a designing, scheming, and dangerous secret political order." Of course, the Democrats made good use of the Americans' bigotry and were always alert to using it politically. John Slidell wrote to a fellow Democrat in Ascension Parish, W. W. Pugh, that the National Know Nothing anti-Catholic plank would prove to be detrimental to the Americans in the heavily Catholic Second Congressional District.[114]

The prejudice of the Know Nothing Party against Roman Catholics was obvious from the bigoted sentiments expressed in its political organs. Therefore, how could some Louisiana Roman Catholics belong to a political party with the avowed objective of carrying on perpetual war on Catholics?[115] In addition to denying that the party proscribed Catholics, many members of the Know Nothing society pointed out that Louisiana was an exception to the anti-Catholicism that characterized Know Nothingism elsewhere. For example, the staunch nativist and Know Nothing representative from New York, Thomas R. Whitney, had nothing but praise for Catholics in

Louisiana.[116] But critics of the party, citing the 1854 elections in New Orleans as an example, alleged that the only reason the Reform ticket had included Roman Catholics was a ruse to attract additional members from the Roman Catholic and Creole areas of the city.[117] However, the most believable reason for Roman Catholic participation appeared in the Creole Catholic newspaper, the *New Orleans Semi-Weekly Creole*. This Know Nothing paper discussed the liberal views of the Creole Catholics of Louisiana who had brought from France "the opinions of the Gallican Catholic Church, which is diametrically opposed to any assumption of political or secular authority by the Pope or by any of his priesthood." The *Semi-Weekly Creole* noted that a vast difference existed between the Gallican and other Catholics.[118] Commenting on the speeches of the converted Catholic Orestes Brownson during his visit to New Orleans, the *Semi-Weekly Creole* demonstrated its liberal Gallican position. It warned its readers that, according to Brownson, "God makes known his authority only through the instrumentality of the Pope—an Italian prince—to the utter exclusion of such plain republicans as Franklin Pierce or Roger B. Taney." According to the *Semi-Weekly Creole*, this belief in papal authority was not consistent with the Americanism of Louisiana Catholic Creoles, who would not permit the pope or his bishops to "interpret their rights as native born Americans." Apparently some Americans on the national level believed the writer since they did distinguish between those Catholics who did accept the pope's temporal power and those who did not. [119]

Of course, the official newspaper of the Catholic diocese, the *Propagateur Catholique*, had no reservations about the anti-Catholic posture of the Know Nothing Party. And Know Nothing denials of bigotry were difficult to believe while Know Nothing papers criticized Roman Catholic priests, attacked Catholic ideology, and referred to Catholicism as anti-republicanism.[120] The *Propagateur Catholique* warned Catholics that they were not allowed membership in the organization, and above all the hatred of Catholicism was paramount among Know Nothing objectives.[121]

THREE

Know Nothingism at Its Peak: 1854–55

By the close of 1854, virtually every part of Louisiana had come into contact with the Know Nothing Party. The party had experienced some local success at the polls, particularly in New Orleans, and numerous Whig newspapers threw their support behind the new movement.[1] The members of the party had every reason to be optimistic for its future. The state elections of 1855 and the 1856 presidential campaign offered the Know Nothings an opportunity to test their strength statewide. The 1854 victory in New Orleans and the widespread newspaper support made the Americans confident that they could win a state election. So confident were they that soon after their success in New Orleans the American press quickly began speculating on prospective gubernatorial and even presidential candidates.

Before the state campaign began, the Americans continued to win at the polls in 1855. In north Louisiana, Americans elected the entire municipal ticket in Farmerville (Union Parish), and the voters of Morehouse Parish, also in north Louisiana, elected a Know Nothing to the state legislature.[2] From Iberville Parish, in south Louisiana, the *Southern Sentinel* reported that "Sam had a glorious triumph" in the Plaquemine municipal election, winning a majority of the positions of selectman. The *Sentinel* also noted that three-fourths of the voters against the American Party had been foreigners.[3] Moreover, the nativists succeeded in the Clinton municipal election, controlled the police juries of East Feliciana and St. Landry parishes, as well as the town government of Washington, and they evenly divided the town government with the Democrats in Opelousas.[4] In addition, the Americans succeeded in electing their candidate, E. T. Merrick, as chief justice of the Louisiana Supreme Court. Know Nothings also won judicial elections on the district level.[5] Finally, the nativist press gleefully reported that Governor Hébert had become disenchanted with his Democratic Party and was contemplating a Know Nothing alliance.[6]

These early victories by the American Party can perhaps best be explained by noting that the Know Nothings capitalized on a general feeling of distrust of the "old politics" in Louisiana. Similar to an anti-party feeling in the nation, many Louisianians believed that the political structure of the state needed reform, and the Know Nothings believed that politicians had abused the naturalization laws and the franchise. They objected to the way both Whigs and Democrats truckled to foreigners. However, Americans singled out the Democrats in particular for their demagogic appeals to, and the manipulation of, the foreign-born to achieve their goals.[7] Know Nothings struck a nerve with their nativist rhetoric and offered Native Americans a return to what they called the purity of former days. William Evitts calls the attraction for the nativists a reaction to the view that "politics continued to be an object of scorn."[8] One American explained the rise of the Know Nothings in the following manner:

> The Know Nothing party was at first a Reform party. The evils to reform were frauds upon our naturalization laws and elective franchise. The party was to elect people to secure a registry law as directed by the state constitution and the eventual repeal of the naturalization laws by Congress. To this end native born Americans are to be voted for. All political wire-working, trickery, and demagoguism were regarded as foreign influence.[9]

From its inception in New Orleans and, with varying degrees of importance, throughout its existence, the American Party continually stressed the necessity to reform the political process and to maintain native control over politics. Historian Frank Towers writes that the American Party's leaders focused on the anti-corruption theme in the South's three largest cities, including New Orleans, and he notes that the American Party was not "old wine in new bottles." Instead, Towers sees a continuity in the leadership of the new party. To Towers, who recognizes the reform mentality in the American Party, the status of party leadership, "the exclusion of poor men and political newcomers from positions of power," continued and was inherited from the Jacksonian era. This was certainly true in Louisiana. At this time, native control over Louisiana politics was assured since there were only two foreign-born members who sat in the Louisiana Assembly.[10]

Of all the early victories, the Americans' greatest success before the state election was in the New Orleans municipal election. In 1854, the Independent Reform movement had made great strides but failed to capture control either of the Board of Aldermen or the executive branch of government. Both parties kept issues at a minimum with the Americans noting the Democratic "fraternization" with the foreign vote while the Democracy accused the so-called reformers in the city council of raising taxes and permitting the bonds of the city to be "dishonored."[11] The Know Nothing Party won the violence-plagued election and each party accused the other of precipitating the violence. The Democrats also charged the nativists with refusing to accept the votes of numerous naturalized citizens. But the Americans ignored this allegation and, with control of the city council, the Know Nothings solidified their position in the city. The Know Nothing-controlled city council then impeached the two remaining Democratic recorders, giving the Americans control of the police as well as the legislative branch of government.[12]

Actually, the Know Nothing victories temporarily overshadowed several weaknesses inherent in the party. In forthcoming campaigns, these weaknesses would be widely publicized by the opponents of the American Party. Certain aspects of the society had been denounced as anti-republican, prescriptive, and deceptive. Opponents continually called Know Nothingism a Whig trick and a movement closely allied with abolitionism in the North. Its secrecy and sophomoric rituals brought ridicule and abuse from the anti-American press. But anti-foreign and anti-Roman Catholic policy, especially the latter, resulted in the most vehement opposition in Louisiana. The nativists attempted to quiet the criticism by compromising some of the major principles upon which the National Order had been founded, but in the process, the state party lost its credibility with the National Council, its own members, and some of the voters of Louisiana.

One continuing problem of the American Party that contributed to its loss of credibility was the Democratic accusation that Know Nothingism was a Whig trick. This was a problem in other southern states, as well. In North Carolina and Tennessee, for example, most of the members of the new party had been former Whigs.[13] In Louisiana, however, across the state Know Nothing newspapers denied the charge and quickly pointed out that their party was composed of both Whigs and Democrats.[14] In fact, Americans noted that the Democratic Party nominated former Whigs. And some Democratic newspapers, such as the *Louisiana Courier*, reported that the anti-Know Nothing movement consisted of both Whigs and Democrats.[15]

Both parties were correct. Whigs and Democrats did join the American movement. The most notable Democrat who joined the Americans was Charles Gayarré. But there were less famous Democrats, such as J. H. Kilpatrick and John Young, both of Caddo Parish. Kilpatrick had been a former Democratic nominee for the state legislature in 1852 and a Franklin Pierce appointee as United States Attorney for the Western District of Louisiana.[16] During the 1855 gubernatorial campaign, the Know Nothings proudly pointed to the four former Democrats on the American State ticket.[17] Also, Democratic allegations that Know Nothingism was a Whig trick became easier to deny when a prominent Whig like Judah P. Benjamin spoke out against the American Party. Benjamin assisted Americans even further in refuting the Whig trick assertion when he drifted into Democratic ranks.[18]

Other prominent Whigs repudiated Know Nothingism. On June 18, 1855, former Whig associate judge of the Louisiana Supreme Court, Pierre A. Rost, addressed the Democratic State Convention in Baton Rouge. He had harsh words for the Americans and soon became involved with the Democratic Party.[19] Know Nothing editors, among them the editor of the *Thibodaux Minerva*, found it difficult to understand why some Whigs opposed the American Party. Identifying the Democratic Party as the foreign party, this editor asserted that Henry Clay, a good Whig, would "stick by the American party"[20] if he were alive. Another Know Nothing editor, this one from Baton Rouge, took the offensive and called the Democratic Party a Whig trick.[21] In the late 1850s, more former Whigs, and for that matter Americans, joined the Democratic Party. However, the desertion to the Democratic Party occurred more as a result of the failure of the Know Nothings to emerge as the majority party. The American Party, however, had never failed before to attract large numbers of former Whigs.[22]

The southern American Party did attract a large majority of former Whigs to its ranks. While the Know Nothing movement was more than "Whiggery in disguise" and there was not "a one-to-one correspondence between Whigs and Know nothings," former Whigs did make up a majority of its membership in Louisiana. The traditional historical interpretation overwhelmingly adheres to this opinion; my quantitative data also support this view. Michael Holt in his *The Rise and Fall of the American Whig Party* agrees as well. For Holt, most of the Whigs in the state "embraced it [the Know Nothing Party] in 1855."[23] When the Whig Party collapsed after 1853, many southern Whigs felt politically stranded. Marc Kruman's North Carolina Whigs also fit into this mold, and he does not even think

North Carolina Whigs necessarily joined the Know Nothings because of American Party ideology but because it was the only alternative to the Democrats. Another historian, J. Mills Thornton, finds the Americans in Alabama did well in the "usual Whig constituencies, the Black Belt and in the southwest parts of Alabama." After having contested the Democratic Party for two decades, the majority of the Whigs in the South and Louisiana refused to join that party, particularly since the Whigs "believed that the foreign-born Irish and other foreigners were being voted against them."[24] For example, Charles Gayareé, a former Democrat, was a vocal critic of the Democratic leadership and its Election Day frauds.[25] Therefore, to remain politically active former Whigs found the American Party a suitable vehicle to oppose the Democracy.

Whether made up of former Whigs, old Democrats, or "new" men, previous historians of the American Party in Louisiana have generally characterized the Know Nothing leadership as representative of the old, wealthy, and slave-owning aristocracy of the state. To these historians, the Americans were the conservative property holders who were first Whigs, then Know Nothings. Or, they were businessmen and lawyers who represented the urban mercantile interests. Conversely, they portray the Democrats as small yeoman farmers or city workingmen.[26]

The career of former Whig Charles Derbigny, who became a Know Nothing, seems to support the suggestion that Americans, like the Whigs, represented the planter and urban and commercial groups with their ties to the legal profession. Derbigny, the son of former Governor Pierre Derbigny, was from an old Louisiana Creole family. Charles studied medicine in Paris, but returned to Louisiana when his father died in an accident. He then studied law and became a member of the state legislature, serving at one time as president of the state senate. In 1845, the Native American Party nominated Derbigny as its gubernatorial candidate. He finished third in a three-way race that year, and lost again in 1855 as the gubernatorial nominee of the American Party. In addition to his legal and legislative career, Derbigny was a sugar planter with large holdings in both Lafourche and Jefferson parishes.[27]

Many leaders of Louisiana's antebellum parties, however, were members of the elite. The careers of many Democrats of this time did not vary much from that of the Whig Derbigny's. Democrats Thomas J. Semmes and G. W. Munday were both distinguished members of the state legislature. Semmes, who moved to New Orleans in 1850, studied at both Georgetown College and Harvard Law School. President James Buchanan appointed him United States

District Attorney for Louisiana in 1858. Munday was a prominent and well-to-do planter of East Feliciana Parish. Starting his business career as owner of a Clinton newspaper, Munday subsequently became deputy sheriff, parish policy juror, and assessor of his parish, in addition to his legislative career.[28]

To be sure, social, economic, and ideological differences did exist between the Know Nothings and Democrats in the 1850s. A recent historian has inferred that the Americans "espoused a social philosophy . . . to which Whigs had been committed for more than two decades" and that was quite different from that of the Democrats' "politics of conflict." For example, one American wrote of his candidate as "a conservative and sincere politician" while the Democrats were "always stirring up storms."[29] If Americans were truly heirs of the Whig Party, this assessment seems to reinforce the opinion of Charles Grier Sellers Jr. In his study of southern Whigs, Sellers writes that the Democratic "measures for extending political democracy, inclined propertied and conservative men to rally to the Whig party as a bulwark against mobocracy."[30] However, were the Americans in Louisiana only facsimiles of the Whigs? Were the members the old, conservative, propertied, and stable crop planters tied to the urban commercial elements of the state pictured by the earlier view, and were the Democrats the small yeoman farmers and men on the make?[31] This characterization of Know Nothings and Democrats is overly simplistic and does not fit the profile of Louisiana's political leaders.

One profession that offered several advantages for an aspiring young man was the law. William Barney, in his study of the political leadership in Mississippi and Alabama in 1860, discusses these advantages in some detail. Generally, as Barney notes, lawyers had access to political and economic information which enabled them to acquire wealth and status in their local areas. As soon as possible, these "lawyer-politicians" invested their money in plantations and slaves, which was the ultimate achievement of most southern men of that day.[32]

However, lawyers clearly favored the Democratic Party to a greater degree than the Know Nothing Party.[33] As one historian has noted, the Democratic Party "promised the most rapid advancement."[34] In Louisiana, the Democrats not only attracted the younger lawyers, who would have been interested in rapid advancement, but it also won more adherents among the lawyers over forty years old than did the Know Nothings. Of the four major occupational classes which I used in this study,[35] the legal profession provided the second largest number of Democrats. Conversely, the members of the American Party found law to be less attractive than the other occupations.[36]

If the earlier view is correct at all, Americans should have had strong support from the town business interests with their connection to northern capital. However, the businessmen and artisans of the towns[37] did not support one party to a greater extent than the other. More of the town middle class supported the Know Nothing Party than the Democratic Party—26 percent as opposed to 23 percent, but the difference is obviously not significant.[38] The only noticeable difference among the town middle class was their place of nativity. Although both parties drew equal support among those born in the Deep South, those party members born in the Upper South and North generally gave greater support to the American Party than to the Democratic Party.[39]

Party leadership in urban New Orleans, with its business interests, cosmopolitan attitude, and large immigrant population, does not completely conform to the earlier view either. Democrats had greater strength among those politicians who were fifty years old and over, and with greater wealth than the Americans. In addition, the Know Nothings, while not attracting older or even wealthier members, did receive support from those of all age groups, but worth less than $25,000. Even though these findings contradict the earlier view, the Democratic Party in New Orleans did have a greater percentage of its political leaders from those younger and less wealthy individuals.[40] Among those politicians for whom data could be found, the Americans engaged more in commerce and industry, with ties to northern capital, than did the Democrats. Both parties in the city had a few foreign-born leaders. However, the Democrats of foreign birth were from Ireland and Germany, while the Americans were from France or former French possessions.[41] Because the American Party had continually disparaged Irish and German immigrants, it is not surprising that the Irish and Germans avoided the Know Nothings.

While it is equally unsurprising that throughout Louisiana slaveholding planters and farmers dominated both parties, further probing of who was a typical leader of the Know Nothings and Democrats does not conform to the traditional view. Of the four major occupation types, planters and farmers who owned slaves constituted 57 percent of the American Party leadership and 49 percent of the Democratic leadership. Know Nothing planters, those who held twenty or more slaves, had a slight edge over the Democrats, 38 percent to 36 percent. Yet these figures hardly reflect the earlier view of Overdyke, Soulé, and Shugg. But more interesting, Know Nothings also led the Democrats in the group of farmers who owned fewer than twenty slaves. According to Shugg, it was this latter group who supposedly favored the

Democratic Party because that party favored an expanding slave economy and the reopening of the African slave trade, all of which better suited ambitious small slave owners since it would reduce the cost of slaves.[42] In addition, the Democrats did well among the older planters (18 percent to 11 percent for the American Party), and the American Party received more support from younger slaveholding planters, those under forty years old—again a group considered partial to the slave expansion rhetoric of the Democrats.[43]

Large slaveholdings and great wealth were not always synonymous with Know Nothingism in Louisiana, as has been traditionally thought. In those Democratic parishes[44] of 1855 with a large concentration of slave ownership, wealthier politicians supported the Democratic Party more than the American Party. Whether young or old, 45 percent of the Democratic leaders in these parishes can be classified as wealthy. On the other hand, Know Nothing success among wealthier politicians was limited to 26 percent of their total leadership in these parishes. This lack of strength among the older wealthy is particularly evident because the largest percentage (43 percent) of the American leadership in these parishes came from those under forty and with personal fortunes valued less than $25,000.[45] In these parishes, the assignment of older wealth to Know Nothings does not stand up.

Americans did do better among older and wealthier politicians in those parishes won by the Democrats in 1855 in which slave ownership was of moderate proportions. Conversely, the Democrats did better among the yeomanry. Older wealth increased significantly for the Americans, 27 percent to 9 percent for the Democrats. The Democratic Party attracted over one-fourth of its leadership in these parishes from those under forty and worth less than $25,000.[46]

Once I disregarded slave ownership, in those parishes carried by the Democratic party in 1855, the preference for the American Party increased with greater wealth. Only in the forty-to-forty-nine-year-old age group did the Democratic leadership outnumber the Americans. The effect of older wealth in this circumstance partially sustains the earlier historical opinion since that group gave solid support to the American Party.[47] However, it is interesting to discover that in those Know Nothing parishes in 1855 older wealth supported the Democracy. It was from the wealthy, younger, and middle-aged political leaders that the Americans received their greatest strength. One possible explanation for this fact is that my findings for Terrebonne Parish indicate that many very young American leaders obviously inherited or acquired great wealth and large numbers of slaves from deceased or older family members.[48] Still, increased wealth among the political leaders in general increased their preference for the American Party.[49]

To further confuse the situation, if the politics of an area is disregarded, younger wealth, surprisingly, tended to support the Know Nothing Party. Know Nothings under forty, and worth over $50,000, constituted 13 percent of the political leaders of their party, while the Democrats in that group accounted for only 2 percent of the total leadership of their party.[50] Nor does older wealth fit the traditional view for Louisiana. First, older wealth was virtually even in its support of Know Nothings and Democrats. Secondly, Democrats actually led in this fifty and over age group with property valued over $50,000 by one percentage point, 11 percent to 10 percent.[51]

Once all variables are excluded, there is little difference in age between the American and Democratic party leadership. Know Nothing political leaders, contrary to the earlier view, were not older than their Democratic counterparts. In fact, what difference in age that did exist statewide runs counter to the earlier view. Know Nothings held a two percent edge in the under-forty age group (43 percent versus 41 percent), while the Democrats in the fifty-and-over group held a one percent margin (27 percent versus 26 percent). In the forty-to-forty-nine age group, the percentage was 31 and 32 for the Know Nothings and Democrats, respectively.[52] Furthermore, the median age for both parties was forty-one. The mean age for both parties also contradicts the earlier view. The average age for the American Party was forty-two, while Democratic leaders on the average were forty-three.[53]

From these statistics, it is readily apparent that political leadership in the state during the existence of the American Party can be characterized quite differently than the earlier held view. The American Party was not simply the party of old, wealthy and large slaveholding planters with their commercial connections. Many Americans did fit this description, but there was not any real difference in age between Democrats and Americans, and significant wealth was not confined to the American leadership. Where older wealth did support the Americans, it was in those areas of Louisiana that did not have large concentrations of slave ownership. Older wealth was virtually even in its support of both parties, and younger wealth (regardless of party strength in the area) tended to support the Know Nothing Party. It is true that the Americans had a slight edge in the planter category, but they also led in the group of farmers who owned fewer than twenty slaves. Also, there was no overwhelming preference among the commercial interests in the state for the American Party, nor did the lawyers of Louisiana clearly favor the Americans.

Charles E. A. Gayarré (Louisiana politician)

Therefore, the broad traditional generalizations used to describe the political leadership in Louisiana during the mid-1850s simply do not apply. The American Party was as successful as the Democrats in recruiting individuals from various social and economic segments of the state.

Even though the strength of the American Party came from no one particular segment of society, all members—whether former Whigs, old or
young, wealthy or not—could and did agree on their dislike of foreigners.
Know Nothings did not compromise this particular principle of their party.
Perhaps it is ironic that a political party that owed its existence to a hatred
of foreigners should achieve its widest acceptance at a time when foreign
immigration declined in the United States and Louisiana.[54] Nevertheless,
the anti-foreignism of the Know Nothings was unremitting, and very likely
was a crucial reason for the existence of the party in the state. On this question of anti-foreignism, Charles Gayarré believed that "the Know Nothing
party had no other ostensible object than that of excluding foreigners from
participating in the administration of the affairs of the country, of securing
the purity of elections."[55]

Gayarré believed, as did the American Party, that the "disorders in the
administration of our public affairs" could be attributed to the constantly
growing foreign influence upon men in public office. The growing political influence of the foreign-born in turn resulted in fraud, corruption, and
intimidation during campaigns, and the subsequent election of dishonest
men. Gayarré concluded that foreign influence had caused the decline in
statesmanship and he often lectured the voters of Louisiana when he noted
that the United States would not have become so corrupt "if you had not
permitted your cradle to become the drain into which has rushed with an
appalling velocity the huge flood of the dregs and impurities of the rest of
the world."[56]

The portrait of the immigrant that appeared in the nativist press of the
state was that of an ignorant, illiterate pauper. One nativist newspaper used
the 1850 census to illustrate that one in every thirty-seven foreigners was
a pauper while only one in every 317 Americans was poverty-stricken.[57]
Nativists also characterized the immigrant as a criminal who filled the prisons, workhouses, and penitentiaries. Nativists thought it was hopeless to
Americanize what they called "the serfs of Europe"; and the immigrant's
inability to appreciate the laws, liberties, and privileges of the nation led to
their corruption by venal politicians.[58]

Much of what the Know Nothing press printed about foreign immigrants and their impoverished condition was true. The assertion that they
made up a disproportionate percentage of the inmates of public hospitals
and prisons was also true.[59] But, according to the anti-nativist press, the
statistics that the Know Nothings paraded in front of the voters misled the
public. What the Know Nothings failed to publicize was that part of the

funding for Charity Hospital came from a tax upon immigrants arriving in the United States. And most of those foreigners admitted to public hospitals, claimed the friends of the immigrants, needed treatment only as a result of injuries or diseases sustained from honest labors.[60]

Not only did the American Party despise the immigrant because of his debased social and economic condition which drained the public coffers, but the party bitterly criticized the political manipulation of the foreign-born. This political manipulation of the foreign-born had been a common complaint of nativists in the past, and the Know Nothing Party believed catering to the foreign-born resulted in the government falling into the hands of foreigners and demagogues. As Gayarré alleged, foreigners received the blame for Election Day frauds and riots whenever and wherever they occurred.[61]

In every election, particularly those which the Know Nothing Party lost, the significance of the foreign vote received constant publicity. New Orleans nativists responded most energetically to what they termed the Democratic fraternization with the large foreign vote. The *Bee* denied that foreign influence was insignificant, as claimed by the anti-nativist press, and it asserted that the foreign vote held the balance of power.[62] Ever alert to the illegal use of foreigners, the American press attacked the Democrats for again "manufacturing voters" in that city.[63] However, Know Nothings in the rural parishes were not unaware of the foreigners' effect on the outcome of elections. Nativist newspapers in Plaquemine and Opelousas reported that local elections in their parishes in 1855 had gone against the Know Nothing Party because of foreigners. In Grand Coteau, the Americans lost to "the anti-American party," and one nativist asserted that it was "a sorry state when native citizens are thrust aside and foreigners preferred." The editor of the *Plaquemine Southern Sentinel* estimated that the foreign vote constituted over 50 percent of the anti-Know Nothing majority in the nativist defeat in Iberville Parish.[64]

The Louisiana Know Nothing Party not only deprecated the debased condition of the foreign-born and the chaos they caused on Election Day, but the nativists, remembering the break-up of the Whigs over the growing sectional controversy and the American Party's focus on the Union, reminded the electorate that the foreign population had an antipathy for the South's peculiar institution. The remarks of the *Daily True Delta* had no foundation, according to the Americans, when that paper stated that "if they [Know Nothings] were deprived of their foreign pauper argument the party would be bankrupt in electioneering capital."[65] The Know Nothings in the state capitalized on the alleged foreign opposition to slavery, and the Americans believed they had ample proof for their claims. One naturalized citizen, who had agreed with the nativists on the wretched conditions of the immigrants, also helped to prove what the local party had reported since it first appeared in the state.[66] This individual advised those contemplating emigrating to the United States to avoid the South since they would have to compete with slave labor, which he thoroughly despised.[67] It was no secret in Louisiana that foreigners, particularly the Germans, avoided the South because of the competition with slave labor. These recently arrived immigrants often became the greatest exponents of free-soil ideas, according to the American press.[68] Even the German immigrants who remained in New Orleans found it difficult to "find a middle path between their natural German abolitionism and their Southern environment." So strong did the Germans feel about slavery that no "German newspaper in South or North accepted advertising dealing with slavery."[69]

As a result of so much attention to slavery, foreigners, free-soilism, and Kansas-Nebraska became inextricably related during the state and congressional campaigns of 1855. Trying to convict the immigrants of the charge of being antislavery, leading Know Nothing spokesmen like B. G. Thibodaux from Terrebonne and Randall Hunt asserted that all foreigners were abolitionists.[70] However, the Democrats, not permitting an opportune issue to escape them, pressed their Know Nothing adversaries hard to explain their opposition to the Kansas-Nebraska Act.

Recent scholarship on northern Know Nothingism demonstrates the liability southern and Louisiana Americans had with the slavery issue. Historians William Freehling, Michael Holt, Leonard Richards, and John Ashworth, for example, all emphasize the anti-Nebraska or antislavery sentiment of many northern Americans during the party's rapid growth. Ex-southern Whigs hoped that their former northern colleagues would embrace any issue other than antislavery. Yet historian Tyler Anbinder writes that the election of Henry Wilson of Massachusetts to the United States Senate showed "the anti-slavery crusade was just as important to northern Know Nothings as nativism." And when southern Americans managed to confirm the Kansas-Nebraska Act at the June 1855 American Party convention, a number of northern delegates bolted.[71]

Keeping up the pressure on the Americans, the Democratic *Baton Rouge Daily Advocate* reported that Know Nothing Congressman T. G. Hunt had voted with the abolitionists against the Kansas-Nebraska Act, and that the Know Nothing candidate for Congress from the Fourth District, W. B.

Lewis, admitted he would have voted against it had he been in Congress.[72] However, it was T. G. Hunt who received most of the Democratic abuse since, as a United States congressman, he had actually voted against the bill. The Democratic press reminded Congressman Hunt that the South opposed the restrictive Missouri Compromise line of 1820 that the Kansas-Nebraska Act repealed. One anti-nativist paper asked Hunt how he could forget his constituents and insult the South by rejecting a bill offered by free-state congressmen that "would put an end to Congressional interference with concerns of the people of the territories over slavery." Because of the way Hunt had voted, claimed the Democratic *Daily True Delta*, every abolition journal in the North "heralds his name with praise." Senator John Clayton of Delaware, another slave-state Whig, demonstrated the pressure that Hunt and other southern Whigs faced over their opposing the Nebraska bill when he asked, "Can a Senator whose constituents hold slaves, be expected to resist and refuse what the North thus and ready offers us . . . ?"[73]

Hunt and the Know Nothing Party, always trying to avoid sectional attacks, denied that his vote had been hostile to the South, arguing that what harmed the South was "the flood of emigrants, opposed to slavery, peopling the territories, which the Democratic party encourages by favoring naturalization of foreigners." Hunt believed the repeal of the Missouri Compromise line, which had silenced outcries of faction and had brought tranquility to the country, could not restore the political equilibrium between North and South. The real purpose behind the Kansas-Nebraska Act was to confer "a political franchise upon foreigners without any condition of residence." Hunt earnestly believed that enfranchising foreigners in turn helped to suppress slavery.[74] Hunt's fellow Know Nothing, and a congressional candidate from the Third District, Preston Pond Jr., agreed with Hunt, predicting that Kansas and Nebraska would be lost to the South as a result of increased immigration that added to the strength of abolitionism. In addition, nativists believed that the land in the territories given away to unnaturalized foreigners should go to natives.[75]

The German immigrants received the brunt of the Know Nothing attack. According to one nativist, the Germans actually believed that all men should be free.[76] The German newspapers in turn warned their readers to have nothing to do with the Know Nothing Party. Prior to the state election of 1855, the *Louisiana Staats-Zeitung* said, "Our Know-Nothings, or, as they call themselves, reformers, are in truth allies of the devil."[77] However, the *Opelousas Patriot* singled out no particular ethnic group when it warned the voters of the state that if they gave foreigners political influence and power "they will not only prevent slavery in the territories, but will call upon Congress to abolish it in the states." To strengthen its case, the *Patriot* quoted articles from the *Chicago Democrat,* a newspaper that favored immigration as a means to abolish slavery.[78]

Despite the concern of Louisiana Know Nothings over immigration and its effect on abolition, the American Party continued to have a difficult time denying the Democratic allegation of being allied with abolitionism. At the Democratic State Convention in Baton Rouge in June 1855, former Whig Pierre A. Rost informed the delegates that the Know Nothing Party in New England was infected with abolitionism. On the same topic, the *Daily True Delta* pondered how Know Nothings in Louisiana could join with "traitors from Maine, Massachusetts and New Hampshire, who are delegated expressly to represent northern fanaticism against southern institutions." In Upper South Virginia, Democratic candidate for governor, Henry Wise was thinking the same thing as Rost. Wise called the Know Nothings soft on slavery because they had allied with anti-southern northerners and that the Massachusetts Senate had just elected anti-southern Henry Wilson to the United States Senate. Historian Elizabeth Varon states that Wise "eviscerated his opponent (Know Nothing Thomas Flournoy) by charging that Know Nothings were lackeys of northern abolitionists . . . and even the minions of British abolitionists."[79]

American Party spokesmen called these Democratic charges "untenable and ridiculous." These supporters denied that their party was tainted with abolitionism and asserted that the American Party stood upon the principle of protecting the constitutional rights of the states in regard to slavery. This absurd charge, Americans reported, originated with the Pierce administration which tried to burden the Know Nothing Party with the stigma of abolitionism.[80]

However, the Louisiana Americans did admit there was "a small and fanatical anti-slavery" element in the party.[81] In fact, despite the Union, and the fact that the Third Degree that demanded Know Nothings avoid sectional issues, northern members increasingly cooperated with the abolitionists. Thus, at the 1855 National Know Nothing Convention a majority of northern delegates refused to accept a pro-slavery platform that endorsed the Kansas-Nebraska Act and they bolted the party.[82] One Louisiana Know Nothing paper absurdly claimed that where free-soilers embraced the American Party they:

harmonize with the men of the South in a determination to support the constitution and the union—in the proposed change of the naturalization—in
placing the control of public affairs in the hands of natives, and in other matters necessary to carry out true American principles.[83]

This same paper did not want to debate an abstraction, and believed the South
had more to fear from the foreign immigrant's opposition to slavery. Finally,
the *Semi-Weekly Creole* pointed out that "Democratic liberality to foreigners
permits them to vote in the territories before they are naturalized, that party is
responsible for the growing balance of power against the South."[84]

According to the Americans, the Democratic attempt to stigmatize the
American Party as antislavery was untenable. Know Nothings claimed
that the attempt of the Democracy to link Know Nothings with abolitionism was "nothing but an 'Old Fogy' trick to scare southerners away
from the American Party."[85] Americans believed that this campaign of the
Democratic Party to stigmatize the American Party as antislavery would
not work since the abolitionist press actually opposed the Know Nothings.[86]
Americans noted that their platform could hardly be antislavery when
numerous northern delegates at the national convention had refused to
sign a document that upheld the rights of the South.[87] The Know Nothing
press of the state agreed with the *Semi-Weekly Creole* that the Democrats
could not awaken any sectional jealousies within the party, and these papers
stressed that the real issue before the country was the alteration or repeal of
the naturalization laws.[88]

Alteration or repeal of the naturalization laws of the country had long
been a panacea of the nativists. The belief that foreigners had increased
their political influence at the expense of natives helped to bring about
this movement to change the naturalization laws. Charles Gayarré, in his
Address to the People of Louisiana on the State of Parties, agreed with other
Louisiana nativists that times had changed and that the immigrants were
"now greedy and half famished, . . . the greater portion have been reared in
brutish ignorance . . . and cannot be expected to understand the complicated machinery of our political system."[89] Of course, the Know Nothing
press belabored the point that these foreigners were unduly influenced by
native demagogues. Nativists also believed foreign interlopers, such as Louis
Kossuth, the Hungarian patriot who unsuccessfully fought for Hungarian
independence from Austria in 1848 and 1849 had too much sway over foreign-born.[90] In addition, with the South always sensitive to any threat to
slavery, the American Party argued that a modification of the naturalization
laws would prevent foreigners from strengthening the abolition cause.[91]

Understandably, Know Nothing speeches and literature stressed the need to extend the period preceding naturalization from five to twenty-one years. In a speech in Houma, congressional candidate T.G. Hunt declared that the extraordinary increase in immigration made the naturalization laws of 1790 obsolete. Hunt did not believe that these recent immigrants, whom he called the "worst classes of the common laborers of the monarchial governments of Europe," could be politically incorporated into the country. If the naturalization laws were not remodeled, the foreigners would soon hold the balance of power in elections, argued Hunt, and "that could be fatal to the liberties of the country."[92]

Nativists recognized the importance of congressional control over naturalization and demanded that that body modify the laws in order to "insure a unity of feeling and sympathy between the foreign and native citizens are the rights of citizenship be conferred."[93] The American Party state platform in 1855 called for "an amendment of the naturalization laws, with proper safeguards to preserve the purity of the elective franchise."[94] The membership of the American Party heartily endorsed this plank at numerous mass meetings and regional conventions throughout the state. One speaker at a New Orleans meeting reminded his audience that the party intended to take away none of the rights or privileges of the foreign-born but only to change the naturalization laws. According to this nativist, the goal of the party was to permit a foreigner to vote only after "he has been, like the rest of us, twenty-one years in the country."[95] Know Nothings believed the intelligent portion of naturalized citizens recognized the need for this change.[96] However, some nativists—"ultraists," as one Know Nothing paper called them—favored total repeal of the naturalization laws. This drastic step received the disapproval of a majority of the American leadership in the state.[97]

The American Party did not convince the anti-nativist press that all they sought was modification of the naturalization laws. The *Daily True Delta* accused the Know Nothing Party of seeking cessation of foreign immigration to the United States. This paper asserted that if the nativists had a real concern for protecting the franchise they would not have removed the 1845 constitutional provision which required a two year state residence before being eligible to vote. This conservative feature would have protected the franchise more effectively than the 1852 Constitution, which the nativists had been instrumental in drafting.[98] Additionally, anti-American spokesmen criticized the Know Nothing attempts to change the naturalization laws because that would have no effect on voting. These critics noted correctly that naturalization did not give a foreigner the right to vote; that right depended on state legislation.[99] Of course, there were those in the Know

Nothing organization who recognized this fact, and as a result they increasingly, if reluctantly, accepted the goal of conferring upon the national government the right to grant aliens the franchise.[100] Obviously, these Know Nothings believed they would have more success in denying the franchise to the foreign-born through congressional action than at the state level.

—◆—

The Know Nothing policy of secrecy received almost as much criticism as did the American position on immigration. To many, secrecy violated the spirit of republicanism, and Democrats attempted to capitalize on this sentiment. Initially, the Know Nothings defended their policy of secrecy. Know Nothing spokesmen denied that the secretiveness of the party was wrong, and they pointed out that the secret features were no different from other parties.[101] The *Clinton American Patriot* stated pragmatically that the party in its initial stages had depended on secrecy; otherwise "it would have been crushed."[102] Charles Gayarré also recognized the necessity for secrecy, but his defense was certainly more eloquent. In response to his question as to who was responsible for the American Party meeting in secret, Gayarré answered:

> Grasping with his right hand the truncheon of demagogism, seated on the throne of party fanaticism, his feet resting on the footstool of immigration, his head crowned with the plunder and spoils of taxation, his temples anointed with the oil of corruption, he bids us hold out liberties at the mercy of his capricious will. The name of that king is Mobocracy.[103]

Others complained that the Democratic press had no right to criticize the Know Nothing secretiveness when the Pierce administration organized foreigners into secret societies, societies which affiliated with abolitionists and caused election frauds.[104]

However, the criticism of the secret rites, and a growing antipathy to the policy on the part of the membership, led to a general call for abolition of the secret features of the party. Agreeing that it once had been necessary, the party press noted it had become "galling and oppressive."[105] In the state campaign of 1855, the American Party held numerous mass meetings while the party organs boasted they did not look like "Hindoos, [*sic*] Dark Lanterns, Assassins, murderers, Cowards, or ruthless proscriptionists."[106] The American Party state convention of 1855 in an official address proclaimed there was no longer a need for secrecy since the party had "attained the vigor of manhood." The convention also released for publication its state platform and policy.[107] Local wigwams gradually followed this lead and abolished all signs, grips, and passwords of the order. The Americans in Louisiana wanted an open order with the only requirement for membership being the approval of the state and national platforms.[108]

Know Nothings' alleged anti-foreignism, abolitionism, and secrecy were frequently overshadowed in the state by the anti-Roman Catholic principle of the American Party. The Know Nothings had made a good case for their opposition to the alien population. In addition, many Louisiana Democrats had once flirted with Native Americanism, and the Know Nothings made good use of that fact. For example, American Party newspapers reported that Thomas Green Davidson and Miles Taylor, successful Democratic congressional candidates in the Third and Second Congressional Districts, respectively, had been prominent in the Native American movement of the 1840s.[109] It was highly improbable that any member of the American Party in the state ever uttered abolitionist principles, although northern members of the party did embarrass their southern brethren. Finally, secrecy, as the Americans agreed, did give their party an initial advantage against the Democrats. Therefore, the anti-Roman Catholic position of the National American Party became perhaps the most serious problem for Louisiana Know Nothings, especially in the early months of the party's existence. Even though the Louisiana party opposed proscription of Roman Catholics and numerous members of the Roman Catholic faith belonged to the American Party, anti-Roman Catholicism furnished the Democrats of Louisiana an effective weapon to use against the Know Nothing movement in the state. At least, Democrat John Slidell thought so. In a letter to a fellow Democrat in Assumption Parish, Slidell wrote that the anti-Catholic plank adopted at the Philadelphia Convention of the National American Party would surely hurt the Know Nothings in the Second Congressional District and produce "good results for the Creole parishes."[110]

The anti-Roman Catholic bias of the National American Party, and local attacks against the papacy and the hierarchy of the church in the state surely weakened the American Party in Louisiana. Early on, Know Nothings throughout the state denied anti-Roman Catholicism was a tenet of Know Nothingism. American Party editors believed these accusations amounted to nothing more than the opposition trying to make political capital. The nativist press alleged that by spreading these false accusations Democrats attempted to influence the Roman Catholics of the state not to become members of the American Party. One Know Nothing editor added that the American people would never make a religious test for office holding.[111]

The American Party tried to convince the nation and the state that they opposed not Roman Catholicism itself, but only the interference of the pope and his priests in the temporal affairs of a country which threatened the United States' republican principles. Nativists charged that the Roman Catholic religion required a belief in the pope's infallibility, and since he interpreted all temporal law he could abrogate it when necessary.[112] Numerous books, pamphlets, and newspaper articles supporting Know Nothingism advanced this thesis, which was designed to allay the fears of Roman Catholics. One pamphlet stated it this way: the American Party only favored "the exclusion of sectarian religion from political influence—the protection of the absolute freedom of thought by vindicating the integrity of the public schools from all sectarian influence, whether Protestant or Papist."[113] Louisiana Americans likewise asserted their opposition to any Roman Catholic encroachment upon political rights or public education.[114]

Louisiana Know Nothings certainly had to be very sensitive to the anti-Roman Catholic issue. A sizable segment of the population of the state belonged to the Roman Catholic Church, and many members of the American Party were Roman Catholics. Therefore, the American Party press made every effort to prevent the Catholic issue from dividing the party in the state.

But there were supporters of the Know Nothing Party, despite party denials of a prescriptive policy against Roman Catholics, who did attack the church and its policies in no uncertain terms. George A. Pike of Baton Rouge, publisher of the *Comet* newspapers, was one of these men. Unlike his colleagues in areas of the state with large Roman Catholic populations who may have exercised restraint because of the Catholic presence in their region, Pike's editorials did little to convince Roman Catholics that his party did not intend to proscribe them. Bishop Hughes of New York, the Society of Jesus (the religious order), and the *Southern (Catholic) Standard* newspaper were the favorite targets of Pike. Pike opposed Bishop Hughes, or any other Roman Catholic bishop, from holding all church property in their name.[115] To Pike and the Know Nothings, ownership of property by a Catholic bishop resulted in the centralization of the Roman Catholic Church with the prospects of the "government . . . soon begging the church for funds to carry on its affairs."[116] Pike's fear of the Jesuits was not an isolated one. Nativists, ironically, characterized that society as "a secret oath bound clan hourly striking death blows at the very foundation of our republic."[117] Finally, the attacks by the Roman Catholic newspaper the *Southern Standard* on the American Party provoked Pike into a rage against it. Calling it a "vile and slanderous sheet," Pike permitted himself to go beyond the bounds of propriety.[118]

If Pike was an embarrassment for the state organization, the National Council proved to be a far greater liability for Louisiana Know Nothings. A Know Nothing delegation from the state traveled to Philadelphia in June 1855 to attend the party's national convention. Immediately, the Louisiana delegates and the convention became involved in a controversy over the seating of the delegation which included the Roman Catholic Charles Gayarré. The convention finally voted to seat only the Protestant members of the delegation, but the Protestant delegates chose not to accept admission under such terms. The convention then proceeded to write its national platform, which included an anti-Roman Catholic plank.[119]

Gayarré's exclusion and the anti-Roman Catholic article (Article 8) of the national platform pleased few Know Nothings in Louisiana. Most Know Nothings papers thought the eighth article ill-advised and regretted the action of the Philadelphia Convention.[120] Rejecting what they termed the anti-republican eighth article, several Know Nothings advised the Louisiana party to "go it alone" and "repudiate their [the Philadelphia Convention's] sentiments and proceedings."[121] Gayarré had intended to address the Philadelphia Convention on the Roman Catholic question had he been seated. He expressed his feelings on the prescriptionist views of the American Party in the following manner:

It was conceived in the womb of ignorance, fathered by prejudice, nurtured by fanaticism, and pushed into the place which it now occupies by the efforts of narrow brained bigots and shallow politicians, who thought it would be an element of success, when appealing to the worst instincts of the human heart.

Is it not worse for you to say to an American—you shall never fill any office of trust or profit in your own country because you are a Catholic, than for the Pope to say to a foreigner: you shall not build a Protestant temple in my dominions?

If your administration should proclaim that all the American Catholics, citizens by birth, are to be excluded from office as dangerous, had not every other government on the face of the earth as strong a right to exclude foreign Protestants from its territory?[122]

At their state convention in July, Louisiana Know Nothings adopted a more conciliatory platform. The state platform, while essentially the same as the one adopted by the national council in Philadelphia, had one important exception. The state convention rejected the anti-Roman Catholic plank since it would not tolerate even an ambiguity which might be construed to deny to any American citizen perfect liberty of conscience, and absolute immunity from legal or political persecution and punishment on account of his religious belief.[123] Shortly after the state convention, over 10,000 persons turned out in Lafayette Square in New Orleans to endorse the state platform.[124]

Thus, the American Party entered the campaign for state and congressional offices with a platform that stood in variance with the national platform when it came to the Roman Catholic question, and with Roman Catholic candidates on its ticket. Throughout the campaign, Know Nothings continually asserted that they opposed religious proscription. They boasted of the three Catholic candidates for high state offices on the American ticket: Charles Derbigny of Jefferson Parish, Louis Texada of Rapides Parish, and J. V. Duralde of West Baton Rouge Parish were the candidates for governor, lieutenant governor, and state treasurer, respectively. The Americans noted that the Democrats had only two Catholic candidates for inferior offices. Therefore, the nativists asked, which ticket was more dangerous to Catholicism?[125] Charles Derbigny, the American gubernatorial candidate, asserted that three-fourths of the Creoles of the state were Americans, and that he expected every Catholic parish in Louisiana to give a majority to the Know Nothing Party.[126]

Derbigny was optimistic because the Louisiana platform had rejected the anti-Roman Catholic plank of the national platform as it applied to American Roman Catholics. In Louisiana, this would permit the native Creole Roman Catholics to sustain the American Party. In addition, the Creoles of Louisiana had denied that the pope had any control over their temporal affairs, and they had always asserted that there was a difference between the Gallican Catholics and other Catholics. Americans throughout the nation also made this distinction. One political pamphlet, which contained Know Nothing principles, supported this distinction among Catholics. Many Native Americans asserted that the Gallican Catholics were liberal and opposed to clerical interference, while the ultramontane papists blindly supported the dictates of the clergy and the papacy.[127]

The Democracy of the state criticized the anti-Roman Catholic plank in the American national platform, while the Catholic press denied there was any such thing as a Gallican Catholic. Democrats noted that even the nativist press opposed the eighth plank of the National American platform, and they ridiculed those Know Nothings who alleged the Roman Catholic test had "crept into the platform" and would be removed.[128] Along with the secular press, the Roman Catholic *Southern Standard* and the *Propagateur Catholique* warned the Creoles to be alert to the real aim of the Know Nothings, the proscription of Roman Catholics. These two Catholic newspapers denied that the Roman Catholic population in Louisiana contained "infidels and apostates." Although these papers admitted that there were some Creole names among the Know Nothings, they claimed these Creoles were simply dupes. The *Southern Standard* denied that Louisiana Americans rejected the Philadelphia Platform; they approved it, the *Southern Standard* claimed, but rejected its application to American Roman Catholics. This newspaper refused to be "humbugged and bamboozled." "We [native Roman Catholics] will stand or fall with our fellow naturalized catholics."[129] Even Charles Gayarré denounced the attempt to differentiate between French Catholics and other Catholics. Although Gayarré admitted that most Roman Catholics in Louisiana did not go to confession or acknowledge papal authority over them, he denied that the Louisiana delegation to Philadelphia supported the proscription of any Roman Catholics. The Louisiana delegation to the 1855 Philadelphia Convention would have accepted no religious test. Gayarré enlightened those who believed that distinctions existed between Catholics in Louisiana.

> But let me tell you, if there is anything which will make us flock to the confessional, it is the intelligence that you dare to interfere with our free action in this matter. I have no hesitation in saying, in the name of my constituents, that latitudinarians as they are in Catholicism, they would shed, if necessary, the last drop of their blood in defence of the creed of their forefathers. . . .[130]

Gayarré referred to some Roman Catholics as latitudinarians. If these were the Roman Catholics who belonged to the Know Nothing Party in Louisiana, the Roman Catholic hierarchy disagreed. If a Catholic belonged to the Know Nothing Party, the Roman Catholic Church asserted that he was one "who has made himself liable to excommunication for not making his Easter duties. Those who are trying to get Catholic support by calling themselves Catholic are not properly calling themselves correctly."[131]

In addition, the *Propaqateur Catholique* claimed that the Creole faction of the American Party did not control the party, and that the Know Nothings bribed them with the offer of places. The *Catholique* concluded that if the Creoles sustained this party "the Creole population would commit suicide."[132] This Roman Catholic newspaper did not accept the concession the Know Nothings of Louisiana pretended to make for Roman Catholics, and concluded that despite the ninth article, which rejected any religious bigotry, the Louisiana party still regarded the Roman Catholic Church as corrupt.[133]

To add to the nativists' problems, the anti-American press charged that predominately Protestant north Louisiana Know Nothings accepted the Philadelphia Platform without reservations. The Democracy exploited this issue during the 1855 campaign.[134] On July 23, 1855, the Bienville Parish Know Nothing Party resolved that the state wigwam had exceeded its authority when it repudiated the eighth article of the Philadelphia Platform. This meeting, held at Sparta, Louisiana, repudiated the state action and affirmed the national platform.[135] The Know Nothing *New Orleans Daily Crescent* denied that the Sparta wigwam typified the Louisiana American Party. These "hot-heads," the *Daily Crescent* charged, numbered only twenty-five or thirty members out of a total of 25,000 persons who accepted the state platform.[136] The *Louisiana Courier* gladly noted the abuse of Roman Catholics in Jackson Parish. The *Farmerville Enquirer* of Union Parish also had an anti-Roman Catholic reputation. This paper believed that Roman Catholic institutions would be better regulated with convents opened to grand juries and habeas corpus extended to them.[137] The correspondent "Justice" in the *Baton Rouge Daily Advocate* reported that a Protestant minister, the Reverend Dr. R. M. Stell, who campaigned for the American Party in north Louisiana, accepted the Roman Catholic test clause of the Philadelphia Platform. Reverend Stell did not stop there; he claimed that the Charity Hospital of New Orleans refused admittance to Protestants. Reverend Stell also referred to the Sisters of Charity, which administered the hospital as "women of easy virtue." In addition, Reverend Stell opposed state appropriations to various charitable causes affiliated with Roman Catholics "as pandering to Catholic influence and Romanish prejudices."[138] Another clergyman joined Dr. Stell in fulminating against Roman Catholics, in north Louisiana. A Protestant minister, simply referred to in the press as Reverend Dr. Harmon, campaigned in the northwestern parishes advancing the claim that Charles Derbigny, candidate for governor, "would rather see his children in their graves than Roman Catholics." This prompted the *Daily True*

Delta to ask the Americans if they were representing their gubernatorial candidate as two different people in two areas of the state.[139]

To further complicate matters in the 1855 campaign, two American tickets appeared. Charles Derbigny headed the ticket nominated in New Orleans in July, but a National American ticket appeared in the fall headed by John Ray of Ouachita Parish in north Louisiana. The Democrats reported that the north Louisiana Americans could not accept the popish candidates and had presented this Protestant ticket. The Democrats denounced the goals of the National American ticket, but argued that the north Louisiana Know Nothings accepted the true principles of the American Party's National Council.[140] The National American ticket quickly acquired the sobriquet Blue Book or Simon Pures. The American press in the state took note of this Simon Pure faction, but only to deny its authenticity. The *New Orleans Daily Crescent* reported that this group, headed by a Charles W. Hardy, had its "dispensation" to establish a state council and subordinate councils revoked in June 1855 by the National Council.[141] Every "regular" candidate nominated by the Simon Pures disassociated himself from the "Bogus ticket," and denounced religious proscription, and they endorsed the "regular" ticket headed by Charles Derbigny. The "regular" Know Nothings called the "Bogus ticket," or, Blue Book ticket, a Democratic trick to confuse the American Party at a late date in the political campaign." Know Nothing and former United States Congressman John Moore forcefully denied that the Know Nothings made religion a test for public office. Yet, it was clear the Americans were on the defensive because of the anti-Catholic plank of the Philadelphia Platform.[142]

The American Party entered the elections of 1855 asserting it was the "only national party to take the high and conservative ground on the slavery question," and decried any persecution of foreigners or Roman Catholics.[143] Although other issues[144] did appear during the campaign, the Democracy's continuous attempts to discredit the American position on foreigners, Catholics, and, in particular, slavery permitted little debate on anything outside of those issues. Not even the American Party's 1855 convention in Philadelphia, which resolved that the existing laws on slavery were "final and conclusive," did much to deflect southern Democratic assertions of Know Nothings being soft on slavery.[145]

When the election returns became known, the Democratic Party had elected all of its state candidates, retained its legislative majority, and won three of the four congressional seats. In the gubernatorial race, the Democrats had increased their 1852 majority by over 9,000 votes. However, the results were much closer in the congressional races, except in the Fourth Congressional District where the Democratic candidate won handily.[146] In the state legislature, although the Democrats maintained their majority, the American Party had not been vanquished.[147] And, in New Orleans, the legislative candidates of the American Party were quite successful. All of their candidates for the state senate won, and they won most of the representative seats.[148]

The election results did bear out various Democratic charges against the Know Nothing Party. The nativists had denied the accusation that the American Party was a Whig trick,[149] but the relationship between the Whig gubernatorial vote in 1852 and the Know Nothing vote in 1855 is certainly apparent. Of the seventeen parishes which the Whig presidential candidate Winfield Scott had carried in 1852, eleven gave majorities to the American Charles Derbigny. In addition, eleven of the seventeen parishes which went Whig in the 1852 gubernatorial election also voted for the Know Nothing candidate for governor in 1855.[150] Some of these parishes which Derbigny carried in 1855 had been thoroughgoing Whig parishes since 1840.[151] These parishes were located in the sugar and cotton areas of the state. Just as the Whig Party had garnered support from these Mississippi and Red River parishes, so did the American Party.

It was clear that Roman Catholics had lukewarm enthusiasm for the American candidates. Both parties attributed the defeat of the Americans to the apprehension that many of the old Whig Catholics had toward the prescriptive policy of the party. The *New Orleans Bee* readily admitted that the Philadelphia Convention's anti-Catholic stand had hurt the party's momentum. This Know Nothing newspaper also reported that the Democrats had used the proscriptive feature well.[152] However, the *Thibodaux Minerva* was only partially correct when it stated that the Creoles were against the American Party "owing to the implied religious test in the national platform."[153] Of those sixteen parishes that returned majorities for Derbigny and the American Party, nine, or more than half, had a significant Roman Catholic population. Yet, during the election, while the Democrats and the Catholic press raised a raucous over the anti-Catholicism of the American Party, many Creole Roman Catholics did not permit the national platform to influence them. In fact, St. Charles, St. James, and St. John parishes—all Know Nothing parishes in 1855—had a church seating capacity that was exclusively Roman Catholic, according to the 1850 United States Census. West Baton Rouge, St. Martin, and St. Mary parishes, which Derbigny carried, had a Roman Catholic church seating capacity of 76, 65, and 44 percent, respectively. Finally, the two "urban" parishes, Jefferson and Orleans, had a Roman Catholic Church seating capacity of 46 and 45 percent, respectively, and both returned American majorities.[154] Even though an argument could be made that in Jefferson, Orleans, and St. Mary parishes the Protestant majority solidly supported the anti-Roman Catholic American Party, it is improbable that the other six parishes with a Roman Catholic majority— ranging from 65 to 100 percent—would have supported a blatantly anti-Roman Catholic party. Only Lafourche, St. Charles, and St. Landry parishes, each with a large Roman Catholic and Creole population, experienced a dramatic decline in support from the Whigs in 1852 to the Americans in 1855, and only Lafourche fell from the Whig-American column in 1855.[155] Since the *Thibodaux Minerva*, published in the parish seat of Lafourche, had reported that the Creoles were against the prescriptive religious test of the American Party, it appears that Creole Roman Catholics in Lafourche believed the Know Nothing Party did not represent their best interests. However, the 1855 election returns indicate that most Creole Roman Catholics who had supported the Whig Party moved over to the Americans or chose not to vote at all.[156] Politically, old Catholic Whigs still supported the Americans because that party gave them the opportunity to continue their political life in a party that was not the Democracy. Catholic Know Nothings in the state also felt strongly about how they believed Irish and German immigrants continued to inflame the sectional controversy over slavery's extension into the territories. Particularly troubling to the Americans was that immigrants to Louisiana also made their way into the Democratic Party.

Therefore, foreigners came in for a great deal of abuse for their alleged role in the Know Nothing defeat. One American editor noted that "five-sixths of the foreigners voted against the Know Nothings."[157] It is unlikely that the non-native-born population supported the anti-foreign Know Nothing Party, and in parishes, such as Jefferson and Orleans parishes, with a significant foreign-born population, that probably had some effect on the vote. Jefferson Parish, a parish which had generally voted Whig in earlier gubernatorial campaigns, increased its majority for the Americans in 1855 by almost ten percentage points over the Whig majority of 1852. Orleans Parish, with a larger number of foreign-born residents than Jefferson, returned an American majority in 1855. This was the first time Orleans Parish had not supported the Democratic candidate for governor since 1842.[158]

In order to have won in New Orleans, the Americans had to overcome the foreign support for the Democrats. The largest concentration of immigrants in that city was in the Third District, known prior to the 1852 consolidation of New Orleans as the Third Municipality. The Irish, the largest immigrant group in New Orleans, the Germans, and the French generally moved into the Third District upon arriving in the city.[159] In previous elections, the Third District had proved itself a Democratic stronghold. For example, in the 1854 municipal election, the Democratic candidate for mayor won the Third District with 75 percent of the vote.[160] If the American gubernatorial candidate was to even have a chance to win the 1855 election, the immigrant vote in the Third District would have to be curtailed. Consequently, the Americans either intimidated Democratic voters at the polls or refused to accept questionable naturalization papers offered by foreign-born voters.[161] As a result, the Third District voters failed to return a majority for the Democratic nominee, Robert C. Wickliffe. In fact, Wickliffe received only 43 percent of the vote in the Third District in 1855. One particular precinct, the Fifteenth, which had given Democratic candidate for Mayor John L. Lewis 557 votes out of a total of 724 cast in 1854, gave Wickliffe only 185 votes in 1855. Meanwhile, the Know Nothing candidate, Derbigny, won that precinct with 295 votes in 1855.[162]

Although the presence of foreigners seems to have affected how nativists voted in 1855, particularly in Jefferson and Orleans parishes, the Democratic charge that Know Nothingism was synonymous with abolitionism in the North appears to have had little impact on the way slaveholders voted. The slaveholding class was not deterred from voting for the American Party. Actually, my quantitative data indicate a tendency of the slaveholding areas of the state to favor the Know Nothing Party in this election. Also, every parish—except for three that voted for the Know Nothing Derbigny—had a slave population of 52 percent or more. Concordia Parish, a wealthy cotton parish situated along the Mississippi River, had a slave population of 90 percent, while 20 percent of the free population of Concordia owned at least one slave, and over 10 percent owned more than twenty slaves. However, Concordia Parish was not the exception. Nine of the sixteen parishes in Derbigny's column claimed 10 percent of the population or more who owned at least one slave.[163]

In spite of Democratic accusations of "Whiggery in disguise," prescriptiveness, anti-republican, and being in league with northern abolitionism, the American Party had done fairly well. However, knowledgeable members of the Know Nothing order recognized that certain changes had to be made, particularly in the national party. These leaders believed that "when everything religious and the secrecy is abolished from the National Organization," the party would meet with little opposition. Nonetheless, the Americans had to make sure Democratic charges that they were soft on slavery could be successfully refuted. It was, of course, the northern wing of the dying Whig Party that had opposed the Kansas-Nebraska bill, and many of those northern Whigs had recently joined the Know Nothings. Additionally, Charles Gayarré's speech that he had planned to deliver before being denied admission to the 1855 American convention not only addressed the anti-Catholic plank, but he made it clear that Louisiana's Know Nothings were also very aware of the slavery issue. If national Know Nothings could threaten the rights of Catholics, Gayarré wondered if the federal government could do that to Catholics, and how long would it be before a northern majority could threaten slavery.[164] For the Americans, the next major test in the state would be in the 1856 presidential campaign.

F̃OUR

The Decline of Know Nothingism: 1856–57

The Democratic victory in 1855 initially left some Know Nothings confused about the continued existence of the party in the state. Although the Democrats had not overwhelmed the Know Nothings,[1] there were those who despaired over the future of the American Party in Louisiana. The editor of the *Plaquemine Southern Sentinel* emphatically announced that only one party existed in the state: the Democratic Party. He believed that the American Party would never rally in the state.[2] However, most Americans remained more optimistic, predicting that only the Know Nothing Party itself could avert a sectional conflict. Even the *Southern Sentinel* soon threw off its negative position and announced that a Know Nothing would succeed Franklin Pierce as president.[3] The faithful claimed that once the national organization removed its objectionable features all Louisianians would march in Know Nothing ranks.[4]

During the 1856 legislative session, however, opposition to the Know Nothings, not solidarity within American ranks, developed as a result of election fraud allegations. Numerous charges of fraud in the recent state election culminated in a legislative confrontation. Most of the fraudulent voting charges originated in New Orleans, the scene of numerous irregularities. The rioting on Election Day was so bad that both parties called upon the legislature to pass a registry law for the city.[5] However, destroyed ballot boxes, intimidation of naturalized citizens, and the rejection of "voters" prompted some Democratic candidates to contest their defeat.[6] The Democratic majority in the state legislature quickly declared vacant the seats of several Americans. Three Know Nothing senators, three representatives, and the sheriff of Orleans Parish were among those who had their elections declared null and void. The American press expected the removals, but expressed disbelief at the haste of the Democrats. One Know Nothing paper bitterly reported that the legislature had "accomplished something for the Democratic candidates that the voters would not do." W. W. Pugh, a Democratic representative from Assumption Parish, had a different view of the legislature's action as he wrote his wife from Baton Rouge that several Americans admitted that Sheriff Joseph Hufty of Orleans Parish "had not been legally elected."[7]

Despite these defeats in the recent state election and in the legislature, Know Nothingism remained a threat to the Democracy. Know Nothings won local election victories in Thibodaux, Washington, St. Landry Parish, Donaldsonville, Bayou Sara, and Minden.[8] Although the Americans did not succeed in the election for selectmen in Baton Rouge, the American candidate for mayor of that city won his election.[9] Nevertheless, the most important test for the American Party prior to the presidential campaign was the municipal elections in New Orleans.

The Know Nothings in the city had the opportunity to capture complete control of the city government. Although they controlled the city council of New Orleans, the Democrats held the mayoralty. In this election, the "reformers" continued to eschew the name "Know Nothing" or "American." Recognizing the hindrance that the anti-Roman Catholic position of the National American Party caused them in heavily Roman Catholic New Orleans, the "reformers" preferred to run on a ticket labeled "Citizens Ticket Irrespective of Party." In addition, Americans hoped the "no-party" label would attract sympathetic Democrats to their cause.[10]

While the Americans stressed the achievements under the reform city council, the Democratic press emphasized the importance the election had for the upcoming presidential campaign. Anti-foreign and anti-Catholic issues received limited attention. The *Louisiana Courier* still bemoaned that "blind" Catholics supported this Citizens ticket, or the Know Nothings.[11] Instead of nativism, the Citizens ticket accentuated the "reformers" accomplishments in extinguishing debts, curtailing expenses, reducing the rate of taxation, and making the wharves of the city profitable. The Democrats, on the other hand, shrugged off these accomplishments, and pointed out the poor condition of the streets and public buildings of the city.[12] The Democratic leadership continued to underscore the importance this election had for the upcoming presidential campaign. The *Louisiana Courier* did not think that enough Democrats were taking the election seriously. It reminded the party that a Democratic victory in New Orleans would "give

Democrats in other states the good promise of Louisiana going Democratic in the national election."[13]

Not unexpectedly, riots and disorder characterized the election. For the Know Nothings, intimidation worked well and, as a result, they won every race. The Americans and Democrats accused each other of being responsible for the violence and murders. Over 4,000 voters stayed away from the polls, and the Democrats alleged it was the result of the citizens' fear of "hired organized bands of ruffians."[14] Know Nothing control of the police force of the city and good discipline at the ward level, "insured large turnouts" for the Americans as well as "domination at the polls." Therefore, the Americans captured, for the first time, both branches of city government.[15] This victory, combined with the earlier rural success, gave the Know Nothing Party renewed hope that it could carry Louisiana in the national election in 1856.

The alleged proscriptive features and abolitionist tendencies of the American Party always remained a favorite target of the anti-American press and, after the 1854 and 1855 northern elections in Massachusetts, New York, and New Hampshire, the Democrats, as historian Michael Holt writes, used the results to "attach the stigma of anti-slavery radicalism to northern Know Nothings." Following the 1855 Louisiana state election, the opposition newspapers continued their attacks on the nativism of the American Party as well as those northern abolitionist leanings. The *Baton Rouge Daily Advocate* reported that an American convention in Cincinnati had adopted a platform which declared that "Congress should refuse to admit into the Union any State tolerating slavery, which shall be formed out of any portion of the territory from which that institution was excluded by the Missouri Compromise."[16] Another anti-American paper felt that the southern Know Nothings had to abandon the "pro-slavery" plank of the Philadelphia Platform in order to succeed in the presidential election. A movement in that direction had already been taken, according to this paper, when Louisiana Representative George Eustis voted for Representative Fuller of Pennsylvania, "a rank anti-Nebraska man," for Speaker of the House. The eventual election of a slavery opponent, Nathaniel Banks, as Speaker, gave the anti-Know Nothing press the opportunity to lay the blame squarely on the southern Americans.[17] In addition, the Louisiana anti-nativist press alleged that the anti-Catholic "Simon Pure" faction of the American Party officially represented the party in the state. The *Catholic Standard* also denied that Roman Catholics harbored anti-republican sentiments or that foreigners could never lose their attachment to their homeland. This paper asserted that no foreign-born Roman Catholic endorsed abolitionism. Instead, those southerners who supported the Know Nothing Party had been "warring on the true friends of southern institutions."[18]

Sensitive to the Democratic charges, the American Party made every effort to allay the fears of those who believed the Know Nothings were prescriptive. Some Americans vowed they would leave the party if the northern wing insisted on the religious question. American Representative Eustis delivered a speech in the House in which he condemned the religious plank of his party and he noted that Louisiana Americans repudiated that plank. At almost the same time Eustis made his speech, Know Nothings in the Louisiana General Assembly supported a resolution which called for the election of a Roman Catholic chaplain for the legislature[19] and the omnipresent Charles Gayarré published another "Address" to the people of the state. In this publication, which dealt with the religious question, the author denied that Roman Catholics sustained any temporal rights of the pope. If the American Party insisted on proscribing Roman Cathlics, Gayarré promised "Louisiana must secede in a body. Louisiana will in 1856 vote for either a Democrat sound on naturalization laws or a candidate of her own."[20]

Gayarré's threat was unnecessary. The American Party presidential nominating convention at Philadelphia in February voted to seat those Louisiana delegates who accepted Catholics in the state order.[21] In addition, the convention moderated its anti-Roman Catholic plank. Article V of the platform stated that "no person should be elected for political station (whether of native or foreign birth) who recognizes any allegiance or obligation, OF ANY DESCRIPTION, to ANY FOREIGN PRINCE, POTENTATE, OR POWER." However, the anti-nativists still claimed this discriminated against Catholics.[22]

Louisiana Americans wanted to forget the recently discarded anti-Catholic plank, but the anti-Know Nothing press refused to cooperate, reminding the voters that proscription of Roman Catholics remained an American goal. The *Louisiana Courier* wondered how an anti-Catholic party could exist in Louisiana. While Americans had in the past differentiated between Gallican and other Catholics, the *Catholic Standard* held fast in its denial of any distinction. Asserting that "all American Catholics agree that beyond his own dominions the venerable head of the Catholic Church has no temporal power," the *Catholic Standard* flatly rejected the American thesis that the pope held any temporal power over Catholics. However, the *Catholic*

Standard did inject itself into the political campaign by endorsing the Democratic Party.[23] Most Americans ignored the *Catholic Standard*. They simply publicized the refusal of the Louisiana delegation at Philadelphia to participate in any proceedings if the national party proscribed Roman Catholics. Of course, the Americans were quick to point out proscription was no longer a feature of the National American Party.

Nevertheless, blatant anti-Roman Catholicism did surface in the 1856 presidential campaign. As in 1855, it was isolated, and limited mainly to the Baton Rouge *Comet* newspapers. The editor continued his attack on the wealth of the church and its foreign hierarchy. According to the *Morning Comet*, the attempts to incorporate Catholic congregations foreshadowed the time when, with government sanction, the church would "strangle the government." This editor did not neglect the *Catholic Standard*, which, according to *Comet* editorials, abused "everything American."[24]

Obviously the American Party in the state, because of the large Catholic population in south Louisiana, felt inclined to reevaluate its immigrant policy. Local wigwams and the state society exhibited a "new look" in 1856. Meeting at Baton Rouge in June 1856, the state convention adopted a resolution which stated: "in political affiliation we reject none, whether native or foreign, whose judgment and sympathies are with us upon the principles we seek to enforce, believing that all interests will be promoted in the end by our success."[25]

This did not please every nativist, however. One editor called it a prostitution of American principles. He did not believe it was good policy, or that it reflected the sentiments of the party in Louisiana. He asked, "Does the American party, now grovel in the dust, and flounder in the political cesspool as other parties have done for power and place?"[26]

Clearly this editor had expressed the sentiments of many Know Nothings. A fellow American from northwest Louisiana simplified, in one sentence, what the election was all about. He thought the main issue was:

whether this country shall be governed by the present race of Pierce office-holders, and their N. York soft-shell freesoiler dependents, aided by "foreign influence," or be restored to its pristine purity and vigor, and ruled by the natives of the land, in accordance with the policy of the immortal "Father of his Country" and the founders of the republic.[27]

Other Americans dragged out the stereotyped foreigner for this campaign. They pictured him living in the poorhouses, asylums, taking up the public domain, and abusing the franchise. Foreign immigration and foreign rule, as the nativists reminded the electorate, had caused the downfall of ancient republics. The *Daily Creole* criticized the Democratic platform which ostracized Americans and cuddled foreigners. The only plank needed in this campaign, asserted the nativists, should call for the entire repeal of the naturalization laws.[28]

Americans in the state also favored the action of their 1856 national convention on the slavery question. In an attempt to unite the northern and southern wings of the party, the convention dropped the pro-slavery plank, and adopted a clause which it hoped would bring the party together. But, as historian William Freehling notes, northern American delegates wanted strong language on the slavery issue, and when it was not forthcoming, forty northern delegates withdrew.[29] The Democrats, however, informed the voters of the state that in place of the pro-slavery plank the Americans had adopted a dangerous principle for the South. The new plank called for "the maintenance and enforcement of all laws until said laws shall be repealed, or shall be declared null and void by a competent judicial authority." Such a principle meant that a law, such as the Fugitive Slave Act, would be obeyed only until abolitionists secured a congressional majority to repeal it, or elected a president who would appoint judges who would declare it unconstitutional.[30]

The Know Nothing Party had to appear strong on slavery in order to help refute Democratic charges that Louisiana Americans were soft on defending the peculiar institution. At the same time, they had to avoid exacerbating the sectional controversy. Therefore, a great deal of Know Nothing literature on slavery centered on the immigrants' alleged hostility to slavery. The recent battle for Speaker of the House in Washington demonstrated that the sectional controversy still raged. George Eustis, remembering the attacks on him because of his vote in the Speaker contest, wrote a fellow Know Nothing that "abolitionism is getting too powerful in this country," As a result, Louisiana Know Nothings came out stronger on slavery, hopefully without agitating the sectional issue. By making the foreigner the scapegoat, Americans believed this would keep their party above the sectional controversy. One determined American editor blamed immigration for all the problems of the country; civil strife in Kansas, disruption of the election process, North versus South, and abolitionism were all directly attributable to the foreign-born. Ultimately an end to slavery would result as the European immigrant continued to increase the political strength of the North. The

Kansas-Nebraska Act received its share of abuse. As in the 1855 state campaign, Know Nothings opposed giving the vote to unnaturalized foreigners
since this would hasten the end of slavery. Americans argued that alien suffrage and squatter sovereignty only perpetrated "an additional wrong on the
South."[31] Their press alleged that the German immigrants exhibited a particularly strong free-soil trait. A free-soil tendency was not only visible in the
free states, but Germans in New Orleans, according to some nativists, supported John C. Fremont, the candidate of the new, antislavery Republican
party. The Bee alleged that the only reason the New Orleans Deutsche Zeitung
did not place Fremont's name at the top of its sheet was that the Republican
candidate could have no electoral ticket in Louisiana.[32]

Generally, Louisiana Know Nothings approved of the national American
platform. The nominations of Millard Fillmore and Andrew Jackson
Donelson for president and vice president, respectively, pleased most members as well. Some nativists withheld their support until they learned what
the platform said on the religious question and whether a southern man
would be on the ticket. One Know Nothing newspaper expressed dissat-
isfaction with the platforms of both parties, but concluded, as did many
Americans, that Fillmore stood on safer ground for the South. In fact, some
non-Americans leaned toward Fillmore. One was Alexander Franklin
Pugh, the brother of Louisiana Democratic representative W. W. Pugh, who
believed the Fillmore platform "seems to be a southern one, but it differs
little from the Democratic on important matters."[33]

The National American Party conducted a conservative and Union
campaign in 1856. Southern delegates ultimately controlled the American
convention following the withdrawal of several northern delegates. But
instead of giving in to sectional jealousies, Know Nothing campaign literature stressed the Union sentiment of the party. Because of this emphasis
on the Union, the Americans also acquired the support of many old-line
Union Whigs in the campaign and, as historian William Freehling writes,
in the South Fillmore represented "a Whig-Know Nothing coalition." As to
be expected, in Louisiana Whigs endorsed the nomination of Fillmore by
the national Whig convention in Louisville. Whig meetings held throughout the state passed resolutions which supported Fillmore and Donelson
and opposed the sectional strife in the country caused by the Democratic
Party.[34] Fillmore pleased old-line Whigs because, as one wrote, he knew
the former president to be "a pure patriot, firm to his duty, a conservative
and sincere politician, and what goes a long way with me a good Whig."[35]
Another former Whig who became a Know Nothing, from the Florida

parishes, reported thousands had turned out for a Know Nothing torchlight parade for Fillmore and that Unionism encompassed everything, while economic issues received short shrift.[36] Americans also practically ignored foreign affairs. Foreign affairs questions that did arise included Cuba and the United States' relations with Spain. The Know Nothings feared that a Buchanan administration perhaps would push "the taking of Cuba." This seemed unusual since many old Louisiana Whigs back in the late 1840s and early 1850s had been supporters of filibustering.[37] Know Nothings hardly neglected nativism, but when mentioned, that subject generally found its way into the conservative and Union rhetoric of the American Party in its attempt to avoid the slavery question.[38]

It was not inconsistent for Louisiana Know Nothings to relegate nativism to a secondary position considering the emphasis given to foreigners in the recent state elections of 1855. Americans in Louisiana were simply following the lead of Fillmore and the party elsewhere, and "confined their campaign literature to pleas for the preservation of the union" and to what one historian has called the Know Nothing Party in the South a Unionist movement. A Louisiana Know Nothing, John Moore, wrote to the Shreveport Fillmore Committee that "lovers of the Union . . . particularly those of the South owe Mr. Fillmore a debt of gratitude that can only be repaid by elevating him . . . to that high station which he filled" and according to Moore, Fillmore knew "no North as against the South." [39] In Louisiana, nativism still commanded some attention, particularly as to how foreigners and slavery were inimical to each other, but "in the heat of the slavery controversy, the American party had conveniently forgotten the issues that gave it birth."[40]

Not unexpectedly, the American campaign centered on Fillmore's Unionism. While the conservatives of the South rallied behind Fillmore, and the preservation of the Union, the Know Nothings alleged the "southern Locofocos . . . are planning the programme of a dissolution of the union in the event of Fremont's election."[41] The *Bee* noted that Fremont appealed exclusively to the North, and Buchanan, although less exclusively, appealed mostly to the South. The election of either Fremont or Buchanan, according to the Americans, meant "the victory of free-soilism and its ascendancy forever, and consequently the division of the Union into anti-slavery and pro-slavery sections." Both candidates were too sectional. As one historian has offered, Fillmore was the alternative to Buchanan in the South. Americans assured the southerners that northern conservatives rejected Buchanan's chances of winning in their region, and, therefore, Americans urged southerners to unite behind Fillmore.[42]

Know Nothings also denied that Buchanan's election would safeguard slavery. Instead, they argued that the only reason the South supported Buchanan was his alleged position favoring the extension of slavery into Kansas. However, the South, to the Know Nothings, ignored squatter sovereignty, "the touchstone of the Democracy," and the Americans called squatter sovereignty inimical to the South. Americans considered squatter sovereignty worse than the Wilmot Proviso. Since Congress did not possess any right either to establish or prohibit slavery in the territories, the Know Nothings rejected giving the people of a territory any such power. This doctrine would in fact stop the extension of slavery. Additionally, the Americans even attempted to prove Buchanan's opposition to the extension of slavery.[43]

In fact, according to the Americans, the Democratic Party as a whole opposed the extension of slavery.[44] The attempts of the Democrats to maintain some semblance of nationality gave the Know Nothings evidence for the allegation. Americans publicized a speech by Buchanan on the Texas admission question in which he stated that his vote for admission actually was a vote against slavery. He had reasoned that with Texas in the Union, Maryland, Virginia, Kentucky, and Missouri would become free. Vice-presidential nominee John C. Breckinridge's Tippecanoe speech also received Know Nothing attention. In that speech, Breckinridge asserted that he opposed the extension of slavery, and Know Nothings even alleged that Louisiana Democratic Governor Robert C. Wickliffe endorsed Breckinridge's speech. Americans charged New York abolitionist Republican Senator Seward himself went no further. In summation of the Democratic position on slavery, the *Bee* reported that they:

> are opposed to slavery in Kansas, to a division of Texas into four more slave states, to the acquisition of Cuba with slavery, and to the maintenance of that equilibrium in the Senate that Calhoun said was necessary to the harmony of the Union.[45]

The Americans charged that southern Democrats supported candidates who opposed the extension of slavery yet these same Democrats were ready to dissolve the Union and fight a civil war if slavery was not extended.[46]

The Democrats of Louisiana responded to their critics. Did not American Congressman Theodore G. Hunt agree with William Seward on the slavery extension issue? Democrats attempted to prove that Hunt believed Congress had the authority to legislate on the question of slavery in the territories. According to the Democracy, this was what Seward had in mind when, in his Albany speech in October, he asserted slavery extension could be stopped in the territories.[47] In regards to the Kansas-Nebraska Act, party spokesmen denied the act contained the principle of squatter sovereignty. That doctrine had no advocates in the South, and the American attack on it was "buncombe." In fact, according to the Democrats, everyone in the South had supported the Kansas-Nebraska Act until Fillmore returned from Europe to the United States. Now Know Nothing politicians believed the repeal of the Missouri Compromise line was unjust. Despite Know Nothing denials, the Democrats charged that Fillmore's election meant the restoration of the line.[48]

Democrats offered additional proof of Fillmore's indifference if not outright hostility to slavery. In his campaign speeches, Fillmore stated Congress had the power to legislate to almost any extent on the subject of slavery. To Democrats, Fillmore's past record on slavery proved his hostility to that institution and they even used an old 1838 Fillmore letter in which he allegedly expressed antislavery views. They charged that he had voted to receive abolition petitions, voted against the admission of Texas, and voted to repeal all laws by which the federal government was bound to protect slavery; moreover, he had doubted the constitutionality of the fugitive slave law.[49]

The Democratic Party, on the other hand, strongly asserted that they defended slavery and denied that their northern brethren, like the Republicans, opposed slavery's spread. Louisiana Democrats supported the Kansas-Nebraska bill and noted that the Americans opposed the bill, which included principles on slavery that the South had a right to demand. Judah P. Benjamin, a prominent ex-Whig and United States senator, defended his conversion to the Democratic Party and summed up the sectional problem in the following manner: "Democrats in Congress, on every question affecting slavery, voted in solid phalanx in favor of the rights of the South, while Whigs and Know Nothings . . . generally voted with the abolitionists." It did not help Louisiana Americans that less than a year before, Know Nothing Tennessee Congressman Felix Zollicofer had accused northern Know Nothngs as being "under the control of Greely and Seward." Nor did two old Whigs in Maryland, a Know Nothing stronghold, who argued that the real choice was between Frémont and Buchanan because "the northern wing of the American party was acting so closely with the Republicans," provide anything positive for southern Know Nothings.[50]

Therefore, despite the emphasis placed on the preservation of the Union by the American Party, the election came down to which party would best serve the interests of the South and Louisiana. Democrats charged that the

Know Nothings favored proscription in the state and that in the North the nativists allied themselves with "freesoilers, abolitionists and negro worshippers."[51] American defenders, while stressing Union and country, alleged that the Democrats had nominated Buchanan because that party needed northern votes and in that section the electorate could picture Buchanan as antislavery. In the past, Buchanan, according to the Know Nothings, had "worn a northern or southern face," depending on the circumstances. They also hoped the walk-out of antislavery northern Know Nothings from the party's 1856 convention would prove Know Nothings' "fidelity to southern interests" so that they could no longer be called "allies of abolitionists." With the sectional crisis so intense, both parties in the state had a difficult time defending the inconsistencies of their party and candidates. As one historian has recently noted, "it was . . . difficult to find a policy on slavery that could be a vote winner on both sides of the Mason-Dixon Line."[52] The voters of Louisiana would have the difficult task of determining which candidate served the best interests of their region and the country.

However, intimidation and fraud, in addition to the growing slavery and immigration issue, was a reality in this campaign. Neither political party was above using fraud or intimidation to win an election. New Orleans, with its large floating population, both native and foreign-born, was the scene of most of the Election Day abuses. The New Orleans municipal election of 1854 had been particularly violent and had set a precedent for the rest of the decade.[53] The Americans controlled the executive and legislative branch of the city government, and the Democrats the judicial branch. Therefore, the Know Nothings appointed the police and the election commissioners. Through the courts in New Orleans, the Democrats issued naturalization papers. Prior to the 1855 state election, the Americans had accused the Democrats of manufacturing voters.[54] On Election Day, the Know Nothing commissioners refused to accept the votes of these naturalized citizens and demanded naturalization papers from many suspect voters.[55] In addition, armed Know Nothings surrounded the polls throughout the city and tried to intimidate citizens to vote for the American candidates.[56] Election Day brought violence at various polling places in the city. Several precincts had their ballot boxes destroyed, votes discounted, or errors made in the tabulation. The Democratic press claimed that several Democratic candidates lost because of these "illegal" acts.[57]

As a result of these past Election Day experiences, the Democratic Party in 1856 was vigilant to the possibilities of fraud and violence. Governor Wickliffe, in an address to the state legislature, recognized that

New Orleans exercises a large control in the legislation of the State, and a
very large influence in general elections; hence, every restriction should be
placed upon her to prevent her corporate power from being abused to promote party purposes.[58]

The country parishes expected to return a large Democratic majority, and
Democrats had no intention of permitting ballot box breaking in New
Orleans to decide the election against their party. The *Calcasieu Press*
reported that the New Orleans vote would not be counted if any fraud
occurred in that city.[59]

Both Americans and Democrats in New Orleans anticipated violence.
The Democratic State Central Committee and the Parish Committee issued
a call to the city Democrats "to register themselves in order to aid in the
maintenance of law and order" on Election Day. The *Louisiana Courier*
could not understand the Americans' chagrin over this call since the Know
Nothings' "Union Hussars will doubtless prove themselves in November
an effective bodyguard of the Union."[60] However, the Americans took no
chances, and the Know Nothing mayor, Charles M. Waterman, ordered a
search for arms at the Charity Hospital and the offices of the Democratic
Louisiana Courier.[61] Although election violence did occur, it was compara-
tively mild. The *Daily True Delta* reported that "brass knuckles were more
frequently, the knife less commonly, employed upon citizens who desired
to vote the Democratic ticket. . . . Of course nobody expected protection
from the police, and nobody was disappointed" as the police simply did
nothing to preserve the peace.[62] If the violence was mild, intimidation must
have been effective. A Democratic majority in the 1852 presidential election and a small Know Nothing majority in the 1855 gubernatorial election
became a 3,400-vote American majority in 1856.[63] Nevertheless, as far as the
Democrats were concerned, the violence that did occur did not affect the
outcome of the state election.

In the state vote, the Know Nothings lost by approximately 1,400 votes.
The Americans carried fourteen parishes in 1856 as compared to sixteen parishes in the 1855 gubernatorial election, and seventeen carried by the Whigs
in the 1852 presidential election. Even though the Americans experienced
a decline in the total number of parishes carried in 1855, as well as in the
number the Whigs won in 1852, the Democratic majority hardly changed.
The Democratic majority in 1856 increased by only sixty-three votes from
that in the 1852 presidential election and actually dropped from 1855 by over
1,400 votes. This latter phenomenon is explained to a great extent by the

large majorities the Americans received in Orleans and Jefferson parishes. In 1855, New Orleans voters gave the American candidate for governor only a 400-vote majority, whereas in 1856 Fillmore carried that city by over 3,300 votes. The situation was comparable in Jefferson Parish. The Know Nothing majority was almost 200 votes in 1855 while in 1856 it had increased to over 800 votes.[64]

Despite the nomination of Fillmore by the national party, old-line Whigs in Louisiana showed less enthusiasm for Know Nothingism than in 1855. The relationship between the Whig presidential vote of 1852 and the Know Nothing vote of 1856 is not as significant as it had been in 1855. A parish-by-parish analysis demonstrates that the American Party suffered some of its worst defeats in former Whig parishes. Clearly, to some extent, the Democratic attacks on the Know Nothings' anti-Catholicism took its toll, particularly in some south Louisiana parishes.[65] Two former Whig parishes, St. John and St. Charles, deserted the Know Nothings in 1856. The Whigs in 1852 had carried St. John Parish with a majority of more than 55 percent of the vote in the presidential election and more than 53 percent in the gubernatorial election of the same year. In the 1855 gubernatorial election, the American Party carried St. John Parish with 53 percent of the vote. However, in 1856 the parish went Democratic by over 52 percent of the vote.[66] More dramatic was the vote in St. Charles Parish. The Whigs carried that parish in the 1852 presidential election with 72 percent of the vote and 79 percent in the 1852 gubernatorial race. The American Party barely carried St. Charles Parish in the 1855 gubernatorial election, and then received only 39 percent of the vote in the presidential election in 1856.[67] The most noticeable reversal occurred in Lafourche Parish. Returning a Whig majority of 83 and 82 percent in the 1852 presidential and gubernatorial elections, respectively, Lafourche Parish voters went Democratic in the 1855 gubernatorial race by 66 percent. Lafourche Parish supported Buchanan in 1856 with a 72 percent majority.[68]

However, what Whig apathy that did appear in 1856 for Fillmore did not result in a mass desertion of Whigs to the Democratic Party. Many former Whigs and Know Nothings, frustrated by repeated losses, most likely stayed at home during the presidential election. At the same time, there was no significantly visible movement of Whigs to the Democratic side from the 1852 election to the 1856 vote.[69] In addition, the Know Nothing majorities in the old Whig parishes of Madison, St. Martin, St. Mary, and West Baton Rouge remained relatively strong. Although these parishes had decreased majorities in 1856 as compared to 1855, all four returned a majority for Fillmore in excess of 53 percent of the total votes. Also, the Americans were victorious in the old Whig parish of Morehouse in 1856. That parish had recently voted Democratic in the 1855 gubernatorial campaign.[70]

Apparently, as in the 1855 gubernatorial election, neither party convinced slaveholders that one party would better protect slavery. Although slavery had played an important role in this campaign—in fact, the Democratic *Louisiana Courier* had called it the "great and pervading issue"—slave owners did not disproportionately support one or the other party. Even owners of twenty or more slaves, those with a greater vested interest in the institution, failed to support either the Democrats or Americans exclusively.[71] Despite a loss of some parishes with a large percentage of slaves, Lafourche, St. Charles, and St. John parishes, the Know Nothing Party still won majorities in others with equally as large slave populations. In West Baton Rouge, St. James, and St. Martin parishes, the American majority was over 56 percent of the total vote and those parishes had slave populations of 73, 70, and 58 percent, respectively. Of the fourteen parishes carried by the Know Nothing Party, eleven had a slave population of at least 52 percent, while half had a slave population of over 60 percent.[72]

In addition to slavery, the preservation of the Union ranked high among the issues of the campaign. The Union, and its maintenance, influenced a large number of those who voted for Fillmore. One Louisiana Know Nothing said that Fillmore was the only candidate who would "restore harmony . . . to our divided land." By using the election figures of 1856 and 1860, there is a strong connection between the 1856 American vote and the Constitutional Union Party vote in 1860. The American Party still attracted the conservative, Union-loving voter.[73] Evidently, while some Whigs either voted Democratic or simply did not vote, the American Party even garnered some support from Union Democrats. Of the three "new" parishes added to the American ranks in 1856, St. Helena Parish, before 1855, had consistently voted Democratic and St. Bernard Parish had often voted Democratic.[74] Conservatism and Unionism received favorable responses from the voters of the state because Louisiana had strong economic and social ties to the rest of the nation. "The Mississippi Valley fed its commerce, a tariff protected its sugar industry, and the North furnished many of its leading citizens." Typical was James Robb, who hoped railroads would provide the "iron bonds of mutual interest . . . to soften the asperities and prejudices that too often alienate and divide the citizens of our common country." Yet, Robb, although elected to office, acted similarly to other politician-businessmen unwilling to "surrender their business activities in the behest of office," and often resigned.[75] Even as late as the fall of 1860, Union men were being advised to "look to your business interest," and to avoid the secessionist impulse and, as historian Charles B. Dew believes, "Louisiana seemed the most firmly attached to the Union in 1860." Dew also notes that New Orleans' business leaders had a number of prominent northern-born members who were "lukewarm to the secessionist cause."[76]

Historian Michael Morrison describes the Know Nothing ticket in the South as a Unionist movement. Clearly, Louisiana fit this description. To a large degree, the conservatism and Unionism of the American Party was also a legacy of Whiggery. During the campaign, the Americans had stressed that Fillmore would be satisfactory to the South, particularly since he had signed the 1850 Compromise measure which "left things in a state of peace for Pierce." Know Nothing campaign material pointed out that Whig compromises "have repeatedly saved the Union—A Whig administration quelled sectional strife. . . ."[77] Then, when the old-line Whig movement organized in July, it endorsed the American candidates and their conservative and Union rhetoric.[78]

The reality of the current sectional politics surely influenced the conservative and Union stand taken by the Know Nothing Party. Because the Democratic Party talked about the danger of Union and constantly brought forward the Americans' alleged lack of concern for southern rights, the Know Nothings felt they had to make a strong case for the Union. When Judah Benjamin finally came out as a Democrat and included in his letter to another Democrat the following, "it is inconceivable that there can exist two parties now in the South," the Louisiana Know Nothings were enraged. It did not help the Americans that Benjamin continued his discourse on the election with "a vote for Fillmore . . . was a vote for Fremont." The *Louisiana Courier* entered the fray by criticizing the Americans' focusing on immigrants when slavery was the issue. In reaction to all of this, Americans stressed that the "conservative men of the South are rallying to elect Fillmore to preserve the Union, while Southern Locofocos . . . are planning the programme of a dissolution of the Union in the event of Fremont's election."[79] Although these conservative and Union men worked hard for Fillmore's election, they did not believe the Union would be dissolved even if Fremont was elected.[80]

For all of these reasons—economic self-interest, the Whig legacy, and plain politics—the massive swing over to the Democracy that occurred in the slave counties throughout the South was not as great in Louisiana as in some other southern states.[81] However, a detection of a movement to the Democracy does help explain why American majorities eroded in certain areas of the state.

There were other important groups in the state, in addition to New Orleans businessmen, who had an interest in the future of the Union, as well as the institution of slavery. Sugar cane and cotton planters both had a crucial interest in the future of the Union and slavery. But no planter group, whether sugar cane or cotton, expressed any unusual affinity for a particular party.[82] The American Party captured five cotton-producing parishes and seven sugar-growing parishes. Still noticeable, although to a lesser extent, was the support given the American Party in wealthy sugar and cotton parishes along the Red and Mississippi rivers. While the farmers in the hill country (the stronghold of the Democratic Party in the state) continued to support the Democracy, some sugar and cotton parishes lined up behind Buchanan.[83] The cotton parishes that voted for Fillmore were Caddo in northwest Louisiana, Morehouse, Madison, and Concordia in northeast Louisiana, and St. Helena in the Florida parishes. The Fillmore sugar parishes were Jefferson, St. Bernard, St. James, St. Mary, St. Martin, Terrebonne, and West Baton Rouge in the southeastern part of the state.[84]

Whether natives believed immigrants were antislavery or not, nativism did have an impact on Louisiana voters. Regardless of the American state policy to proscribe no citizen, the proximity of a large foreign-born population influenced Native Americans to support Fillmore.[85] The greatest concentration of foreign-born individuals was in Orleans, Jefferson, and St. Bernard parishes. All three parishes supported Fillmore, but the percentage in Jefferson and Orleans was extremely high, 88 and 69 percent, respectively.[86] James Broussard argues that despite the few immigrants in the South, the insistence of the American Party that northern immigrants were endangering slavery influenced southern voters.[87] Although this reasoning may have influenced some Louisiana voters, a more probable reason for the significant correlation between the American vote and a large percentage of foreign-born residents appeared often in Know Nothing newspapers. Charles Gayarré summed it up in his 1855 *Address*, noting that the immigrants are "now greedy and half famished—the greater portion have been reared in brutish ignorance . . . and cannot be expected to understand the complicated machinery of our political system." Like many other nativists, Gayarré had no objection to denying foreigners the right to office and he believed that "in this time of national crises only Americans should decide the country's fate."[88] Apparently nativists, particularly in the New Orleans area, felt threatened by the large number of immigrants and on Election Day agreed with Gayarré's assessment.

The anti-foreign-born attitude of the American Party affected the vote in 1856, while the earlier anti-Roman Catholic stance of the national American

Party apparently had less of an impact. The Democrats and the Roman Catholic newspapers of the state still could not convince Louisiana Roman Catholics of the dangers of Know Nothingism. Although the Americans failed to retain four heavily Roman Catholic parishes which the Whigs had won in 1852, Roman Catholics across the state showed no clear hostility to Fillmore's candidacy. Even in south Louisiana, which had a greater number of Catholics, Buchanan failed to receive an overwhelming mandate from the Catholics.[89] Know Nothing parishes such as Terrebonne, St. Martin, West Baton Rouge, and St. James had Catholic Church populations ranging from 61 percent of the church population to 100 percent.[90]

Therefore, in Louisiana the American Party continued to draw support from Whig areas of the state, areas with strong Union sentiment, a large foreign-born population, and even large numbers of Roman Catholics.[91] The perceived threat to slavery, promoted by the Democrats such as Benjamin and the editor of the *Louisiana Courier*, did not result in a solid Democracy in 1856, although movement in that direction was noticeable. The American Party had done fairly well in Louisiana, and many Americans remained buoyant after the defeat. They considered the Know Nothing Party as a viable alternative to the Democrats in Louisiana and the nation. One American newspaper even predicted that the American Party would have a national candidate in the field in 1860 for president.[92]

Regardless of the scattered post-1856 election optimism, the American defeat finished the party in the nation and Louisiana, except for New Orleans. National party members had hoped to throw the presidential election into the House. But the Americans had captured only the electoral votes of Maryland. In Louisiana, Know Nothings had fewer explanations for defeat in 1856 than in the past. A feeling of resignation set in. One editor lamented that he felt outnumbered. Or, in the words of another, the Know Nothings failed because of the lack of patriotism in their age.[93]

Buchanan's election, and Fremont's strong showing, sobered many Know Nothings. This turn of events left one American "no longer sanguine about the fate of the Union." Surely the rejection of Fillmore, who the Americans called the only national candidate, and the strength of the Republicans meant the continued agitation of the slavery question. These unionists asked, what could the country expect in 1860 from the black Republicans?[94] Despite Fremont's strength, Union-loving men in Louisiana could still be found. The *Bee* even found hope in Buchanan's election. Although dejected over Fillmore's defeat, it saw the election of Buchanan less a party victory than a triumph of Union-loving men of all parties who had united in an effort to defeat Fremont.[95]

Generally, the Americans hoped Buchanan would rid the country of sectionalism.[96] Some still thought the repeal of the naturalization laws, with Democratic assistance, would help.[97] Many refused to fight sectionalism with sectionalism, calling upon Union men everywhere to unite.[98] But a growing sense of helplessness led some Americans to advocate southern unity.

Know Nothing solidarity for Union had begun to crumble. A Plaquemine American believed all past political ties had to be forgotten. "A solid southern phalanx to combat the rising tide to preserve the union" had to be found. According to this disappointed unionist, a "Union of the South for the sake of the Union would protect inviolate the constitution and Union, stop northern fanaticism and sectionalism, and develop southern manufactures." This American editor of the *Southern Sentinel* denied his program was sectional and he argued that "the union of the southern people, then, for the purpose of effecting a great national end, is not of necessity a 'Southern Party.'"[99] While this attitude became contagious in the state, in the opinion of another American newspaper editor, the number of Union men in the South, though still a majority, daily declined.[100]

Southern unity continued to attract Know Nothings in 1857. Early that year, two Know Nothing editors,[101] opposed to sectionalism in principle, advocated a southern party for "the protection of constitutional and legal rights.[102] To some former Americans, continued support of the American Party would only aid the Republicans. The Democratic Party, according to these recent converts to southern rights, deserved the approbation of all southern men. They declared that the members of the American Party would vote only when capable Democrats were presented.[103]

Democrats had to appreciate such declarations. Members of the Democracy agreed that all southern Know Nothings should abandon their party for the Democratic Party. Democrats warned that Buchanan's election had only postponed the dissolution of the Union. If the Democracy failed to defeat Republicanism the South would seek to dissolve the Union. The Democratic *Baton Rouge Daily Advocate* agreed with the Know Nothing *Southern Sentinel* of Plaquemine that "an unbroken southern phalanx" would protect the interests of the South.[104]

However, numerous Americans vehemently opposed any talk of disunion.[105] Some expected to "sweep Louisiana in the upcoming fall elections."

A Know Nothing from the Florida parishes wrote, "Let our party be quiet, purge itself of all its bad doctrine and machinery, and remain at the same time true to the Union and the South."[106] Even that recent convert to sectionalism, the *Southern Sentinel,* vacillated between unionism and sectionalism.[107]

Neither unionism, sectionalism, nor nativism garnered much support among Louisianians in the 1857 judicial and local and parochial elections. Except in New Orleans, the Democracy had its way in these elections.[108] The Democrats had hoped to control the New Orleans elections through the artifice of a partisan election law passed by the Democratic controlled legislature in March 1857. When the Democrats introduced the bill, the Americans in the legislature called it revolutionary and tyrannical. It created an Election Board presided over by a Superintendent of Elections, appointed by the governor. Know Nothings objected to the summary arrest power the bill gave the superintendent. After the passage of the election law, the Americans questioned the constitutionality of the law. They believed it violated Article 124 of the state constitution which gave the citizens of New Orleans, not the governor, the right to appoint the police officers of the city.[109] However, the law did not become operative immediately. As a result, the Democrats called for a nonpartisan judicial race and offered no organized opposition in either election.[110] Taking advantage of their dominant position in New Orleans, the Americans won all judicial races.[111] The Native American goal to control the judicial branch of government in New Orleans had succeeded in this election. Former Democratic justices had illegally granted naturalization papers in the city, Americans alleged, and now the American Party leaders believed they could put an end to such demagogic practices. Immigrants would no longer be made "citizens" on the eve of elections to swell Democratic majorities. In the aldermanic contest, the Democrats could only criticize the extravagance of the American administration, as well as its anti-foreign attitude.[112] In the absence of their election law, the Democrats watched the Know Nothings sweep the election.

The state elections of 1857 would be the last major campaign for the American Party in Louisiana. However, in some areas of Louisiana the membership hardly acted like defeated men. Optimism abounded in some parish conventions. Ouachita Parish Know Nothings, for example, resolved that though defeated the Americans of Ouachita were not conquered.[113] Delegates nominated at these parish meetings went on to the state convention at Baton Rouge in June. There the party nominated their congressional and state candidates.[114] The state convention approved an address protesting immigration, and criticized the Democratic Party for its failure to protect the rights of the South in Kansas. The delegates also adopted resolutions critical of state Democrats for wasting public lands, neglecting the public schools, assailing the rights of popular suffrage, and bankrupting the state treasury. There was even the brief reappearance of the tariff issue.[115] But in this state campaign of 1857, both Know Nothings and Democrats, out of necessity, worked hard to demonstrate that their party best protected the South.

Even though the Americans had claimed in the 1856 election that the Democrats raised the bar on the sectional tension, the crisis continued. Ironically, but not unexpectedly, Know Nothings adopted a more southern posture. Officially the party still affirmed its conservative and Union goals, but during a time of heightened tension, Know Nothings chose a more distinct southern image. The overriding issue by 1856 and 1857 was a strong commitment to southern rights. With state offices at stake, along with the congressional positions, the American Party concentrated on national affairs. It was on national issues that Americans obviously hoped to expose what they considered the anti-southern attitude of the national Democracy. By this time, the politics of slavery had become too attractive to the Americans; as one recent scholar has remarked, "Not even southern nativists could escape the lure of the slavery issue's electoral power."[116]

Obviously, nativism, unless attached to disfranchising immigrants, received less attention in this campaign.[117] Know Nothings instead attacked the anti-republican and antislavery attitude of immigrants. Since the politics of slavery had become attractive to the American Party, the disfranchising of a large bloc of a growing northern electorate had a strong political appeal. Know Nothings, therefore, alleged that both black Republicans and northern Democrats struggled to acquire the alien vote that their section of the country hoped would help overcome southern power. In particular, the Know Nothings remained adamantly opposed to alien suffrage and squatter sovereignty. The *Daily Creole* thought it strange that the state rights men did not see the danger of alien suffrage and squatter sovereignty. According to the *Daily Creole*, the American Party would:

> arrest . . . the assaults which have been made upon the constitution by the fanaticism of the times. First, by arresting the growing power of foreign influence upon our government; and second, by uniting all American hearts to resist . . . aggression upon state rights.

Of course, the panacea of repealing the naturalization laws still received the approval of Louisiana Know Nothings.[118] One American newspaper demonstrated the importance of the foreign-born issue to all nativists when it declared that only when "the principle that Americans Shall Rule America is acknowledged throughout the country will the reason for the Know Nothing party cease."[119]

Americans injected President Buchanan's domestic and foreign program into the state campaign. Know Nothings agreed with the southern rights-oriented *New Orleans Daily Delta* that in both areas Buchanan had shortchanged the South.[120] For example, Americans wondered if Buchanan intended to continue former President Pierce's anti-filibustering policy in Central America. There was even some Democratic support for these overseas adventures. Many Louisiana Democrats and old Whigs had been supportive of these ventures in the late 1840s and early 1850s. As a result, the American Party believed it was "the natural destiny of Anglo-Americans to overrun Central America," and Americans made good use of this issue. Despite some concerns about violating international law, the Know Nothings made use of President Pierce's dismissal of Democrat Pierre Soulé from his post in Spain because of Soulé's expansionist views on Cuba. [121] Know Nothing newspapers also approved of General William Walker's Nicaraguan expedition and they believed that "the course of Americanism in Nicaragua is now bright." To many Know Nothing papers, Buchanan's support of Commodore Hiram Paulding's capture of William Walker in November 1857, made the American Party the "more reliable proslavery party."[122]

But Kansas became more important than Nicaragua during the campaign since filibusterer William Walker's rule had been overthrown before the campaign really intensified. Know Nothings found the idea of submitting the constitution of Kansas to a popular ballot obnoxious. President Buchanan's governor in Kansas, Robert Walker, had taken sides with the free-state party, according to the nativists, and approved of submitting the constitution to the actual residents.[123] To the Know Nothings, such a plan would be detrimental to the South. The American Party asked how the Democratic press could propose that all parties unite behind Buchanan when his administration followed policies so adverse to the South. Americans alleged that Buchanan's failure to remove Walker proved the president unfaithful to the South. In addition, the American Party press demanded to know why Democratic Senators Benjamin and Slidell, as well as the Louisiana Democratic congressional candidates, had not denounced Buchanan and Walker. The Know Nothings also pointed out that the address of the Democratic State Central Committee failed to censure either the president or Governor Walker. [124] As promising as Buchanan's and Walker's actions or inaction in Kansas appeared to be during the campaign, "Bleeding Kansas" predictably threatened what was left of any unity among northern and southern Know Nothings. William Freehling writes that, without Bleeding Kansas, maybe northerners would have "seen the Pope as the worst enemy to American republicanism."[125]

Of course, the Democrats of the state defended themselves, denying that Buchanan supported Governor Walker's actions. The southern Democracy, said Louisiana Democrats, condemned Walker, noting that President Buchanan rebuked the Kansas governor. The Democrats also claimed that Walker abandoned his earlier position of submitting the constitution to a popular vote and Senator Benjamin, addressed in a speech what southerners now questioned, the widespread antislavery sentiment in the free-states. To Benjamin and other southerners, the lack of equality over the admission of Kansas made it impossible for Kansas to ever "be admitted as a slaveholding state." The *Baton Rouge Daily Advocate* also believed it was the American opposition to the Kansas-Nebraska Act that was more dangerous than recent Democratic policy regarding Kansas. Additionally, according to this Democratic newspaper, the Know Nothings still favored the Missouri Compromise, "or some other measure restricting the institution of slavery." [126]

Meanwhile, the American Party found it difficult to maintain unanimity on the issue of Unionism as opposed to sectionalism. The issue of southern unity, which began soon after the 1856 defeat, continued in 1857. Despite their state convention resolution upholding the constitution and the Union,[127] a noticeable spirit of sectionalism crept into the editorials of some Know Nothing newspapers. Even pro-Democratic rhetoric could be found in some former American papers. For example, the *Plaquemine Southern Sentinel* and the *New Orleans Daily Crescent* advocated a united South "to preserve the Union."[128] The *Southern Sentinel*, soon after the American convention, decided that to support the American Party was hopeless. Other Know Nothings criticized this defeatist attitude and denied the people wanted a southern party.[129] But late in the campaign, even the staid and conservative *New Orleans Bee* conceded the reality of the death of the American Party in Louisiana. This newspaper urged the South to choose the lesser of two evils: the Democrats over the black Republicans.[130]

Because of these defections, the American candidates suffered another defeat. The Democrats won all three state offices. However, the American Party continued its predominance in New Orleans, despite the operation of the election law. But success in the city, and a few other local victories, did not halt the continued Know Nothing decline. The Democratic Party not only held its legislative majority, it increased that majority from seven to eleven in the House and from twelve to thirteen in the senate.[131]

The Know Nothings did no better in the congressional elections. Know Nothing strength in these elections centered mainly in the First and Second Congressional Districts (of which Greater New Orleans was a part).[132] With Greater New Orleans in the makeup of these two districts, the Americans had hopes of possibly capturing both the First and Second Congressional Districts. The voters of the First Congressional District did return Know Nothing George Eustis to Congress, but the party lost the other three congressional races. Despite the American majorities in Jefferson and Orleans parishes in the Second District, several of the country parishes returned large Democratic majorities to defeat the American candidate George W. Watterson in that district. They even failed to take advantage of a division within the Democracy in the Third District between the followers of John Slidell and the more state's-rights wing of the Democrats. This division had given the American Party faithful a glimmer of hope throughout the state. With Greater New Orleans a stronghold of the Know Nothings and the city, a part of both the First and Second Congressional District, they did have a reasonable expectation to capture both districts. Americans even joined forces in the Third District with the states'-rights Democrats, led by Pierre Soulé, in their criticism of the regular Democrats led by John Slidell. Slidell came under heavy criticism from the American press as a wire-puller and a northern-born, absentee politician whose southern loyalty came into question. Despite the discord within the Democratic Party, which the Know Nothings believed would benefit them, nothing worked in the end. The Know Nothings lost the Third District by over 700 votes.[133] Outside of the New Orleans area, and the parishes of Concordia, Madison, St. James, and St. Martin, the Democratic majorities increased significantly over the 1855 congressional elections.[134]

A strong, continuing relation between the American congressional vote in 1857 and the Constitutional Union Party vote in 1860 continued to point to a relationship between conservative and Union men and the Know Nothing Party. Increased emphasis on southern rights by the Americans apparently did not deter many of these "Union-loving" men from voting for the American candidates. Union men still believed the American Party offered the better choice. Investors in manufacturing, with their ties to northern and European capital, likewise supported the American Party.

But wherever strident state rights attitudes prevailed (based on a relationship between the 1857 Know Nothing congressional and the 1860 Southern Democratic presidential vote), the Know Nothings received less support than the Democrats.[135] Old Whig cotton and sugar parishes along the Red and Mississippi Rivers, as well as the sugar parishes of St. Martin and Terrebonne, returned Know Nothing majorities. Even though the American Party held its own in the old Whig area of the state, former members of that party showed no preference for the Know Nothings as they had in previous elections in the state.[136] But Whigs did not overwhelmingly defect to the Democrats.

Nativism and slave ownership influenced few Louisianians to vote for Democratic or American candidates. Again, the alleged anti-Roman Catholicism of the American Party had no major effect on the vote in 1857. As in previous elections, parishes with large Catholic majorities continued to vote for the Know Nothing congressional candidates, albeit, to a lesser degree.[137] Nor did slave owners believe that the Americans would better protect the institution of slavery than the Democrats.[138] However, Americans did do well in some of the large slaveholding parishes, including Caddo, Concordia, Madison, St. James, and West Baton Rouge. All of these parishes had a slave population comprising at least 60 percent of the total population.[139] Therefore, slave owners apparently thought little of the continuing Democratic allegation that Know Nothingism was synonymous with abolitionism. Additionally, as in the case of religion, neither did the planters of the state vote for either party in a discernible bloc.[140] Finally, the presence of a large foreign-born population, by this time in the late 1850s, failed to have any significant effect on the voters across the state.[141]

In the final analysis, the nativism of the American Party meant less to the voters of the state and to the Americans themselves, than it had previously. Protection of southern rights and the preservation of the Union became the leading issues of the day. The American Party, in its fight against the sectionalist impulse, sought to preserve the Union. Yet, the Americans' desire for victory in Louisiana led them into some apparent contradictions. Although in favor of the Union, Know Nothings took an increasingly stronger prosouthern position. There were simply too many slaves in the state with too many Louisianians committed to slavery, and the politics of slavery clearly affected the Know Nothings.[142] However, to the Americans there was nothing inconsistent with standing up for the South and preserving the Union. These two goals were not incompatible. Americans believed that the nation, the South, and the state needed office holders who would not exacerbate the sectional controversy. In 1856, they had stressed that Fillmore was such a man. He was the only national candidate and was, therefore, the best qualified to protect the interests of the South. The repeal of the Missouri Compromise line, the Kansas-Nebraska Act, and doctrines like "Popular Sovereignty" had been the machinations of the Democratic Party. All had led to the civil strife in Kansas and agitation in Congress, none of which helped the South or the Union. However, after 1857 in Louisiana, all of the American program and goals became moot, since that party, as such, would not offer another candidate for state or congressional office.

Party unity and voter appeal for the Americans had centered on either nativism or the preservation of the Union. State issues provided little help in either party cohesiveness or voter appeal. State campaigns dealt mainly with national political issues. In some fashion, as one historian has said, a "commitment to slavery had become the single litmus test for candidates."[143] Americans denounced the foreign-born and Roman Catholics, and devoted their energy to changing the Naturalization Laws of the United States. Know Nothings always found it propitious to demonstrate that the naturalization laws affected other national policies and institutions. For example, matters such as Kansas-Nebraska, slavery, free-soilism, and homestead legislation always found their way into the debates over immigration and the naturalization laws. Since a large number of the immigrants were Roman Catholics, the anti-Catholic bias of the American Party received considerable attention during the 1850s. This emphasis on national issues and the problem of naturalization pushed further into the background the issues over which Whigs and Democrats had traditionally opposed each other. Issues like railroads, internal improvements, and banking no longer remained as divisive in Louisiana. Indicative of the problem was the plea of the *New Orleans Daily Delta* in 1855 to keep federal politics out of local affairs.[144] However, few heeded this advice to any great extent.

As a result of the emphasis on nativism and national politics, state issues and the meager American state program received little attention or support.[145] One plank in the American Party platform of 1855—"Reform of abuses, and retrenchment in our State expenditures"—was so vague that the party hardly addressed itself to that issue. Another plank, "Education of the youth of the country in schools established by the State," had little meaning in Louisiana. The state spent only $300,000 annually on public education. This limited financial support prompted the Superintendent of Public Education to report that "there really is not a single feature of the system anything approaching what it ought to be."[146] In Louisiana, Democratic and American legislators primarily opposed each other over questions of fraudulent voting, contested elections, and a registry law and election law for the American stronghold of New Orleans.

The Democratic legislators from 1856 to 1858 used their majorities in both houses of the General Assembly to weaken the American Party in the legislature and in New Orleans. The first order of business for the 1856 legislature was the removal of Know Nothing Sheriff Joseph Hufty, of New Orleans, and of three American senators and several representatives from that city. The *Louisiana Courier* reported that the votes on these removals were strictly partisan actions, referring to the unseating of the Americans as "another great work on the part of the majority."[147] The final senate vote on an "Address" to remove Sheriff Hufty from office clearly demonstrated the partisanship involved. The vote was nineteen to twelve, with every American present voting no.[148]

The struggle for political dominance continued in the legislature with the introduction in 1856 of a bill to register voters in New Orleans and an election bill in 1857. The former bill actually received the support of both parties, but the Democrats claimed they had always feared they might be "interfering with free suffrage" if such a law passed.[149] Know Nothings, however, attributed the Democratic reluctance to pass such a law to partisan politics. A. G. Brice, a Know Nothing representative, believed a registry law would mean a loss of money to the Democratic State Central Committee. A registry law would end the election frauds in New Orleans, and the Democrats, according to Brice, could no longer buy and sell the several "offices of emolument."[150] Americans and Democrats divided over whether naturalized citizens should "show more proof of citizenship" in order to register. The Americans favored a strict proof of citizenship, but the Democrats were opposed. A vote on one section of the bill requiring a strict proof of citizenship resulted in eight Know Nothings, along with two Democrats, voting yes, with only one American and thirteen Democrats voting nay.[151]

The election law passed in 1857 was also a partisan piece of legislation aimed specifically at weakening the Americans in New Orleans. According to the *New Orleans Bee*, this law removed from New Orleans officials:

all control over the arrangements for elections, the appointment of Commissioners, and the establishment of places for voting, and vests those powers in an irresponsible Board and an Executive officer who is clothed with absolute authority.[152]

The bill passed the senate by an eighteen-to-ten vote—all Democrats in favor and all Americans opposed.[153] In the House, the vote was thirty-six to nineteen in favor. Again, as in the senate, not a single American Party member voted for the bill.[154]

Beyond these questions of power politics,[155] there was little partisanship on substantive issues. State aid to railroads, internal improvements, and more liberal banking laws no longer excited the party struggles as they did during the Whig-Democratic era. Leasing of the state penitentiary and the importation of free black laborers, which received limited attention in the 1850s, likewise failed to divide state legislators along partisan lines. Both political parties to a greater or lesser extent supported these programs. Two issues on which the Americans gave the appearance of presenting a clear alternative to the Democrats were a constitutional organization of the Swamp Land Commission and an efficient Internal Improvement Department. However, even on these two issues party unity disappeared in the General Assembly.

Long before the appearance of the Know Nothing Party, Whigs and Democrats had recognized the advantage of state aid to railroads. The Whig-controlled constitutional convention of 1852 restored to the legislature the authority to grant aid of the state to railroad ventures. Then, the Democratic General Assembly in 1853 voted state aid to three major railroads: the Vicksburg, Shreveport, and Texas Railroad Company, the New Orleans, Opelousas, and Great Western Railroad Company, and the New Orleans, Jackson, and Great Northern Railroad Company. Democrats had been instrumental in prohibiting such aid in the old 1845 State Constitution. However, in the 1850s Democratic newspapers found great virtue in the state subscribing to private railroad companies stock. The Democratic *Courier* believed the Vicksburg, Shreveport, and Texas railroad would increase the population of north Louisiana and would help "counteract the diversion of trade from New Orleans which railroads of the North and West had done."[156] The *Baton Rouge Daily Advocate* hoped that the legislature could provide "amply" for another railroad venture: the Baton Rouge, Grosse Tete, and Opelousas Railroad.[157] This latter railroad company and the New Orleans and Baton Rouge Railroad Company received support from both

Know Nothings and Democrats. Both won state aid in the legislature, and the New Orleans and Baton Rouge line secured the endorsement of the Democratic governor.[158] The final senate vote on the bill granting aid of the state to the New Orleans and Baton Rouge Railroad Company was twenty-two in favor and five opposed. Of the five opposed, four were Democrats and one, William M. Kidd, was a Know Nothing.[159]

The only real political feud that developed during the debates over state aid to railroads was state sectionalism, or north Louisiana legislators versus south Louisiana legislators. During the discussion of the New Orleans and Baton Rouge railroad bill, Francis Oliver, a Democrat who represented the north Louisiana parishes of Catahoula, Caldwell, and Franklin, opposed this bill because his home parish of Catahoula had no railroad tracks in it, yet that parish would be taxed to pay for the interest on state railroad bonds.[160] This issue of sectionalism in the state would not come to fruition for a few years, but the argument did point out that opposition to this bill, including William Kidd's, appears to have been based not on any ideology or a party position but more on a sectional bias.[161]

The question of internal improvements also elicited support from most legislators and the press of the day. When opposition did arise to internal improvements, it concerned the creation of a new Board of Public Works, speculation and waste in the management of the state swamp lands, or which section of Louisiana received its fair share of tax dollars for internal improvements.[162] The American Party introduced a controversy by supporting what they called "a constitutional organization of the Swamp Land Commissioners" during the 1855 state campaign. The controversy continued in Louisiana until 1859, centering on the 1852 state constitution provision for an elective Board of Public Works to supersede the old Swamp Land Commission. However, the Democratic governor continued to appoint the members of the Swamp Land Commission. While the Know Nothing Party regularly attempted to capitalize on the refusal of the Democrats to create the elective Board of Public Works, nativism and naturalization always dominated the American Party platform and editorials.[163] In addition, not every Know Nothing agreed with the necessity of an elective board. Duncan Kenner, an American from Ascension Parish, did not believe the Louisiana Constitution mandated the legislature to create an elective Board of Public Works. He thought it was just "directory." In fact, Kenner voted with the Democratic majority to repeal those sections of the constitution which created so much controversy over whether an elective Board of Public Works should be established.[164] Actually, the Americans received more cooperation from certain Democrats on this issue than from Kenner. Whereas Kenner voted against his party, Democrat Adam Beatty from Terrebonne Parish favored following up the constitutional requirement. In addition, four other Democrats during this same 1856 legislative session voted against a move to recommit a bill which did provide for the creation of an elective Board of Public Works.[165]

Know Nothings again demonstrated their inconsistency and lack of unity when legislation concerning internal improvement projects came up for consideration in the General Assembly. Even though the American Party approved of internal improvements, several Know Nothings opposed any project which would be funded from the Swamp Land Fund of the state. These party diehards refused to vote affirmatively on any such funded project until "there was a constitutional organization of a Board of Public Works."[166] This issue was an integral plank in the 1855 American Party's state platform. However, soon after one Know Nothing senator outlined this party policy for the legislature, six Americans voted along with eight Democrats on a senate bill which authorized an appropriation for $130,000 to construct a levee in Madison Parish with money from the Swamp Land Fund.[167] Know Nothing policy fared no better in the legislative sessions of 1857 and 1858. A bill to construct levees in Catahoula Parish with appropriations from the Swamp Land Fund passed the senate with the help of six Americans. In 1858, Know Nothing Senator Joseph M. Ducros, a member of the Committee on Swamp Lands, introduced a bill (subsequently passed by the senate) which appropriated $25,000 from the Swamp Land Fund "to finish work in progress in the Second Swamp Land District."[168]

Know Nothings had even less success in achieving unity over the management of public lands in Louisiana. During the 1855 state campaign, the American Party included in its state policy the pledge of "a more efficient administration of the Internal Improvement Department, with a view of improving our inland navigation."[169] Throughout the 1855 campaign, the state campaign of 1857, and as late as 1858, American Party newspapers accused the Democrats of squandering state land, speculating with state land, and mismanaging swamp land funds.[170] Nevertheless, when an American senator from New Orleans attempted to amend a levee construction bill (the amendment provided against speculation), several Know Nothings deserted him. The amendment would have required anyone purchasing land affected by the proposed levee to take an oath that "he does not apply to purchase any portion of said lands for the purpose of speculation." Additionally, the amendment limited the number of acres that could be purchased. The chair ruled his amendment out of order, and five American senators helped sustain the ruling.[171]

The absence of American unanimity on public lands continued throughout the 1858 legislature. The Know Nothing *New Orleans Daily Crescent* had complained about the high cost of reclaiming swamp land and the low price for which it sold.[172] Yet, only three Know Nothing senators in 1858 voted against the sale of one million acres of swamp land at one dollar and twenty-five cents per acre. At least five Americans in the senate voted for the land sale.[173]

Know Nothing senators continued to split their votes on the subject of state lands, while Americans in the House of Representatives demonstrated little enthusiasm for the Know Nothing position on alleged Democratic mismanagement of state lands. Even though American newspapers in Baton Rouge and New Orleans detailed the abuses in the First Swamp Land District of the state, a majority of the American representatives failed to vote on crucial bills concerning that district.[174] In 1856, at least twenty-one American representatives were absent when the house passed a bill appropriating $32,000 for work in the First District. Shortly after that vote, just nineteen representatives voted against an appropriation of $250,000 "to be placed at the disposal of the commissioners of the Swamp Land Districts for drainage and reclamation."[175] Considering the low opinion the American Party had for the Swamp Land Commission, a larger number of American representatives in attendance should have been expected for this vote on such a large appropriation.

On the financial front, the American Party remained silent in 1855 and 1856 on the issue of banks and banking. However, during the financial panic of 1857, and the state campaign of that year, the Know Nothings spoke up. In an "Address to the People of Louisiana," the Know Nothings charged that "the action of the Legislature with respect to the banks, has been illiberal and injudicious." The "Address" continued with the assertion that "restriction should not be imposed upon the banks which operate as obstruction to trade and commerce."[176] Specifically, the American newspapers noted that the Democratic legislature had been illiberal in refusing to charter new banking institutions.[177]

⋯⋯⋯⟨◆⟩⋯⋯⋯

The *Louisiana Courier* felt it was absurd for the Americans "to come out at this time when the business of the whole country is shaken to its very centre in consequence of privileges unjustly and injudiciously extended to moneyed corporations." According to the *Courier*, "the banks of Louisiana are sound because the Legislature of Louisiana resisted interested appeals for their indefinite multiplication, and carefully restrained their operations within the bounds of safety."[178]

The banking issue once again received the attention of the legislature in 1858. Americans and Democrats found themselves at odds when the Joint Committee on Banks and Banking of the two Houses of the General Assembly, in a lengthy report, recommended in part that "no more banks shall be created under the Free, or General Banking Law."[179] Know Nothing Senator Edward Delony from East Feliciana Parish opposed that part since he believed it conflicted "with the intent and spirit of the article of the Constitution authorizing Free Banking."[180] Although several Americans advocated more banks, Know Nothing solidarity also fell apart on this question. During the 1858 legislative session, the senate debated a bill which would prohibit the future establishment of any banks or banking corporations under the provisions of the Free Banking Act of 1855. A motion to lay the bill indefinitely on the table (which would have in effect killed the bill) came up for a vote late in the session. Not all the Americans voted yes on the motion, as might have been expected. Of the six Americans voting, three voted to kill the bill and three against. The senate killed the bill, but it required the efforts of several Democrats who voted to lay the bill indefinitely on the table.[181]

The 1857 and 1858 legislative sessions dealt not only with the banking question, the leasing of the state penitentiary and the importation of free black laborers were two other measures that created a slight stir. Because the election bill of 1857 and the question of creating more banks in the midst of a financial crisis occupied much of the legislators' time, the penitentiary and black laborer problems received less attention from the General Assembly. Members of both parties spoke for and against legislation concerning these two issues. Neither political party appeared to take a definitive stand, and individual legislators voted without party discipline. The American Party certainly had no official opinion on either question. Know Nothing Joseph Chew, senator for Concordia and Tensas parishes, spoke out against leasing the penitentiary. He believed that "in leasing it you may aid in enriching one or two favorite individual citizens." However, two of his fellow American senators disagreed and voted for leasing while four others were absent for the vote. The division of the party continued as four other Americans joined Chew in opposing the leasing agreement which passed by a fifteen to eight vote.[182]

The 1858 bill to import free black laborers, or, as it was more popularly known, the "African Apprentice Bill," also received divided support from both political parties. Actually, the bill was nothing more than a disguise that would provide for the reopening of the African slave trade.[183] On a test vote to adopt section one of the bill, five Americans voted in favor while three opposed. The test vote was tied when the Democratic President of the senate, C. H. Mouton broke the tie by voting yes. However, the bill became so controversial that the legislature later postponed it indefinitely.[184]

A final insult to what little party unity existed among the Americans came in the 1859 legislature when party members failed to vote unanimously for Randall Hunt in his bid for United States senator. Hunt, former Know Nothing candidate for attorney general in 1855, secured only five votes from Americans. The *Louisiana Courier* reported that Know Nothings voted in greater numbers for the two Democratic candidates. Judah P. Benjamin received six or seven American votes, Henry Gray received twenty or thirty, and Hunt five.[185] Of course, this was simply consistent with what Know Nothings had been doing with their votes throughout the 1850s. Initially, the Americans had presented what appeared to be a united party. However, the problem was the inability of Know Nothing state legislators to achieve party unity within the General Assembly. This lack of unity, along with the growing need to present a stronger southern rights stand, helps to account for the weakening of the Know Nothing Party in the state.

FIVE

Nativism Struggles: 1858–60

The defeat of the American Party in 1857 surprised few Know Nothing supporters. According to one Know Nothing newspaper, the inaction of American candidates and the lethargy of the leaders of the party throughout the state caused the defeat.[1] One American wrote that since all their "friends" were defeated, "we must submit."[2]

But pockets of Know Nothing resistance persisted in the state, most notably in New Orleans, and American candidates elsewhere did continue to offer themselves for local public offices. In addition, some of the ideology of the American Party persisted. Nativism remained part of the American rhetoric, particularly in the Baton Rouge area, but its importance declined. Toward the end of the 1850s, those newspapers that had supported American principles of nativism and republican values centered their attention more upon the problem of the preservation of the Union. As historian John Bladek has written, when the national American Party divided, the old Whigs pushed their agenda of Unionism. These adherents of Americanism continued to oppose what they perceived to be a growing demand for "anarchical extreme southern rights; a Great Southern Party and a dissolution of the Union."[3] Therefore, they grasped at any chance to oppose disunionist sentiment. With the national American Party gone, and its anti-Roman Catholic rhetoric less of an issue, many old-line Whigs were less hesitant to join with Americans in their attempt to preserve the Union. Of course, it was in vain, but these Know Nothings and former Whigs continued to hope Unionism would prevail.

However, these Americans and former Whigs had to decide to what party they could turn to accomplish their goal. The American Party press recognized both its own weakened position and the Democrats' lack of opposition in the South.[4] Desertions from the Know Nothings occurred too frequently. Many Know Nothing voters and newspapers either joined the Democracy or urged cooperation with the Democrats. The Know Nothing *Plaquemine Southern Sentinel* became the Democratic *Gazette and Sentinel* in early 1858, announcing that the "Democratic party has swallowed up or destroyed all opposition." According to the editor, the paper changed its affiliation because the Democratic Party could check northern fanaticism. Even the *New Orleans Bee* at one point advocated cooperation with the Democrats rather than remaining neutral. One Know Nothing withdrew from the party citing the contamination of his party with abolitionism and black Republicanism. However, many of the defections could be attributed to the failure of the American Party to become a national party and its failure to achieve its main goal of reforming the naturalization laws of the country.[5] American legislative strength by 1859 was barely existent, and those in the legislature who called themselves Americans sometimes supported sectional legislation which hardly aided the American goal of Unionism.[6]

As a result, the American Party existed only on the local level, and even there its existence remained precarious. One American paper claimed the Know Nothings possessed a majority of the Iberville Parish Police Jury, but opponents claimed these alleged Know Nothings were in fact Independents.[7] Further proof of the weakness of the American Party, outside of Greater New Orleans, was evident in the Baton Rouge municipal elections of 1858 and 1859. In 1858, the Americans managed to win only three of the nine positions in the municipal election; so hopeless did the situation appear that the Know Nothing candidate for mayor withdrew in favor of an Independent candidate. The Democrats charged that the ticket had been presented for appearances only. And by 1859 Know Nothings in Baton Rouge failed to present a ticket.[8]

Even in the citadel of Americanism, New Orleans and its surrounding area, the party no longer presented a unified front. In the 1858 municipal election, an Independent movement appeared. The *Daily Crescent* called the Independent ticket a John Slidell trick and an aristocratic movement.[9] The Democrats presented no formal ticket, generally supported the Independent candidates and hoped their sponsored election law would control Know Nothing violence. However, Democrats denied the American charge that the Independents constituted a Slidell trick. Indeed, some Know Nothings, opposed to the continuing violence involved in the elections of the city, also supported the Independents. According to one supporter of the independent ticket, bullies and cutthroats had taken over the American Party. The *Plaquemine Gazette and Sentinel* wrote about how the Independents wanted to combat "years of thuggery, disorder, outrage, and unchecked assassination." Therefore, some of the propertied Know Nothing merchants, tired of the violence and how the labor wing of the American Party had become more assertive, threw their support behind the Independents. One historian notes that the moneyed merchants of the city supported the Independents' mayoral candidate while the working-class natives felt businessman mayor, Charles Waterman, no longer protected natives' interest. These working men believed they had taken all the risks in the past and they now moved to take over the party in the city. Class tension had taken precedence over nativism in the city.[10]

For mayor, the Independents nominated a political novice and military man, P. G. T. Beauregard, who campaigned for reform of the city government. But Beauregard also introduced a national issue into the city campaign, announcing that although he supported the Union he did not intend to sacrifice the rights of the South.[11] Focusing on the local campaign, some of Beauregard's supporters, in order to insure a peaceful election, formed a vigilance committee, took over a state arsenal, and manned barricades around Jackson Square. Not to be outdone, the Know Nothings organized an opposition force, held Lafayette Square in the "uptown" area of the city, and the city prepared for the coming battle. A last-minute compromise allowed the election to be held rather peacefully; many voters fearing violence avoided the polls. Not even with the new Democratic orchestrated election law, could the Know Nothings be denied. They carried the election, but the Democratic *Louisiana Courier* boldly declared Know Nothingism in New Orleans dead.[12]

The announced death of the Americans in New Orleans was somewhat premature because in the 1859 and 1860 elections factionalism again surfaced. Another Independent Citizens ticket made its appearance in the city in 1859 and the dissident Americans organized a Citizens ticket in 1860. By 1859, according to one Democratic paper, the Know Nothing Party in New Orleans had become so disorganized that it now had to woo some of the very people it had formerly criticized, the German voters of the city. The Americans succeeded in the New Orleans elections of 1859 and 1860, but once again, the party had not presented a unified front and a Baton Rouge Democratic paper, reported, apparently erroneously, that the American Party in New Orleans had succumbed and "gone into line with the only national party," the Democrats.[13] In these municipal elections in New Orleans, the issue of nativism no longer played a major role. Nativism had apparently become obscured by a struggle between the financial "haves and have-nots." From accounts in the New Orleans press, the moneyed faction in 1858, 1859, and 1860 had become disillusioned or, as one historian has said, frightened by the violent aspects of the Know Nothing Party in the city. As one critic of the Know Nothings put it, the "proper members, not being able to correct things dropped away."[14]

Despite its continuation in New Orleans, the American Party had little success in the more rural parishes of the state. Its failure to win on Election Day led Americans to admit that the party had disbanded in every parish except Orleans. One American, at this late date, wrote the party was now "without any head and front."[15]

Although the American Party had virtually disbanded in the state, many former Whigs and Know Nothings refused to permit the Democrats to go unchallenged. In March 1859, old Whig and Know Nothing members of the Louisiana General Assembly announced their intention to reorganize the Whig Party. According to the Whig "Address to the People of Louisiana," northern Democrats were adverse to slavery and opposed its extension. The "Address," in some respects attempting to revive some of the old issues of the 1840s and perhaps with a feeling of desperation, noted that the national Democratic Party failed to present a unified program on the tariff, internal improvements, the acquisition of Cuba, a Pacific railroad, state rights, and the African slave trade. The *New Orleans Bee* did not find this Whig resurgence surprising. In Louisiana, dissension continued among the Democrats, particularly between the Slidell and Soulé wings of that party in the state, as well as, on the national level, and the *Bee* alleged the Democratic troubles were the result of the failure of the Buchanan administration.[16]

The Whig intention to reorganize, however, did not receive unanimous support. Many Whigs and Know Nothings expressed the conviction that both the state and nation needed an alternative to the Democratic Party. But the confused state of the American Party and the politics of the day prompted a mixed reaction to the news of a Whig reorganization. The Know Nothing *Daily Crescent* pronounced the Whig Party dead. Any resurrection would be impossible and no good would come from this, argued that newspaper, since the Democratic Party had appropriated many of the Whig principles.[17] Another American Party paper, the *Shreveport South-Western*, exhibited more enthusiasm. The editor of the *South-Western* reported that Caddo Parish would be well represented at the Whig convention in New Orleans in June.[18] As expected, the Democrats referred to the Whig effort as hopeless, while the *Louisiana Courier* specifically labeled it as an attempt to "disguise the Know Nothing cat with Whig meal."[19]

As the 1859 gubernatorial election approached, opponents of the Democracy urged some kind of organized political opposition to the Democrats in Louisiana. The remnants of the American Party showed no inclination to field a state ticket. The Know Nothing Party did offer candidates for local offices and legislative positions. One Know Nothing, Dr. Thomas J. Buffington, ran for state senator in East Baton Rouge Parish with no party backing, and in Avoyelles Parish, Colonel Fenelon Cannon ran for the General Assembly as an American Democrat.[20] Most American candidates for local offices were seen in Caddo, Rapides, Terrebonne, and Orleans parishes. Caddo and Terrebonne parishes had been consistent Whig and Know Nothing parishes, while Orleans Parish claimed the only well-organized American Party wigwam. The continued existence of the American Party newspaper, the *Alexandria American*, certainly aided the Know Nothings of Rapides Parish in south-central Louisiana. However, the fragmentation of the American Party weakened the efforts of the Know Nothings in the local campaigns. The Caddo Parish Americans eventually dropped the name American in favor of the label Opposition Party, and in Rapides Parish the Know Nothings included two Democrats on their ticket.[21]

Statewide opposition to the Democratic party received little support. The recent Whig call had largely gone unheeded, and most Whigs and Know Nothings believed further attempts to revive it would fail.[22] The *Shreveport South-Western* urged opponents of the Democratic Party to form an opposition party.[23] However, the *Bee* believed that the only opposition would probably come from the discontented portion of the Democracy.[24]

Many discontented Democrats had been around since the state's-rights Democrats had failed to defeat Slidell's choice for Congress in the Third Congressional District in 1857, and by 1859, the Slidell-Soulé division brought out more rebellious Democrats. The "Regular," or Slidell Democrats, charged that these dissidents, or "Purifiers" as they were called, intended to defeat the Democrats and would accept "all aid, even from the followers of 'Rip Sam.'"[25] Some Know Nothings did endorse this dissident Democratic movement, and the *Baton Rouge Advocate* reported that a meeting in Plaquemines Parish resulted in a coalition between the Know

Nothings and "Purificators." East Feliciana Parish Know Nothings also endorsed the "New Line," or Soulé Democrats.[26] Additionally, the *Advocate* charged that Know Nothings had aided the "Purifiers" in appointing their delegates who would nominate state candidates.[27] However, John Slidell, the Democratic administration leader in Louisiana, showed little concern over this movement which had been organized by Pierre Soulé. Slidell informed President Buchanan that despite Soulé's determination to bring disaffected Democrats and Know Nothings together, the old-line Democrats had a decided majority, and would control the nomination of the state ticket.[28]

Soulé's inability to control the Democratic Party in naming a state ticket, as well as the weakness of the American Party, led to increased speculation that Soulé dissidents intended to bring about a Know Nothing-Soulé fusion to carry the state.[29] The Soulé "New-Line" Democrats, at a hastily called meeting in early April 1859, called for Whigs, Know Nothings, and Democrats to support former Democratic Representative Andrew Herron for governor. Although the *Bee* believed Soulé's Independent Democrats and the Know Nothings could cause trouble for the regular Democrats, the *Bee* was distressed that the Democrats would probably go unopposed in the elections.[30] The *New Orleans Commercial Bulletin* reported that the country press also called for opposition to the Democrats. The Know Nothing *American* of Rapides Parish hoisted the name of Thomas J. Welles of Rapides as its choice for governor in opposition to the regular Democratic nominee. Yet the *Commercial Bulletin* thought it useless to contest the Democratic nominees. Only in the Second Congressional District did the *Commercial Bulletin* believe the Know Nothings had a chance since the Democratic incumbent, Miles Taylor, had supported the purchase of Cuba which would hurt him with the state's sugar interests located in that congressional district. Although disaffected Democrats continued to correspond "with those belonging to other parties," the *Commercial Bulletin* noted that little progress had been made.[31]

Opponents to the regular Democratic ticket did meet in New Orleans in September to nominate candidates for state office.[32] The convention consisted of several former Know Nothings and Pierre Soulé Democrats, and according to the *New Orleans Bee*, the convention did not amount to anything. The opponents had waited too long to present a ticket, and success for an Opposition Party appeared dim since only five parishes had sent representatives to the convention.[33] The Know Nothing press of Baton Rouge also objected to the name "Opposition Party." The *Baton Rouge Weekly Gazette and Comet* suggested the party be called the Democratic

Know Nothing Party or the American Democratic Know Nothing Party. In addition, this newspaper bemoaned what it called the incorporation by the Democrats of all the best Know Nothing principles and leaders.[34] But with little hope of the now disbanded Know Nothing Party presenting its own ticket, the weekly *Gazette and Comet* pleaded with Americans and Independent Democrats to vote the Opposition ticket and defeat "King Caucus." [35] Another Know Nothing paper was conflicted between supporting the Soulé or the Slidell Democrats, but the *West Baton Rouge Sugar Planter* finally came out for supporting the Slidell Democrats. Other former Know Nothings objected to the influence of disgruntled Democrats in the party, especially Soulé. One old Whig who had serious objections to Slidell nonetheless said that Slidell was "a safer man than Pierre Soulé."[36]

Not every American or disgruntled Democrat despaired of the chances of the Opposition Party. The *New Orleans Daily Crescent* claimed it had met with an encouraging reception. Alexandria Know Nothings predicted that Democrats and Americans alike would vote for the nominees of the Opposition Party. According to the *Alexandria American*, the people of Louisiana "have become tired of seeing fools and knaves foisted into office."[37] And the editor of the *West Baton Rouge Sugar Planter* refused to vote for the Democrats just because they represented, at the time, the only obstacle to black Republicanism. This writer believed that the Opposition Party was greatly underrated, and that that party offered a viable alternative on Election Day.[38]

Democrats, however, thought little of the Opposition Party. They dismissed it as a group of old Know Nothings simply seeking to hold office, and the *Louisiana Democrat* of Alexandria characterized the convention which nominated the Opposition ticket as "a body consisting of a New Orleans Know Nothing delegation and such straggling Samuelites or sore-headed Democrats as may have been in town at the time."[39] According to the *Louisiana Democrat*, the Opposition had adopted no platform, only resolutions written by one member of the New Orleans Know Nothing wigwam. That newspaper also charged that the delegation from Rapides Parish represented only a single precinct. The New Orleans American Party, the *Louisiana Democrat* asserted, organized the Opposition movement to appear as a statewide party, and not a spoils party.[40]

Despite Democratic allegations to the contrary, the Opposition Party did adopt a platform. In fact, there were some former Americans who objected to the last clause of the platform which invited "all citizens" to cooperate with the Opposition Party.[41] Indeed, these old nativists had to be chagrined since the issue of nativism was conspicuously absent from this campaign and "all citizens" seemed to be a call even to the foreign-born. More prominent in this platform was a denunciation of the Buchanan administration. According to the Opposition Party, the national administration had not fulfilled its pledges to the people. Primarily the Opposition charged Buchanan with wasting public money, conducting a cowardly foreign policy, and exacerbating sectionalism. Not surprisingly, state issues received a secondary position in the platform. According to the Opposition press, Democrats of the state had overspent public funds, mismanaged public lands, and burdened the citizens with high taxes.[42] The Opposition Party alleged that the Democrats "stood not on their merit, but on their merit as supporters of the Buchanan Administration." Opposition candidates criticized the Democratic unwillingness to discuss state policy, but because of the heightened sectionalism both parties stressed national issues, and neglected state affairs.[43]

Unsurprisingly, the 1859 state campaign launched the 1860 presidential election campaign for both the Democrats and their opponents. During this state campaign, editorials appeared in the Opposition Party press warmly receiving the possible candidacy of Stephen A. Douglas, while the administration Democrats attacked the senator from Illinois at every opportunity.[44] The *New Orleans Bee*, with the national American Party disbanded, referred approvingly to Douglas's principles as moderate, "which avoided the extremes of either side."[45] Although the *Bee* criticized "hot-headed politicians of the South, who are the chief culprits in fostering dissension," a former American but now Democratic newspaper, the *Gazette and Sentinel* of Plaquemine, urged the old Americans to throw their support to the Democrats in 1860.[46]

In the final analysis, the 1859 campaign created less excitement than any campaign during the decade of the 1850s. Because the American Party had gone the way of the Whigs, opponents of the Democracy drifted aimlessly. The *Bee* had been correct when it reported earlier in the campaign that the opponents of the Democratic Party had waited too long to present a ticket.[47] The Democratic *Daily Delta* of New Orleans reported what everyone expected; except in New Orleans, the Democrats anticipated little opposition.[48]

The results of the election confirmed the prediction of the *Daily Delta*. The Democratic candidate for governor, Thomas O. Moore, defeated his Opposition Party rival by almost 10,000 votes. The Democrats succeeded in three of the four congressional races, losing only in the First Congressional District to Know Nothing John E. Bouligny.[49] The Opposition ticket won majorities in only two parishes, Terrebonne and Orleans. Voter interest was so low in this election that the total vote failed to exceed that of the 1855 gubernatorial election. Democrats had been confident of success throughout the campaign, and many citizens obviously failed to vote. Neither did last-minute enthusiasm for the Opposition Party convince enough dissident Democrats, old Whigs, or Know Nothings that the regular Democratic ticket could be defeated.

The bulk of the support for the Opposition Party candidates did come from former Whigs and Know Nothings.[50] Old Whig parishes, such as Caddo and Concordia in north Louisiana, and the sugar parishes of St. Charles, St. James, St. Martin, Terrebonne, and West Baton Rouge, managed to give 40 percent or more of their vote to the Opposition gubernatorial candidate.[51] The same was true of those parishes which had supported Know Nothing candidates in the mid-1850s—Caddo, Catahoula, Concordia, East Baton Rouge, Jefferson, Madison, Orleans, Rapides, and the sugar parishes. All Know Nothing parishes showed remarkable support for the Opposition Party.[52] Some Whigs and Know Nothings probably voted for Democratic candidates, but most either supported the Opposition ticket or simply stayed home on Election Day.

The continuing theme of nativism, which had heightened many an argument in the 1850s, played much less of a role in the 1859 election. Nine of the twenty-four strongest Opposition Party parishes had a Roman Catholic population of 50 percent or more. Five others had a Roman Catholic population of at least 25 percent. Although the parishes with the largest foreign-born population also supported the Opposition Party, the great majority had few non-native-born Americans. In addition, Plaquemines and St. Bernard parishes, which had a noticeable community of foreign-born inhabitants, went overwhelmingly Democratic.[53]

Despite the intense sectionalism of the day, slave ownership also failed to overwhelmingly sway Louisiana voters in this election. Nineteen parishes that returned strong support for the Opposition Party had slave populations which accounted for more than half of the total population. West Baton Rouge, St. James, St. Charles, Madison, East Feliciana, and Concordia parishes had a slave population of better than 70 percent. Concordia and Madison parishes had slave populations of 90 and 88 percent respectively, These strong Opposition parishes also had several planters who could be classified as large slaveholders. Therefore, many slaveholders, even at this late date, did not necessarily believe the Democratic Party better protected the interests of slaveholding in Louisiana or the South.[54]

Neither the wealth of a parish nor the type of agriculture which predominated in a parish affected the outcome of the election. The wealthy parishes of Ascension and Concordia, and the poorer parishes of St. Helena and St. Tammany, all leaned toward the Opposition Party. The Democrats also received support from both wealthy and poorer parishes, but that party did have poorer parishes in its column. Finally, both sugar and cotton parishes went for the Democratic and Opposition parties.[55]

Whereas nativism, the belief that one party better protected slavery, wealth of a parish, and the type of agriculture of a parish apparently did not seem to significantly influence those who voted for the Opposition Party, a genuine fear for the Union did. As previously noted, the election data illustrate that a majority of old Whigs and Know Nothings still found it difficult to vote for a Democrat. Therefore, most supported Opposition candidates. Whereas the Democrats had made more significant gains in "strong" Whig parishes in 1855, they had less success in 1859.[56] However, the fear of any continued agitation of the slavery question united these supporters of the Opposition ticket more than a general antipathy toward the Democrats. The Opposition Party platform during the campaign had stressed national issues, and the first plank deprecated further agitation of the slavery question. The second plank accused the Buchanan administration of fostering "mischievous sectional action."[57] Throughout the campaign, Opposition spokesmen had continually called for the preservation of the Union. And despite the seemingly hopeless situation of the Opposition Party, and the lethargy of former Whigs and Know Nothings, over 37 percent of the voters responded to the conservative appeal of the Opposition Party. The presidential election of 1860 would prove that most Louisianians would reject a sectional candidate and remain conservative on the question of the Union as this 1859 election forecast.[58]

Ever since the 1856 presidential election, Democratic and opposition newspapers, whether formerly Whig or Know Nothing, had printed little political news that did not relate to the 1860 election. The presidential election of 1860 had intruded upon the recently concluded state campaign with both parties conducting their campaigns with an eye on 1860. The Buchanan administration received more attention during the recent Louisiana elections than did state and local issues. Free-soilism, Lecompton, Cuba, and Nicaragua were some of the issues seriously discussed by local candidates. Of particular concern was how these problems would affect the status of the Union.

Know Nothing newspapers in the late 1850s reflected this growing concern for the preservation of the Union. From all areas in the state, the theme of Union pervaded the editorials of these papers. The *Shreveport South-Western* blamed the Democrats for the current crisis atmosphere. According to this northwest Louisiana paper, the Democrats were responsible for "the chicanery and intrigues of its free-soil northern managers, and the demagoguism of its pliant southern leaders, who have brought the union to the brink of ruin."[59] Louisiana Americans opposed the rash of retaliatory resolutions offered in the 1858 legislative session against the personal liberty law of Massachusetts. Such sectional measures as these resolutions, which would tax the commodities of that northern state, and the movement for southern Bibles, hymn books, school books, tracts, and literature, met with opposition in the American press. In fact, the *Baton Rouge Daily Gazette and Comet* advocated permitting the reading of all incendiary tracts against slavery, arguing that the institution was just and "the truth can't be corrupted by error."[60] Although the *New Orleans Bee* believed northern meddling in the slave question prompted southern sectionalism that newspaper quickly pointed out that disunion would not solve the problems of the South.[61] Furthermore, Know Nothing sentiment generally rejected the gloomy picture of the future of the Union painted by such southern radicals as Robert Barnwell Rhett. One Louisiana American newspaper asserted that "long after his [Rhett's) bones have returned to their native dust, the Union he so desperately assails will endure to gladden the heart of the patriot."[62] So attached to the Union was the proprietor of the *Baton Rouge Daily Gazette and Comet* that he hoped there would be someone in the presidency as strong as Andrew Jackson if any state attempted disorganization.[63]

Although the Know Nothing press blamed the Democrats for the sectional tension which existed during the 1850s, some state Democrats also recognized the disadvantages of sectionalism. There were those Louisiana Democrats who felt that a southern sectional party would drive northern conservatives away from the state rights Democracy. The Democratic *Louisiana Courier* charged the advocates of a southern party with disunion. As this newspaper saw it, William L. Yancey and his Southern League represented "a movement . . . to distract the Democratic party, and come in direct conflict with the strict adherents to the doctrine of State Rights."[64]

However, unanimity on the question of southern rights, and just what that meant, did not exist among members of the American Party. The disintegration of the Know Nothing Party, and its lack of leadership and direction, prompted contradictory statements from the press and members of the party. Despite the general disapproval of sectional agitation by Americans, several individual Know Nothings did not feel bound to that position. In March 1858 Know Nothing Senator W. R. Adams of New Orleans advocated a sectional party. Opposition to Senator Adams's view, interestingly enough, came from a former Know Nothing newspaper the *Plaquemine Gazette and Sentinel*, which had recently joined the Democratic Party.[65] At the same time, the American Party newspaper, the *New Orleans Daily Crescent*, attempted to prove that a southern confederacy could succeed. This newspaper also refused to support what it called the "Union-at-any-and every price." Despite denials that it supported disunion, the *Daily Crescent* saw little to be optimistic about in regards to northern fanaticism on the slavery issue.[66] This newspaper advocated the preservation of the Union only if it "remains worth preserving."[67] Even the *Bee* in 1858 expressed a similar view. It favored the Union:

> so long as it remains one of even possible justice—so long as the South may continue within it, and not be at once despoiled and dishonored—so long as the rights guaranteed to us by the federal Constitution are respected.[68]

The Know Nothing *Opelousas Patriot* went so far as to support the Southern League of William L. Yancey. This newspaper opposed those "who cry peace when there is none." In addition, it believed any attempt to reorganize the Whig Party in Louisiana and the South would distract southerners "during this crisis." The *Patriot* urged the South to "march in one solid phalanx upon the Black Republican forces of the North and West."[69]

Fragmented and with little direction, some Know Nothings in Louisiana found it expedient to exacerbate sectional tension by attacking the Buchanan administration for its less than enthusiastic support of southern rights. According to these Americans, the president's message in 1857 demonstrated the failure of the national Democracy to treat the South equally. Americans opposed Buchanan's anti-filibustering sentiment since they believed it conflicted with the "manly American principles enunciated in the celebrated Ostend circular." Many southern newspapers favored United States expansion into Mexico, Central America, and Cuba, and even the Democratic *Louisiana Courier* regretted Buchanan's position on Nicaragua in particular.[70] Neither did Buchanan, alleged his Know Nothing opponents, protect southern interests in Kansas. Although the *Bee* believed the president was more pro-southern in regards to Kansas, other Know Nothings noted Buchanan had retained Walker in Kansas long enough to do "all the mischief that he could."[71] Clearly, the anti-foreign-born ideology of early Americanism had disappeared.

Now that the national American Party no longer existed, Louisiana Americans had the additional problem of whom to support in the presidential election of 1860. American newspapers, as well as old-line Whig papers, periodically advanced suggestions as to a possible candidate. These newspapers, despite some of them having contributed to the increased sectionalism, generally sought what they called a "conservative" man, one who opposed further sectional tension. The name which appeared more frequently was that of United States Senator Stephen A. Douglas of Illinois. The *New Orleans Bee* believed Douglas would be the foremost candidate of "conservatives and nationals throughout the Union."[72] Newspapers like the *Bee* questioned the logic behind the attacks on Douglas by the Buchanan administration for the senator's stand on the Lecompton Constitution and the English Compromise. However, the Democrats in Louisiana charged Douglas's action on Kansas ran counter to the best interests of the South, and one Democratic supporter went so far as to offer that he "saw no marked difference between Douglas and Lincoln."[73] But the Know Nothing and Whig newspapers applauded Douglas's defeat of Lincoln for the US Senate in 1858. The *Bee* called it "a victory of National Democracy over the blind and besotted fanaticism of anti-slavery."[74] The *Bee* had become so nationalistic that in 1859 it reported that it would not be alarmed by the prospect of William H. Seward's election to the presidency. Seward, according to the *Bee*, would become more conservative upon taking office.[75]

With the 1859 state election out of the way, many Know Nothings and former Whigs advanced Douglas's candidacy. The *New Orleans Daily Crescent* reported that Democratic congressman Miles Taylor supported Douglas. The *Daily Crescent* agreed with Taylor that Douglas "has at this time full possession of the popular mind of the North which is truly, and on principles, favorable to the maintenance of all of the rights of the South under the Constitution and in the Union."[76] Whigs and Americans looked upon Douglas with favor, claimed one former Know Nothing paper, and another suggested making him the people's candidate if the Buchanan Democrats kept him out of the Charleston convention.[77] In a more practical vein, the *Daily Crescent* queried what other northern man could bring thirty-four votes to the electoral college along with the one hundred and twenty of the South? Of course that man was Stephen A. Douglas.[78]

Yet, many former Whigs and Americans had difficulty supporting a Democrat, and many still hoped for a Union movement. As speculation regarding a national Union party increased, the *Bee* equivocated. It now advocated such a national Union party. Although Douglas had received the approbation of the *Bee*, it preferred the old Whigs John Bell, John Crittenden, or Edward Everett. The problem of accepting these latter individuals, objected the *Bee*, was that they "are men without a party."[79] The dissident Soulé faction of the Democratic Party hoped the disorganization of Americans and Whigs would work to their advantage. Having lost their bid in 1859 to control the state Democratic machinery, Soulé's "Purifiers" once again made overtures to the conservative Whigs and Know Nothings to join them in appointing delegates to the Democratic state convention. But by 1860, a Union movement appeared likely and the conservative *Bee* now cautioned against accepting any overtures from the Soulé faction. Additionally, the *Bee* believed it would be too difficult for Whigs and Americans to "metamorphasize themselves."[80]

Even with the nomination of John Bell and Edward Everett as presidential and vice-presidential nominees of the Constitutional Union Party, Americans and old Whigs equivocated.[81] At first these conservatives counseled a wait-and-see attitude. If the Democrats, after their Charleston debacle, remained divided, the Union movement would have a better chance of success. Union men thought the prospects of the Constitutional Union candidates depended on who the Republicans would nominate.[82] Before the nomination of Bell, the *Daily Crescent* charged that a three-party race would harm the South, and it looked unfavorably upon a Constitutional Union presidential candidate. Even though that newspaper later changed its stance and reported it knew of no better way to defeat the black Republicans, it still refused to commit itself unconditionally to Bell and Everett. The conservative *Gazette and Comet* newspapers of Baton Rouge supported Stephen Douglas and its editorials stood for "union-at-any price."[83] In the final analysis, however, most of the former Whig and Know Nothing newspapers supported the Bell-Everett ticket. In New Orleans, the *Bee, Daily Crescent, Commercial Bulletin*, and the *Daily Picayune* supported the Constitutional Union Party. In the country, the *Shreveport South-Western* and the *West Baton Rouge Sugar Planter* also cast their lot with Bell.[84] The *Daily Crescent* became such an advocate of Bell that it lectured former Whigs and Know Nothings not to forego their principles just because they thought their candidate had no chance of success. Yet, according to the *Daily Crescent*, Bell had a good chance for success.[85]

The Slidell Democrats in the state, naturally, regarded both Douglas and Bell as anathema to the South. The *Louisiana Courier* attacked those Soulé Democrats who supported Douglas's candidacy, and noted that present advocates of the senator had once attacked his principle of squatter sovereignty. In addition, the administration Democrats critically linked Soulé with former Know Nothings in the state. They were also not willing to allow the American-Oppositionists to occupy the Unionist high-ground and applauded Judah Benjamin's speech in Congress when he said, "we fight to preserve the constitution, and, in so fighting, fight to preserve the Union."[86] Nor did the *Courier* have kind words for John Bell, whose past record on slavery matters received detailed scrutiny. The Breckinridge Democrats reviewed Bell's career beginning in 1837, and listed several instances in which Bell had opposed the institution of slavery.[87] In addition, these Democrats did not take seriously the talk of fusion between the supporters of Douglas and Bell. The *Daily Delta* charged they loved "their political chief more than they do their country and this glorious union."[88]

This presidential campaign temporarily resurrected the old nativistic issue as well. After the demise of the national American Party, anti-Roman Catholicism and anti-foreignism received little attention in Louisiana. Defeated and disorganized, Louisiana Know Nothings, with few exceptions, no longer found it expedient to harangue the public on the problems of foreign immigration. Only the *Baton Rouge Gazette and Comet* continued to agitate for a change in the naturalization laws. The failure of President Buchanan to mention anything about naturalization in his 1857 message to Congress disturbed the editor of the *Weekly Gazette and Comet*. He believed native demagoguism would continue "as long as there is a growing foreign element in our midst whose first and only lesson in republicanism is that 'Liberty is License.'"[89] Prior to the 1860 presidential election the *Baton Rouge Daily Gazette and Comet* attacked the Democratic party for "cow-towing" to foreigners, and blamed the dissolution-of-the-Union talk on foreigners.[90] Some Louisiana nativists also opposed any federal homestead legislation because it would favor foreigners. However, nativist and southern Democrats did come together in opposition to homestead legislation because it would also favor speculators and black Republicanism.[91]

The nativism of John Bell, the Constitutional Union candidate, was an issue in Louisiana during the campaign of 1860. Democrats not only attacked Bell for his alleged opposition to slavery, but they also accused him of opposing Roman Catholics and naturalized citizens. The *New Orleans Catholic Standard* reported that, although Bell never joined the American Party, he reportedly endorsed its prescriptive principles.[92] To substantiate this charge, the *Baton Rouge Daily Advocate* printed excerpts from a speech delivered by Bell in 1860 in Knoxville, Tennessee, in which he stated that he favored "a little bloodletting in order to avoid future blood-letting between Native Americans and foreigners when aliens, if not checked, flood the land."[93] Had nativism been more of an issue in the campaign, the Democratic *Louisiana Courier* could have caused some embarrassment for the Democrats in the state when it attacked the German newspaper the *Louisiana Staats Zeitung* of having abolitionist leanings.[94]

Nativism was, nevertheless, a virtual afterthought in this election. Three occurrences, no doubt, contributed to the decline in nativist sentiment. First, the disintegration of the Know Nothing Party had a significant impact on all Americans. Newspapers that had been leading exponents of immigration restriction practically eliminated all articles relative to antiforeignism. The defeats in 1856 and 1857 confused many Americans and they simply lost their direction. Secondly, immigration to the United States continued to decline in the late 1850s. In both Louisiana and the United States, the number of immigrants who arrived between 1853 and 1856 had declined by 50 percent and the numbers continued to decline for the rest of the decade.[95] Therefore, with the source of friction drying up, nativists became more restrained. Finally, the sectional controversy overshadowed other issues and subsumed nativism. Louisiana nativists, as well as other Louisianians, were engrossed in what most of the citizens thought to be the more critical issues of preserving the Union and maintaining southern rights. It was clear that many nativists and Know Nothings were increasingly convinced that southern rights were critical.

Therefore, the major issue for the conservatives and Union men in 1860 was the preservation of the Union.[96] Whether they supported Douglas or Bell, the conservative and Union newspapers displayed virtual unanimity on the question of preserving the Union. Further discussion of the slavery question received no support from Union men. Conservative men, whether old Whigs, Americans, or Democrats, regretted the southern Democrats' attempt to insert a congressional slave code into their party platform. According to one former Whig and Know Nothing, "slavery is decided by soil and climate not legislation or judicial decisions."[97] One loyal Unionist charged that issues arising from this slavery agitation endangered the Union and the South by "washing away and undermining those fraternal bonds which are the ligaments that bind together the Union."[98] The *Bee*, more optimistic in 1860, did not even consider the election of a Republican cause for dissolving the Union.[99] But the supporters of John Bell warned the voters that the Breckinridge Democrats threatened secession if Lincoln was elected. These conservative proponents of Bell charged the Democrats with attempting to nullify federal laws and to violate the United States Constitution. Historian John Sacher's view of Louisiana's "Old Line" Democrats holds that they "sought to attract voters by emphasizing the politics of slavery," and one Unionist paper wrote that the Democracy plainly threatened the Union while another said the Democrats' policy was an "eternal agitation of the slavery questions."[100]

Union meetings and conventions throughout the state urged the people to rally behind the Union. Unlike the state Opposition Party convention in 1859, the state convention of the Constitutional Union Party packed the Hall of Representatives in Baton Rouge. Almost every parish sent delegates to this convention, which resolved to uphold the federal constitution and Union. After the convention the leadership of the state Constitutional Union Party strengthened their organization. Every parish but one, Carroll, had a parish committee. The organization included a state central committee, a finance committee, and a committee of arrangements. The party also began publication of a special party newspaper in New Orleans, the *Louisiana Signal*.[101] So intense did some of these conservative Bell men feel about the Union that several came out for the Union-at-any-price. From a distance, former Whig and railroad executive James Robb echoed the concern of the pro-Union conservatives. Now residing in Chicago, Robb wrote a friend that the South would reap economic disaster if it should secede. Following Lincoln's election, Robb also wrote his new father-in-law in Georgia urging the people of Georgia to heed the conservative logic of Alexander Stephens; Robb further offered father-in-law Alonzo Church that the Union must be preserved at all costs. A former American Party paper that supported Douglas in this campaign, the *Baton Rouge Weekly Gazette and Comet*, was "willing to go as far as Old Hickory went into South Carolina, to teach the sisters of the confederacy, what they owe to the Constitution."[102]

Breckinridge Democrats scoffed at the Union-at-any-price men in the South. However, the supporters of Breckinridge denied they were for dissolution of the Union. They did believe "that the continued repetition of intentional and unwarranted violations of the Constitution may, and ultimately will effect [*sic*] the dissolution of the Confederacy."[103] What these Democrats desired was the right to take their slave property into the territories without "their rights, either of person or property, being destroyed or impaired by Congressional or Territorial legislation."[104] As for Bell, the Democrats criticized his "opposition to the natural and constitutional extension of slavery under any form." To the Southern Democrats Bell's conservatism was "a strange conservatism," and they made it known that they would "prefer Yancey's conservatism."[105]

Although the sectional candidate Breckinridge carried the state, he did not gain the majority in Louisiana. Bell and Douglas, supported by the conservative Whigs, Know Nothings, and Democrats who had campaigned on a Union platform, received a majority of the votes of Louisiana.[106] Even though the Southern Democrats had agitated the slavery question during the campaign,[107] slaveholders, large and small, showed no preference for Breckinridge over Bell and Douglas. Both the conservative candidates and Breckinridge received about the same support from the large planter class of the state.[108] Breckinridge managed to do well in some of the richest black belt parishes, but so did Bell and Douglas. While there is no significant relationship between the wealth of a parish and the election results, Breckinridge did win in more of the poorer parishes, and the conservative candidates, particularly Douglas, did better in the more wealthy parishes.[109]

William Barney, in his study of the 1860 election in Alabama and Mississippi, found that particular areas of those states supported one of the candidates who spoke most directly to "[their] needs and aspirations."[110] In Louisiana, there was a similar relationship between a particular candidate and areas of the state. Breckinridge's strength in Louisiana centered in those areas where planter agriculture was expanding or in areas of predominately small white farmers. Generally, the strong Breckinridge parishes in the state experienced more growth in the slave population, the white population, and showed an increased number of acres of improved farmland. Of the twenty-nine parishes returning a majority for Breckinridge, twenty had an increase in the slave population during the 1850s. The only Breckinridge parish that had a decrease in the white population was West Feliciana Parish. All the others registered increases during the decade with Bienville, Calcasieu, Caldwell, Franklin, Rapides, Tensas, Carroll, and Claiborne parishes experiencing a white growth rate of over 60 percent. Finally, with the exception of Plaquemines and West Feliciana parishes, every Breckinridge parish had an increase in the number of acres of improved farmland. Several had outstanding increases. DeSoto Parish had an increase in the number of acres of improved farmland from 37,520 acres in 1850 to 96,591 in 1860. Tensas went from 59,391 acres of improved farmland to 117,355 acres in the same period. On the other hand, the Bell and Douglas parishes were generally more static. Of the eighteen Bell and Douglas parishes, nine had an increase in the slave population. The remaining nine either declined in the total number of slaves or remained about the same. Whites were not moving into these conservative and Union parishes either. The white population of Ouachita and St. Tammany parishes declined by 21 and 15 percent, respectively. East Feliciana showed no change in the white population from 1850 to 1860. St. James and St. Mary parishes had only a one percent increase and St. Martin and West Baton Rouge parishes registered an increase in their white populations of only 5 and 2 percent, respectively. Only Morehouse and Terrebonne parishes had an increase in the total white population of more than 50 percent. Then, while the number of acres of improved farmland did increase in the Bell and Douglas parishes, the increases were smaller than in many of the Breckinridge parishes.[111]

The anti-Breckinridge forces in Louisiana were in the old Whig heartland, whether sugar or cotton areas, and in the towns.[112] Results from south Louisiana Whig and sugar parishes, like Iberville, St. Mary, and Terrebonne, indicate that Breckinridge had made inroads there. But his strength centered mainly among the cotton planters of north Louisiana[113] and the Red River region, and southwest Louisiana.[114] In many of the old Whig parishes that went for Bell and Douglas, the plantation economy had matured.[115] Most notable was the static condition of agriculture in the sugar parishes which opposed Breckinridge.[116] In Ascension, Assumption, and Lafourche, parishes where the production of sugar had barely increased during the 1850s, Douglas won with a plurality. In addition, town Democrats went for Douglas.[117] In the urban parishes of Orleans and Jefferson, Douglas outpolled Breckinridge, and in Plaquemines Parish the Illinois Senator won almost 30 percent of the vote.[118] Finally, most of those late members of the American Party in the state, many of whom were old Whigs, also opposed Breckinridge's candidacy.[119]

The election in Louisiana had, therefore, revolved around two issues. The maintenance of the Union, supported by the conservative Bell and Douglas men, and the determination of Breckinridge's followers to protect what they believed to be in the best interests of the South—an expanding slave system. Similar to the situation in Mississippi and Alabama, it appears the conservatives wanted to preserve what they possessed. Thus, the Southern Democrats in Louisiana and the South spoke to the aspirations not of the planter class as a whole, but to the rising planter class.[120] Nevertheless, the results of the election in Louisiana demonstrated that "the majority of the people were still conservative and union-loving."[121]

<hr>

After the defeat in 1857, no Know Nothing ran for a state office in Louisiana on the American Party ticket. The party had been reduced to its original nucleus in New Orleans. However, even in the Crescent City, the party lacked unity, and Independent movements challenged the Americans' dominance. So different had the Know Nothing movement become by 1859

The Honorable George Eustis Jr., Louisiana Know Nothing Representative, Thirty-fourth and Thirty-fifth Congresses; Courtesy Tulane University, Rare Books Department

The Honorable John Edward Bouligny, Louisiana Know Nothing Representative, Thirty-sixth Congress; Biographical Directory of the United States Congress

that its members appealed to the German voters of New Orleans for support. It was no wonder, then, that in 1859 no American ticket opposed the Democrats and the remnants of the party, along with dissident Democrats formed an Opposition ticket. Finally, in 1860 the majority of old Know Nothings supported either Stephen A. Douglas or John Bell in the presidential election. Former American Party members virtually abandoned their own nativist rhetoric in these later years, but some never completely lost sight of their conservative and Union goals. Bell and Douglas outpolled Breckinridge in the presidential election of 1860 by more than 10 percent.

Some former leaders of the Know Nothings in the state bravely responded in positive ways for the Union. James Robb, predicting disaster if the South seceded, left Louisiana. Robb did return to New Orleans in 1866 and organized the Louisiana National Bank. He retired to Ohio in 1871, where he died in 1881.

John Edward Bouligny, elected as the American Party candidate to the Thirty-sixth Congress (March 4, 1859–March 3, 1861), branded himself pro-Union by opposing secession, retaining his seat in Congress after Louisiana seceded. He remained in the North, where he died on February 20, 1864.

On the other hand, Bouligny's Know Nothing predecessor for the First Congressional District of Louisiana, George Eustis Jr., who served in the Thirty-fourth and Thirty-fifth Congress, March 4, 1855–March 3, 1859, supported the Confederacy and became the private secretary to Democrat John Slidell, the leading light of Louisiana Democrats and chief of the Confederate Mission to France. Eustis remained in France after the Civil War and died in Cannes on March 15, 1872.

And in the heart of anti-foreign sentiment, New Orleans, the Know Nothing Mayor John T. Monroe would surrender his city to Union General Benjamin Butler in May 1862. Embroiled in controversy, Monroe was later imprisoned until after the war ended.[122] In 1866, he won reelection, resumed the mayor's office, and became entangled in Reconstruction politics. He died in Savannah, Georgia, in 1871.

E̦PILOGUE

Political nativism in the 1850s was nothing new in Louisiana. In the 1830s and 1840s, ethnic tension existed in Louisiana. For instance, Creole-American tensions crackled during the Jacksonian Era. By the 1840s, the immigration of a large number of foreigners to the state, particularly to New Orleans, resulted in political and social allegations against foreigners and Roman Catholics. Protestant fears of papal power and an alleged anti-republicanism among these new residents helped to explain the rise of nativism in the state. Both Whigs and Democrats were guilty of strong negative attitudes toward foreigners and Catholics, with the Whigs being more adamant in their hostility. This nativistic sentiment contributed to an early formation of a Native American association in Louisiana.

In part, these nativist beginnings, inherited mostly from the old Whigs, allowed the nativistic and new American or Know Nothing Party to supplant the Whig Party in the state, and to achieve an early political success in 1854. Soon after its formation, the Know Nothing Party in Louisiana demonstrated that it could effectively contest the rival Democrats. However, the party faced challenges in overcoming several weaknesses. Opponents took aim at the easy targets—secrecy and bigotry. Although the Know Nothings abandoned the secrecy that had surrounded it, the initial stigma left the impression among some Louisiana voters that the party was anti-republican. Also, except for New Orleans, there simply were not enough immigrants in the rest of the state to excite many of the voters in order for them to fully embrace the Know Nothings' nativist arguments. Yet, those outside of Greater New Orleans could not help but be concerned about how the influx of immigrants into Greater New Orleans might affect the outcome of statewide elections. Furthermore, expressing anti-Roman Catholic positions continued to plague members of Louisiana's American Party. Even so, many Roman Catholics joined the Know Nothings. But the evidence shows how Catholic Whigs never pledged their support for the movement to the extent that they had adhered to their old Whig Party. The Catholic Know Nothings, like the former Democrat and writer Charles Gayarré, were relatively successful in parrying the anti-Catholic attacks by claiming that Louisiana's Gallican Catholics were different from the recent Catholic immigrants in their understanding of republicanism.

But some Louisiana Catholics recognized that there was an anti-Catholic bias within the state's American Party, particularly in north Louisiana and in Baton Rouge, where some members of the party made no distinction between the liberal native-born Catholics and the more recent-to-arrive foreign-born Catholics. There is little substantive evidence that most Catholics stayed away from the Americans because of the religious bias; undoubtedly, the bigotry of the Americans kept some Catholics from actively siding with them. The inability of the Americans to achieve party unity on issues they advocated also hurt their cause in the state. Louisiana Know Nothings' acceptance of Catholics within their ranks obviously made their party very different from Know Nothings in the northern states and those American parties in the other southern states. Louisiana Know Nothings also had to answer the Louisiana Democratic charges that the national party would not recognize Louisiana's Catholic Know Nothings. Many Catholics in the state remained committed to the Know Nothings; still, Catholic support waned with persistent Democratic allegations.

Another charge leveled by its opponents was that the new party basically was only "warmed-over" Whiggery in disguise. Political tension increased when Democrats accused the new party of simply providing a haven for Whiggery. The fact was that many ex-Whigs decided they had no other place to go after their party collapsed.[1] Many of the new party's members were old Whigs, and they received their main support from the old Whig areas of the state, similar to Know Nothings elsewhere. However, Louisiana Know Nothing leaders differed sharply from the traditional view of other southern Know Nothings. This study uses quantitative and qualitative data to demonstrate that many of the leaders of Louisiana's Know Nothing Party not only came from the old Whig Party, but in attempting to determine the socioeconomic background of these Louisiana Know Nothings, the data shows that they were not simply the wealthy slave owning aristocracy portrayed by earlier historians. Nor were Louisiana's American Party members primarily businessmen or lawyers representing mercantile interests, as the old consensus contends. Instead, what the evidence for Louisiana shows is that many Democrats were, during the 1850s, similar in wealth, age, and occupation to the leaders of the American Party. Nor in the citadel of Americanism, New Orleans, does the older view hold up. For example, this study demonstrates that the Democrats had greater strength among older politicians with greater wealth, a group the earlier historians ascribe to the Know Nothings. Additionally, the Americans received support from men casting ballots for the first time, as well as older voters. And throughout the state, slaveholding planters and farmers dominated both parties, and among planters with more than twenty slaves, the Know Nothings only had a slight edge, but they also found support among farmers who owned fewer than twenty slaves. The first category was traditionally thought to be strongly indicative of the leaders of the Know Nothings, and the second group was traditionally thought to be dominated by Louisiana's Democratic leadership. What additional research reveals is that the Louisiana Know Nothing Party generally did not conform to those earlier views of the party in Louisiana, in other southern states, or in the nation. Therefore, this study offers a different and new perspective on a state where the members, leaders, and goals of the American Party were often unique.

In the nation, the Know Nothings failed to become a national party and were not successful in reshaping the naturalization laws of the United States. Such change had been the panacea of the party throughout its existence. Additionally, despite its conservative goals and support for the Union, the national party was also unable to alleviate the sectional tension of the 1850s. Like the American Party elsewhere, and as historian Tyler Anbinder argues, Louisiana Know Nothings' leadership by 1856 had come under the control of conservative ex-Whigs who had moved toward a defense of the Union rather than to continue to make nativism its primary focus. Ironically, the Know Nothings in Louisiana came to a point where they argued they could better support southern rights within the Union and, in their own way, they actually contributed to the sectional tension of the 1850s almost as much as did the southern-rights Democrats. The Know Nothings simply failed to overcome or to quell the sectional tension of the time.

It was the sectional crisis that not only ended the political life of the Know Nothing Party in the nation; it also ended it in Louisiana. Early nativist and republican rhetoric had proved crucial in the party's early success in the state, and the Louisiana Know Nothings remained committed to their nativism. Stigmatizing foreign-born Irish and Germans as anti-republican, paupers, and an easily misled voting bloc gave the Know Nothings significant victories in 1854. That commitment became less prevalent in the party's rhetoric, slipping to the level of a strategic political device rather than a hardened ideology. Nativism and the anti-foreign sentiment grew inextricably with the question of slavery. The American Party in the state blamed the foreign-born for the increased sectional tension over the slavery issue. Nativists contended that if only the foreign-born could be prevented from swelling an antislavery population in the territories, sectional tension would abate.

At the same time, however, the Americans had to defend themselves from Democratic allegations of their close relationship with northern abolitionist Know Nothings by promoting how they were better in protecting southern rights. Sectionalism now mushroomed, growing so dominant that the national American Party, by that point, also emphasized conservatism and the Union more than nativism, dividing the party into northern and southern branches. At the national convention in Philadelphia in 1855, many northern delegates walked out of the meeting over the pro-slavery stance forced on the party. Then, in 1856 northern Know Nothings refused to support any candidate for president who did not support congressional action intended to bar slavery from the territories, putting them in line with the upstart Republican Party. When this move failed, an additional number of northern delegates bolted the convention. These departures left southerners virtually in control of the party. Although southerners predominated, the American Party still offered itself as the compromise national party and it hoped to avoid the slavery issue. As a result, Know Nothings in the nation, and in Louisiana, continued their appeal to the idea of conservatism and Union. This was at a time when only sectional issues assured mass political allegiance. Louisiana Know Nothings had largely neglected the issues that had given them their early success in the state and, instead, insisted that only they were the ones to avert a sectional conflict and possible secession. Therefore, like the Whig Party before, and the Democratic Party in 1860, the American Party succumbed to the "politics of slavery" and the sectional crisis.[2]

Know Nothings in the state had struggled to save the Union. In this struggle, the American Party in Louisiana can perhaps be viewed as desperate to defend southern rights. Yet, they failed to calm the growing sectional conflict and they were unsuccessful in preserving the Union. In Louisiana, during their party's last days, they appealed to the German immigrants in New Orleans. In the end, the American Party lost its nativistic focus and many were willing to embrace a sectional party. The sectional tension that Americans had originally opposed ironically had been exacerbated by Louisiana's Know Nothings. All that remained was a shadow of a party struggling to remain viable, to some extent, in New Orleans up to the Federal occupation of the Crescent City in April 1862. It was no wonder that, statewide, the Know Nothings did not run a candidate in the 1859 state elections nor did the Americans offer a candidate in the 1860 presidential contest. Instead, along with dissident Democrats in 1859, they formed an unsuccessful Opposition ticket. Finally, in 1860 the majority of old Americans supported either northern Democrat Stephen A. Douglas or Constitutional Unionist John Bell in the presidential election. They had abandoned their early reform and nativistic ideology, they defended the Union, and they attempted instead to answer the Democratic charges that they, the Know Nothings, had flirted with abolitionism. They argued that only they could better protect southern rights. Once Know Nothings did that, Louisianians focused more on protecting the South as their primary goal. The Know Nothings' legacy was more of the same; like Southern-Rights Democrats, many embraced the politics of slavery. While the Union still meant a great deal to some of them, the appeal for Union fell off and the old hallmark of nativism virtually disappeared, overwhelmed by the politics of slavery.

APPENDIX A

TABLE 1						
PARTY MEMBERSHIP OF SLAVEHOLDERS BY AGE AND OCCUPATION						
Occupation	Party	Under 40	40–49	50 & Over	Total	
					N	%
Planters	Know Nothing	11%	16%	11%	26	38
	Democrat	2	16	18	14	36
Farmers	Know Nothing	6	7	6	13	19
	Democrat	0	11	2	5	13
Lawyers	Know Nothing	10	6	1	12	17
	Democrat	13	11	2	10	26
Town Middle Class	Know Nothing	13	4	9	18	26
	Democrat	16	5	2	9	23

TABLE 2						
PARTY MEMBERSHIP IN NEW ORLEANS BY AGE AND WEALTH						
Age	Party	Under $25,000	$25,000 – $49,000	$50,000 & Over	Total	
					N	%
Under 40	Know Nothing	11%	0%	0%	2	13
	Democrat	37	6	0	7	44
40-49	Know Nothing	33	20	11	10	67
	Democrat	12	0	6	3	19
50 & Over	Know Nothing	11	7	0	3	20
	Democrat	12	6	18	6	37

TABLE 3					
POLITICIANS—DEMOCRATIC PARISHES WHERE SLAVE OWNERSHIP WAS SIGNIFICANT Party Membership by Age and Wealth					
Age	Party	Under $25,000	$25,000–$49,000	$50,000 & Over	Total	
					N	%
Under 40	Know Nothing	43%	3%	9%	19	55
	Democrat	25	5	10	8	40
40-49	Know Nothing	9	0	14	8	23
	Democrat	20	5	25	10	50
50 & Over	Know Nothing	17	3	3	8	23
	Democrat	0	0	10	2	10

TABLE 4					
POLITICIANS—DEMOCRATIC PARISHES WHERE SLAVE OWNERSHIP WAS MODERATE Party Membership by Age and Wealth					
Age	Party	Under $25,000	$25,000–$49,000	$50,000 & Over	Total	
					N	%
Under 40	Know Nothing	18%	3%	12%	11	33
	Democrat	26	4	0	7	30
40-49	Know Nothing	9	6	15	10	30
	Democrat	26	0	17	10	43
50 & Over	Know Nothing	3	6	27	12	36
	Democrat	13	4	9	6	26

		TABLE 5				
	**PARISHES CARRIED BY THE DEMOCRATIC PARTY IN 1855** Party Membership by Age and Wealth					
Age	Party	Under $25,000	$25,000 –$49,000	$50,000 & Over	Total	
					N	%
Under 40	Know Nothing	31%	3%	11%	29	45
	Democrat	26	5	5	15	35
40-49	Know Nothing	9	5	13	17	26
	Democrat	23	5	21	21	49
50 & Over	Know Nothing	11	2	16	18	28
	Democrat	7	2	7	7	16

		TABLE 6				
	**PARISHES LOST BY THE DEMOCRATIC PARTY IN 1855** Party Membership by Age and Wealth					
Age	Party	Under $25,000	$25,000– $49,000	$50,000 & Over	Total	
					N	%
Under 40	Know Nothing	24%	3%	15%	30	42
	Democrat	36	7	0	24	44
40-49	Know Nothing	18	7	13	27	38
	Democrat	15	2	5	12	22
50 & Over	Know Nothing	8	6	6	14	20
	Democrat	16	5	13	19	34

TABLE 7					
LOUISIANA POLITICAL LEADERS Party Membership by Age and Wealth					
Age	Party	Under $25,000	$25,000–$49,000	$50,000 & Over	Total	
					N	%
Under 40	Know Nothing	27%	3%	13%	59	43
	Democrat	33	6	2	42	41
40-49	Know Nothing	14	5	12	42	31
	Democrat	17	4	10	29	32
50 & Over	Know Nothing	11	5	10	34	26
	Democrat	12	4	11	26	27

TABLE 8			
ANNUAL REPORTS, BOARD OF ADMINISTRATION OF THE CHARITY HOSPITAL			
Year	No. of Irish Admitted	No. of Foreign-Born	Total Admitted
1850	11,130	16,598	18,476
1851	11,655	16,503	18,420
1852	10,195	16,141	18,031
1853	7,217	12,333	13,759
1854	5,491	11,606	13,192

	TABLE 9				
BRECKINRIDGE PARISHES—1860 PRESIDENTIAL ELECTION 1850 Census Data					
Parish	White Population	Number of Acres Improved Farm Land	Percent Slaves	Cane Sugar 1,000 lbs. Hogsheads	Ginned Cotton Bales of 400 lbs. each
Avoyelles	4,059	33,898	55.3	4,481	3,538
Bienville	3,623	18,015	34.2	--	1,648
Bossier	2,504	40,284	64	--	4,181
Caddo	3,634	44,174	58.6	--	4,819
Calcasieu	2,718	8,542	24.5	460	122
Caldwell	1,584	12,081	43.7	--	1,570
Carroll	2,336	47,701	73.3	--	15,544
Catahoula	3,585	26,077	49.5	--	6,648
Claiborne	4,949	31,971	33.8	--	2,483
Concordia	823	50,059	89.4	33	18,297
DeSoto	3,549	37,520	55.5	2	2,995
Franklin	1,664	14,443	48.4	--	3,044
Iberville	3,568	46,050	70.1	23,208	64
Jackson	3,406	18,621	38.8	--	1,394
Lafayette	3,390	24,448	47.2	2,629	2,500
Livingston	2,524	9,163	24.9	120	265
Natchitoches	5,466	70,784	55.4	4	15,574
Plaquemine	2,221	39,774	64.7	16,835	60
Pointe Coupee	2,968	43,010	68.9	8,560	1,622
Rapides	5,037	69,653	68.5	4,613	4,222
Sabine	3,347	18,254	25.9	1	1,107
St. Bernard	1,406	11,435	61.1	4,367	--
St. Helena	2,354	21,913	48.1	--	1,284
St. Landry	10,140	87,584	48.9	5,951	3,920
Tensas	900	59,391	90	--	21,665

TABLE 9 (Continued)					
BRECKINRIDGE PARISHES—1860 PRESIDENTIAL ELECTION 1850 Census Data					
Parish	White Population	Number of Acres	Percent Slaves	Cane Sugar	Ginned Cotton
		Improved Farm Land		1,000 lbs. Hogsheads	Bales of 400 lbs. each
Union	4,778	45,135	41.8	--	5,213
Vermillion	2,328	5,913	31.3	871	45
Washington	2,367	13,071	30.4	--	693
W. Feliciana	2,473	76,311	80.5	4,767	18,291

TABLE 9 (Continued)					
BRECKINRIDGE PARISHES—1860 PRESIDENTIAL ELECTION 1860 Census Data					
Parish	White Population	Number of Acres	Percent Slaves	Cane Sugar	Ginned Cotton
		Improved Farm Land		1,000 lbs. Hogsheads	Bales of 400 lbs. each
Avoyelles	5,904	58,078	54.6	4,445	20,068
Bienville	5,900	No Data	45.5	No Data	No Data
Bossier	3,348	91,583	70.5	--	40,028
Caddo	4,733	98,928	72	--	9,385
Calcasieu	4,451	8,621	19.8	34	640
Caldwell	2,888	21,468	40.2	--	7,296
Carroll	4,124	118,116	72	91	84,165
Catahoula	5,492	54,413	52.5	--	23,564
Claiborne	8,996	114,699	46.6	--	18,893
Concordia	1.242	87,406	90.9	--	63,971
DeSoto	4,777	96,591	64	--	16,554
Franklin	2,758	34,138	55.2	--	9,307
Iberville	3,793	62,523	72.8	10,828	179
Jackson	5,367	70,873	43.3	--	10,687

TABLE 9 (Continued)					
BRECKINRIDGE PARISHES—1860 PRESIDENTIAL ELECTION 1860 Census Data					
Parish	White Population	Number of Acres	Percent Slaves	Cane Sugar	Ginned Cotton
		Improved Farm Land		1,000 lbs. Hogsheads	Bales of 400 lbs. each
Lafayette	4,307	111,375	49.6	1,003	11,530
Livingston	3,120	10,537	29.6	3	1,563
Natchitoches	6,304	80,616	56.5	--	36,887
Plaquemine	2,595	28,975	63.4	12,607	
Pointe Coupee	4,094	82,932	72.8	12,187	28,947
Rapides	9.711	105,839	60.6	12,087	49,168
Sabine	4,115	26,350	29.4	--	5,052
St. Bernard	1,771	No Data	55	No Data	No Data
St. Helena	3,413	37,458	52	--	6,484
St. Landry	10,703	93,292	49.5	3,437	21,198
Tensas	1,479	117,355	90.8	--	141,493
Union	6,641	82,791	36	--	10,843
Vermillion	3,001	85,753	30.4	1,550	14,405
Washington	2,996	22,177	35.9	--	2,735
W. Feliciana	2,036	71,539	82	5,705	21,331

TABLE 10					
UNION PARISHES—BELL AND DOUGLAS—1860 PRESIDENTIAL ELECTION 1850 Census Data					
Parish	White Population	Number of Acres	Percent Slaves	Cane Sugar	Ginned Cotton
		Improved Farm Land		1,000 lbs. Hogsheads	Bales of 400 lbs. each
Ascension	3,340	28,346	67.6	13,438	406
Assumption	5,170	31,361	50.7	17,160	130
E. Baton Rouge	5,347	37,535	53	7,074	1,346

TABLE 10 (Continued)					
UNION PARISHES—BELL AND DOUGLAS—1860 PRESIDENTIAL ELECTION 1850 Census Data					
Parish	White Population	Number of Acres Improved Farm Land	Percent Slaves	Cane Sugar 1,000 lbs. Hogsheads	Ginned Cotton Bales of 400 lbs. each
E. Feliciana	4,060	82,936	70	1,105	9,967
Jefferson	18,046	22,430	24.7	8,897	
Lafourche	5,142	40,268	45.8	10,055	
Madison	1,416	56,619	83.8	--	12,771
Morehouse	1,877	15,895	51.3	--	3,303
Orleans	91,431	4,844	15.1	1,495	
Ouachita	2,292	20,373	54.1	--	3,486
St. Charles	867	20,596	80.7	10,206	
St. James	3,285	41,905	69.8	21,670	
St. John	2,586	22,285	62	11,935	
St. Martin	4,743	35,971	55.2	4,188	4,073
St. Mary	3,423	43,051	71.9	24,765	84
St. Tammany	3,642	5,824	37.1	20	41
Terrebonne	3,305	18,706	56	9,171	
W. Baton Rouge	1,815	25,775	69.4	7,920	262
Winn	(not a parish in 1850)				

TABLE 10 (Continued)					
UNION PARISHES—BELL AND DOUGLAS—1860 PRESIDENTIAL ELECTION 1860 Census Data					
Parish	White Population	Number of Acres Improved Farm Land	Percent Slaves	Cane Sugar 1,000 lbs. Hogsheads	Ginned Cotton Bales of 400 lbs. each
Ascension	3,940	42,666	64.2	16,087	684
Assumption	7,189	57,886	52.6	17,707	619
E. Baton Rouge	6,944	55,220	53.4	5,477	11,621

			TABLE 10 (Continued)		
		UNION PARISHES—BELL AND DOUGLAS—1860 PRESIDENTIAL ELECTION 1860 Census Data			
Parish	White Population	Number of Acres	Percent Slaves	Cane Sugar	Ginned Cotton
		Improved Farm Land		1,000 lbs. Hogsheads	Bales of 400 lbs. each
E. Fe1iciana	4,081	96,728	72.1	1,013	23,332
Jefferson	No Data	24,148	33.3	9,467	
Lafourche	7,500	40,555	45.5	14,736	476
Madison	1,640	104,383	88.3	--	44,870
Morehouse	3,784	52,988	63.4	--	20,982
Orleans	149,063	5,749	8.3	2,050	400
Ouachita	1,887	25,881	60.1	--	8,639
St. Charles	938	29,969	79	7,067	
St. James	3,348	45,166	70.4	13,736	
St. John	3,037	32,481	57.9	4,981	
St. Martin	4,984	42,870	58.1	7,499	4,717
St. Mary	3,475	78,389	77.6	30,731	142
St. Tammany	3,153	6,126	34.1	--	200
Terrebonne	5,131	38,816	56.1	17,022	195
W. Baton Rouge	1,859	32,044	73	10,176	1,405
Winn	5,480	20,617	19.7	10,822	2,993

APPENDIX B

ASCENSION PARISH						
NAME	AGE	OCCUPATION	PROPERTY		SLAVES	PLACE OF BIRTH
			Real	Personal		
Know Nothings						
1. Duncan Kenner	47	Sugar Planter	$190,000	$250,000	473	Louisiana
2. L. D. Nichols	34	Lawyer	--	$24,000		Louisiana
3. A. F. Rightor	62	Surveyor	$40,000	$12,000	13	New York
4. Phillip Winfree	37	Editor	$2,000	$2,000	2	Louisiana
Democrats						
1. John F. Ayraud	48	Recorder	$0	$0		Louisiana
2. Albert Duffel	47	Supreme Court Judge	$0	$10,000	5	Louisiana
3. Trasimon Landry	64	Sugar Planter	$540,000	$275,000	316	Louisiana
4. W. C. Laws	31	District Judge	$0	$0		Louisiana

ASSUMPTION PARISH						
NAME	AGE	OCCUPATION	PROPERTY		SLAVES	PLACE OF BIRTH
			Real	Personal		
Know Nothings						
1. John Dalferes	33	Sugar Planter	--	--	15	Louisiana
2. Dr. E. E. Kittredge	61	Sugar Planter	$330,000	$300,000	177	New Hampshire
3. R. C. Martin	47	Sugar Planter	Not given	($50,000) est.	91	N. Carolina

ASSUMPTION PARISH						
NAME	AGE	OCCUPATION	PROPERTY		SLAVES	PLACE OF BIRTH
			Real	Personal		
4. F. W. Pike	41	Sugar Planter	$30,000	$72,000	4	New Hampshire
5. Walter Pugh	30	Sugar Planter	$70,000	$96,500	62	Louisiana
6. James Wilson	50	Manager	$50,000	$45,000	123	Maryland
Democrats						
1. W. W. Pugh	49	Sugar Planter	$300,000	$210,000	161	N. Carolina
2. Miles Taylor	55	Sugar Planter	$100,000	$90,000	92	New York

AVOYELLES PARISH						
NAME	AGE	OCCUPATION	PROPERTY		SLAVES	PLACE OF BIRTH
			Real	Personal		
Know Nothings						
1. John Aymond	33	Farmer	--	$45,500		Louisiana
2. Adolphe D. Coco	35	Farmer	--	$7,600		Louisiana
3. Lucien D. Coco	47	Farmer	$100,000	$3,500	58	Louisiana
4. Henderson Taylor	56	Lawyer	--	$25,000		S. Carolina

BOSSIER PARISH						
NAME	AGE	OCCUPATION	PROPERTY		SLAVES	PLACE OF BIRTH
			Real	Personal		
Democrats						
1. John Sandidge	62	Planter	$120,000	$219,000	193	S. Carolina

CADDO PARISH						
NAME	AGE	OCCUPATION	PROPERTY		SLAVES	PLACE OF BIRTH
			Real	Personal		
Know Nothings		-				
1. L. P. Crain	42	Lawyer	--	$20,000		N. Carolina
2. George Dillard	31	Editor	$0	$8,000		Kentucky
3. L. Dillard	66	Printer	$0	$8,000		Virginia
4. B. W. George	45	Planter	--	$22,000		Tennessee
5. Colonel B. L. Hodge	36	Lawyer	$40,000	$75,000		Tennessee
6. H. Iles	35	Farmer	$18,000	$1,000		Louisiana
7. John McCain	36	Farmer	--	$1,350		N. Carolina
8. Thomas M'Call	65	Farmer	--	$400		Georgia
Democrats						
1. A. D. Battle	31	City Marshall	$3,000	$500		Georgia
2. Dr. M. Estes	54	Physician (editor)	$15,000	$1,000		Virginia
3. Roland Jones	46	Lawyer	$0	$0		N. Carolina
4. A. Slaughter	30	Lawyer	$40,000	$4,000	4	Kentucky

CLAIBORNE PARISH						
NAME	AGE	OCCUPATION	PROPERTY		SLAVES	PLACE OF BIRTH
			Real	Personal		
Democrats						
1. J. W. Barrow	27	Farmer	$2,000	$6,000		Georgia
2. J. W. Berry	41	Farmer	$15,000	$40,000	3	Indiana
3. Colonel J.W. McDonald	46	Farmer	$15,000	$70,000		
4. Isaac Miller	46	Farmer	$3,000	$8,000	9	
5. T. Vaughn	26	Lawyer	$2,000	$1,500		Ohio

EAST BATON ROUGE PARISH						
NAME	AGE	OCCUPATION	PROPERTY		SLAVES	PLACE OF BIRTH
			Real	Personal		
Know Nothings						
1. F. Arbour	56	Saw Mill Owner	--	$37,650	33	Louisiana
2. T. J. Buffington	39	Physician	$7,000	$30,900		Virginia
3. Dennis Daigre	40	Farmer	$28,000	$40,500	33	Louisiana
4. A.M. Dunn	53	Lawyer	$8,000	$18,000	25	S. Carolina
5. John R. Groom	43	Farmer	$0	$11,233	23	Virginia
6. Paul Kleinpeter	48	Farmer	--	$48,000	28	Louisiana
7. J. C. Knox	47	Farmer	$10,000	$42,500		Mississippi
8. J. H. Matta	33	Merchant	$0	$11,000	1	Louisiana
9. Joseph Monget	63	Commissary-Market	--	$11,000	8	Mississippi
10. Dan Morgan	40	Farmer	--	$15,000	13	Louisiana
11. James Morgan	48	Farmer	$1,200	$19,500		Louisiana
12. Fergus Penniston	33	Farmer	$90,000	$194,500	151	Louisiana
13. Charles B. Pipes	35	Farmer	$4,000	$19,800	17	Louisiana
14. A. B. Vail	32	Farmer	--	$22,100		Louisiana
15. William B. Walker	45	Farmer	$134,600	$250,000	169	Virginia
Democrats						
1. Thomas Bynum	28	Editor	$25,500	$20,900		Louisiana
2. Edward Cousinard	40	City Marshall	$1,100	$300		Louisiana
3. A. DeLaroderie	75	Saw Mill Owner	$13,050	$10,400		France
4. Emile Droz	26	Farmer	$3,050	$300		Louisiana
5. James C. Elam	29	Mayor of Baton Rouge	$1,500	$7,000		Louisiana
6. J. F. Glover	41	Physician	$0	$32,000	28	Virginia
7. Andrew S. Herron	36	Lawyer	$0	$7,400	11	Tennessee

EAST BATON ROUGE PARISH						
NAME	AGE	OCCUPATION	PROPERTY		SLAVES	PLACE OF BIRTH
			Real	Personal		
8. H. J. Hyams	32	Editor	$0	$300		N. Carolina
9. L. A. Latil	62	Gunsmith	$0	$500		Louisiana
10. John F. Piker	42	Parish Assessor	$0	$8,000	5	Louisiana
11. J. M. Taylor	29	Editor	$1,100	$19,000	4	Alabama

EAST FELICIANA PARISH						
NAME	AGE	OCCUPATION	PROPERTY		SLAVES	PLACE OF BIRTH
			Real	Personal		
Know Nothings						
1. R. J. Bownman	38	Lawyer	$22,000	$39,350		Mississippi
2. W. W. Chapman	41	Merchant	$20,000	$50,000	15	Louisiana
3. J. O. Fuqua	38	Lawyer	$8,000	$3,000		Mississippi
4. M. W. Hughes	56	Blacksmith	--	$6,000		Virginia
5. O. P. Longworthy	34	Physician	--	$7,300		
6. P. Pond Sr.	54	Physician	$3,000	$4,000		New Hampshire
7. P. Pond Jr.	35	Lawyer-Planter	$10,000	$30,000		New Hampshire
Democrats						
1. John McVea	39	Judge	$44,125	$101,300	97	Ireland
2. General G. W. Munday	44	Planter	$10,000	$40,000	42	Louisiana

IBERVILLE PARISH						
NAME	AGE	OCCUPATION	PROPERTY		SLAVES	PLACE OF BIRTH
			Real	Personal		
Know Nothings						
1. W. P. Bradburn	44	Editor	$0	$8,000		Tennessee
2. Samuel Matthews	36	Lawyer	--	$4,000	6	Alabama

IBERVILLE PARISH						
NAME	AGE	OCCUPATION	PROPERTY		SLAVES	PLACE OF BIRTH
			Real	Personal		
Democrats						
1. P. O. Hébert	48	Planter-Lawyer	$200,000	$10,000	94	Louisiana
2. E. W. Robertson	37	State Auditor	--	$16,200		Tennessee

JEFFERSON PARISH						
NAME	AGE	OCCUPATION	PROPERTY		SLAVES	PLACE OF BIRTH
			Real	Personal		
Know Nothings						
1. E. Merrick	46	Supreme Court Judge	$10,000	$4,000	5	Virginia
2. E. M. Moise	49	Lawyer	$12,000	$12,000	5	S. Carolina
3. Christian Roselius	56	Lawyer	$150,000	$50,000	9	Germany

LAFAYETTE PARISH						
NAME	AGE	OCCUPATION	PROPERTY		SLAVES	PLACE OF BIRTH
			Real	Personal		
Democrats						
1. Charles H. Mouton	58	Planter	$18,000	$27,000		

LAFOURCHE PARISH						
NAME	AGE	OCCUPATION	PROPERTY		SLAVES	PLACE OF BIRTH
			Real	Personal		
Know Nothings						
1. Captain R. G. Darden	49	Farmer	$75,000	$75,000		N. Carolina
2. P. H. Gary	51	Foundry Keeper	$70,000	$70,000	22	Virginia
3. T. Harang	35	Lawyer	--	$50,000	6	Louisiana

LAFOURCHE PARISH						
NAME	AGE	OCCUPATION	PROPERTY		SLAVES	PLACE OF BIRTH
			Real	Personal		
4. John C. Ragan	43	Farmer	--	$21,600		New York
Democrats						
1. L. S. Allain	34	Clerk of District Court	$3,000	$5,500	7	Louisiana
2. E. G. Robichaux	31	Sheriff	$2,000	$4,100	3	Louisiana
3. J. A. Robichaux	29	Parish Assessor	$2,000	$2,700	2	Louisiana
4. Valmond D. Terrebonne	41	Lawyer	$1,500	$2,800	2	

LIVINGSTON PARISH						
NAME	AGE	OCCUPATION	PROPERTY		SLAVES	PLACE OF BIRTH
			Real	Personal		
Democrats						
1. Thomas G. Davidson	55	Farmer	$100,000	$25,000	94	Mississippi

MADISON PARISH						
NAME	AGE	OCCUPATION	PROPERTY		SLAVES	PLACE OF BIRTH
			Real	Personal		
Democrats						
1. William S. Parham	46	Lawyer	$100,000	$5,000	81	Virginia

MOREHOUSE PARISH						
NAME	AGE	OCCUPATION	PROPERTY		SLAVES	PLACE OF BIRTH
			Real	Personal		
Know Nothings						
1. Robert B. Todd	35	Lawyer	$3,400	$18,000	16	Missouri

MOREHOUSE PARISH						
NAME	AGE	OCCUPATION	PROPERTY		SLAVES	PLACE OF BIRTH
			Real	Personal		
Democrats						
1. Dixon Hall Jr.	40	Farm Manager	$1,000	$6,000	5	Georgia
2. Jacob Mathews	37	Lawyer	$30,000	$6,000		Ohio
3. W. H. Wadlington	41	Judge-Farmer	$18,000	$31,654		Kentucky

NATCHITOCHES PARISH						
NAME	AGE	OCCUPATION	PROPERTY		SLAVES	PLACE OF BIRTH
			Real	Personal		
Democrats						
1. Julius Somparac	39	Planter	$24,000	$4,000	40	Louisiana

ORLEANS PARISH						
NAME	AGE	OCCUPATION	PROPERTY		SLAVES	PLACE OF BIRTH
			Real	Personal		
Know Nothings						
1. Henry Bebee	40	Sugar Broker	$60,000	$10,000		Louisiana
2. James E. R. Chisholm	40	Parish Assessor	$0	$300		Alabama
3. Ben Campbell	48	Merchant	--	--	4	New York
4. E. G. Delile	49	Cotton Press Owner	$0	$100,000		Pennsylvania
5. John Dolhonde	48	Accountant	$12,000	$2,500		Louisiana
6. Adolphe Dupre	53	Bank Clerk	$14,000	$2,900		Louisiana
7. George Eustis	39	Congressman	$10,000	$8,000		Louisiana
8. Hippolyte Fortier	31	Tax Collector	$0	$5,000		Louisiana
9. Randall Hunt	47	Lawyer	$20,000	$10,000		S. Carolina
10. Thomas G. Hunt	54	Judge	$0	$10,000		S. Carolina

ORLEANS PARISH						
NAME	AGE	OCCUPATION	PROPERTY		SLAVES	PLACE OF BIRTH
			Real	Personal		
11. George W. Lewis	46	Clerk of Court	$7,500	$1,700		Louisiana
12. F. A. Lumsden	49	Editor	$40,000	$8,000		S. Carolina
13. James McFarlane	60	Physician	$30,000	$10,000	5	N. Carolina
14. James Phelps	46	Merchant	$12,000	$25,000	2	New York
15. E. H. Wilson	42	Commission Merchant	$10,000	$5,000		Kentucky
Democrats						
1. Donatien Augustin	65	Lawyer-Judge	$15,000	$3,000		Louisiana
2. John B. Cotton	37	Lawyer	$4,000	$10,000	7	Georgia
3. W. R. Crane	51	Lawyer	$25,000	$7,000		Dist. of Columbia
4. Dr. H. Edwards	55	Physician	$10,000	$2,500		Connecticut
5. P. A. Guyol	47	Federal Officer	$6,000	$1,500		Louisiana
6. John Hughes	54	Master Shipwright	$40,000	$50,000	7	New York
7. H. M. Hyams	55	Lawyer	$400,000	$30,000	20	S. Carolina
8. D. C. Jenkins	35	Editor	$0	$0		Massachusetts
9. Dr. John Ker	45	Physician	$10,000	$1,000		Pennsylvania
10. Jacob J. Lugenbuhl	39	Lawyer	$800	$250	2	Germany
11. John Pemberton	40	President Insurance Co.	$45,000	$25,000		Louisiana
12. Charles S. Reese	35	Lawyer	$10,000	$1,500		Georgia
13. Thomas J. Semmes	35	Lawyer	$24,000	$13,000		Dist. of Columbia
14. John Slidell	64	Lawyer-US Senator	$150,000	$6,000		New York
15. John Sullivan	33	Custom House Officer	$0	$500		Ireland
16. Paul E. Theard	31	Lawyer	$12,000	$3,000		Louisiana

OUACHITA PARISH						
NAME	AGE	OCCUPATION	PROPERTY		SLAVES	PLACE OF BIRTH
			Real	Personal		
Know Nothings						
1. W. J. Q. Baker	31	None listed	$100,000	$111,000	53	Ohio
2. Arthur H. Harris	28	Lawyer	$7,500	$500	4	Tennessee
3. John T. Ludeling	32	Lawyer	$71,200	$1,800		Louisiana
4. John Ray	44	Lawyer	$15,000	$2,000		Mississippi
5. Robert Ray Sr.	30	Lawyer	$10,000	$1,000	5	Missouri
6. S. L. Slack	39	Lawyer	$10,000	$4,000	6	Ohio
7. H. H. Slaughter	34	Merchant	$55,000	$80,000	67	Alabama
8. O. D. Stillman	50	Lawyer	$5,000	$1,500		Rhode Island

PLAQUEMINES PARISH						
NAME	AGE	OCCUPATION	PROPERTY		SLAVES	PLACE OF BIRTH
			Real	Personal		
Know Nothings						
1. Dr. David R. Fox	36	Physician	$5,000	$2,500	6	Mississippi
2. Martial Lafrance	59	Rice Planter	$10,000	$9,000		Louisiana
3. Edmond Martin	52	Rice Planter	$10,000	$6,000	8	Louisiana
4. Ferdinand Martin	57	Planter	$5,000	$3,500		Louisiana
5. Simeon Martin	30	Sheriff	$1,000	$800		Louisiana
6. Hypolite Ragas	35	Planter	$1,000	$1,200		Louisiana
7. John C. Rapp	32	Justice of Peace	$0	$0		Louisiana
8. Victor Reaud	35	Parish Recorder	$2,500	$2,000	3	Louisiana
9. Dr. J. B. Wilkinson	43	Planter	$13,000	$0		Mississippi
Democrats						
1. Oscar Arroyo	38	Clerk	$3,000	$4,000	6	Louisiana
2. Charles J. Villere	30	Attorney	$60,000	$45,000	89	Louisiana

POINTE COUPEE PARISH						
NAME	AGE	OCCUPATION	PROPERTY		SLAVES	PLACE OF BIRTH
			Real	Personal		
Democrats						
1. Alcide Bondy	40	Planter	$23,000	$8,000		
2. A. D. M. Haralson	43	Lawyer	$11,500	$500		Virginia
3. Ovide LeJeune	40	Planter	$100,000	$45,000	77	Louisiana

RAPIDES PARISH						
NAME	AGE	OCCUPATION	PROPERTY		SLAVES	PLACE OF BIRTH
			Real	Personal		
Know Nothings						
1. C. W. Boyce	33	Printer	$5,000	$15,000	2	Massachusetts
2. O. N. Ogden	42	Lawyer	$86,000	$3,500	44	N. Carolina
3. Louis Texada	41	Farmer	$123,500	$8,760	61	Louisiana
4. Colonel T. J. Wells	54	Farmer	$20,000	$10,800		Louisiana
Democrats						
1. Thomas O. Moore	55	Governor-Planter	$320,000	$24,300	226	

ST. BERNARD PARISH						
NAME	AGE	OCCUPATION	PROPERTY		SLAVES	PLACE OF BIRTH
			Real	Personal		
Democrats						
1. Antoine Marrero	40	Planter	$35,000	$65,000	71	Louisiana

ST. CHARLES PARISH						
NAME	AGE	OCCUPATION	PROPERTY		SLAVES	PLACE OF BIRTH
			Real	Personal		
Democrats						
1. P. A. Rost	60	Planter-Retired	$600,000	Not given	133	France
2. F. B. Trepagnier	56	Manager of Plantation	--	$25,000	5	

ST. HELENA PARISH						
NAME	AGE	OCCUPATION	PROPERTY		SLAVES	PLACE OF BIRTH
			Real	Personal		
Know Nothings						
1. G. P. McMichael Sr.	59	Farmer	$33,570	$47,550	15	S. Carolina
2. James Strickland	63	Farmer	$20,000	$2,000	12	Georgia
3. J. A. Williams	44	Clerk of Court	$5,000	$11,740	10	
4. A. B. Womack	40	Farmer	$10,000	$37,750	37	Louisiana
Democrats						
1. F. H. Hatch	43	Farmer	$3,000	$1,000		
2. G. W. Hatch	40	Farmer	$5,000	$11,000	14	

ST. JOHN THE BAPTIST PARISH						
NAME	AGE	OCCUPATION	PROPERTY		SLAVES	PLACE OF BIRTH
			Real	Personal		
Democrats						
1. Andre Deslondes	76	Planter	$200,000	$450,000	119	Louisiana

ST. LANDRY PARISH						
NAME	AGE	OCCUPATION	PROPERTY		SLAVES	PLACE OF BIRTH
			Real	Personal		
Know Nothings						
1. Alphonse Deboillon	42	Planter	$500	$2,500	5	Louisiana
2. Francois Devilliers	60	Planter	$22,600	$48,600	34	
3. Albert DeJean	30	Lawyer	$0	$0		Louisiana
4. Cyprien Dupre	58	Planter	$20,000	$200,000	25	Louisiana
5. J. B. A. Fontenot	65	Farmer	$5,800	$64,000	48	Louisiana
6. Elbert Gantt	42	Planter	$40,000	$30,000	51	
7. J. A. Glaze	24	Planter	$3,400	$2,250		
8. Solomon B. Harman	52	Planter	$12,500	$27,400		Louisiana
9. Thomas H. Lewis	58	Lawyer-Planter	$28,000	$40,000	33	Louisiana
10. Dr. D. W. Martin	38	Planter	$20,000	$200,000	32	Kentucky
11. Joseph Moore	36	None Listed	$13,000	$7,500		Louisiana
12. Francois Robin	50	Planter	$20,000	$80,000	75	Louisiana
13. Louis Stagg	27	Merchant	$2,200	$2,000	1	Georgia
14. Elois Vidrine	42	Planter	$8,000	$26,000	20	Louisiana
15. A. Webb	38	Planter	$80,000	$100,000		Louisiana
Democrats						
1. T. S. Hardy	30	Manager	$0	$0		Maryland
2. Villeneve Joubert	50	Parish Assessor	$0	$6,000		Louisiana
3. G. W. Marsh	51	--	$0	$0		
4. William Offutt	52	Farmer	$6,000	$6,000		
5. Pierre Pitre	45	Planter	$4,000	$15,000		
6. Raphael Smith	55	Planter	$12,000	$49,000	33	
7. Andrew Thompson	45	Clerk	$2,000	$5,000		Missouri

ST. MARTIN PARISH						
NAME	AGE	OCCUPATION	PROPERTY		SLAVES	PLACE OF BIRTH
			Real	Personal		
Know Nothings						
1. Dr. A. Duperier	32	Planter	$195,000	$15,000		Louisiana
2. John G. Harry	47	Planter	$7,500	$1,000		Louisiana

ST. MARY PARISH						
NAME	AGE	OCCUPATION	PROPERTY		SLAVES	PLACE OF BIRTH
			Real	Personal		
Know Nothings						
1. Joseph V. Fourmy	38	Secretary, Ins. Co.	$8,000	$6,000	6	Louisiana
2. Wilson McKerall	46	None Listed	$6,000	$20,000	6	
3. Adolphus Olivier	26	Lawyer	$4,500	$15,000	4	Louisiana
4. J. W. Walker	50	Lawyer	$10,000	$7,000	10	Louisiana
Democrats						
1. Joseph Gautreaux	30	Asst. Marshall-Census	$6,000	$8,000		
2. A. L. Tucker	41	Lawyer	$4,000	$2,500	1	

ST. TAMMANY PARISH						
NAME	AGE	OCCUPATION	PROPERTY		SLAVES	PLACE OF BIRTH
			Real	Personal		
Democrats						
1. Anatole Carrière	36	Brickyard Owner	$2,000	$25,000	31	Louisiana
2. Nicholas Galatas	44	Sheriff	$1,000	$13,000	18	Louisiana
3. M. G. Penn	61	Miller	$12,000	$18,000		Virginia
4. Henry Spring	31	Farmer	$220	$100		Louisiana
5. William Tally	33	Farmer	$640	$222		Louisiana

NAME	AGE	OCCUPATION	PROPERTY		SLAVES	PLACE OF BIRTH
TERREBONNE PARISH						
			Real	Personal		

NAME	AGE	OCCUPATION	Real	Personal	SLAVES	PLACE OF BIRTH
Know Nothings						
1. William Bisland	34	Planter	$112,500	$148,000	113	Mississippi
2. Aubin Bourg	28	Sheriff	$1,000	$5,000	2	Louisiana
3. Albert Cage	32	Planter	$190,000	$307,000	110	Mississippi
4. Duncan Cage	35	Planter	$190,000	$307,000	437	Mississippi
5. Henry F. Collins	29	Planter	$50,000	$76,000	59	Louisiana
6. G. F. Connely	43	Planter	$66,000	$208,000		Kentucky
7. A. J. Delaporte	27	Parish Recorder	$0	$3,000		Louisiana
8. Jouachaim Gueno	36	Planter	$85,000	$85,150	63	Louisiana
9. William H. Knight	26	Lawyer	$0	$1,200		Louisiana
10. G. S. Lester	35	Planter	$26,000	$17,000		Mississippi
11. William J. Minor	25	Planter	$340,000	$440,000	349	Louisiana
12. Henry Newell	32	Clerk of Court	$2,000	$6,000	6	New York
13. J. C. Potts	52	Planter	$91,000	$95,000	72	New York·
14. N. H. Rightor	28	Lawyer	$0	$0		Louisiana
15. Colonel J. B. Robinson	54	Planter	$120,000	$157,600	89	Mississippi
16. W. A. Shaffer	64	Planter	$156,000	$173,000	118	S. Carolina
17. W. L. Shaffer	24	Planter	$73,000	$55,000		Louisiana
18. J. J. Shaffer	28	Planter	$69,000	$41,000	17	Louisiana
19. Charles Tennent	38	Merchant	$4,000	$10,000		Delaware
20. B. G. Thibodaux	47	Planter	$63,000	$110,000	32	Louisiana
Democrats						
1. H. Arceneau	50	Farmer	$6,000	$7,000		Louisiana
2. R. R. Barrow	65	Planter	$1,062,000	$545,000	399	Louisiana
3. M. Daigle	62	Farmer	$7,000	$1,800		Louisiana
4. Charles L. Ducroy	60	Merchant	$3,000	$5,000		France

TERREBONNE PARISH						
NAME	AGE	OCCUPATION	PROPERTY		SLAVES	PLACE OF BIRTH
			Real	Personal		
5. Frank Gagne	39	Merchant	$6,500	$15,000		Canada
6. J. A. Gagne	34	Physician	$1,200	$10,700	6	Canada
7. F. S. Goode	29	Lawyer	$7,000	$6,800	6	Alabama
8. Surville Labit	40	Farmer	$800	$500		Louisiana
9. Dr. William M. Mercer	32	Physician	$0	$3,500		Kentucky
10. Adolphe Peregrin	51	Farmer	$5,000	$900		Louisiana
11. A. Verret	41	Planter	$72,000	$103,000	107	Louisiana
12. J. P. Vigurie	32	Planter	$12,900	$12,000		Louisiana

WEST FELICIANA PARISH						
NAME	AGE	OCCUPATION	PROPERTY		SLAVES	PLACE OF BIRTH
			Real	Personal		
Democrats						
1. James R. Marks	34	Editor-Mayor Bayou Sara	$1,500	$2,500		Georgia
2. R. C. Wickliffe	35	Lawyer	$1,000	$1,500		Kentucky

APPENDIX C

The American National Council met in Philadelphia February 19, 1856. All the States, except four or five were represented. E. B. Bartlett, of Ky., President of the National Council presided, and, after a rather stormy session of three days, devoted mainly to the discussion of a Party Platform, the following, on the 21st, was adopted:

AMERICAN PLATFORM

1. An humble acknowledgment to the Supreme Being, for his protective care vouchsafed to our fathers in their successful Revolutionary struggle, and hitherto manifested to us, their descendants in the preservation of the liberties, the independence, and the union of these States.

2. The perpetuation of the Federal Union and Constitution, as the palladium of our civil and religious liberties, and the only sure bulwarks of American Independence.

3. Americans must rule America; and to this end native-born citizens should be selected for all State, Federal and municipal offices of government employment in preference to all others. Nevertheless,

4. Persons born of American parents residing temporarily abroad, should be entitled to all the rights of native-born citizens.

5. No person should be selected for political station (whether of native or foreign birth), who recognizes any allegiance or obligation of any description to any foreign prince, potentate or power, or who refuses to recognize the Federal and State Constitutions (each within its sphere) as paramount to all other laws, as rules of political action.

6. The unqualified recognition and maintenance of the reserved rights of the several States, and the cultivation of harmony and fraternal good will between the citizens of the several States, and to this end, non-interference by Congress with questions appertaining solely to the individual States, and non-intervention by each State with the affairs of any other State.

7. The recognition of the right of native-born and naturalized citizens of the United States, permanently residing in any territory thereof, to frame their constitutions and laws, and to regulate their domestic and social affairs in their own mode, subject only to the provisions of the Federal Constitution, with the privileges of admission into the Union whenever they have the requisite population for one Representative in Congress: Provided always, that none but those who are citizens of the United States, under the Constitution and laws thereof, and

who have a fixed residence in any such Territory, ought to participate in the formation of the Constitution, or in the enactment of laws for said Territory or State.

8. An enforcement of the principles that no State or Territory ought to admit others than citizens to the right of suffrage, or of holding political offices of the United States.

9. A change in the laws of naturalization, making a continued residence of twenty-one years, of all not heretofore provided for, an indispensable requisite for citizenship hereafter, and excluding all paupers and persons convicted of crime, from landing upon our shores; but no interference with the vested rights of foreigners.

10. Opposition to any union between Church and State; no interference with religious faith or worship, and no test oaths for office.

11. Free and thorough investigation into any and all alleged abuses of public functionaries, and a strict economy in public expenditures.

12. The maintenance and enforcement of all laws constitutionally enacted until said laws shall be repealed, or shall be declared null and void by competent judicial authority.

13. Opposition to the reckless and unwise policy of the present Administration in the general management of our national affairs, and more especially as shown in removing "Americans" (by designation) and Conservatives in principle, from office, and placing foreigners and Ultraists in their places; as shown in a truckling subserviency to the stronger, and an insolent and cowardly bravado toward the weaker powers; as shown in reopening sectional agitation, by the repeal of the Missouri Compromise; as shown in granting to unnaturalized foreigners the right of suffrage in Kansas and Nebraska; as shown in the vacillating course on the Kansas and Nebraska question, as shown in the corruption which pervade some of the Departments of the Government; as shown in disgracing meritorious naval officers through prejudice or caprice; as shown in the blundering mismanagement of our foreign affairs.

14. Therefore, to remedy existing evils, and prevent the disastrous consequences otherwise resulting there-from, we would build up the "American Party" the principles herein before stated.

15. That each State Council shall have authority to amend their several constitutions, so as to abolish the several degrees and to substitute a pledge of honor, instead of other obligations, for fellowship and admission into the party.

16. A free and open discussion of all political principles embraced in our Platform.

On the following day (Feb. 22,) the American National Nominating Convention, composed mostly of the same gentlemen who had deliberated as the National Council, organized at Philadelphia with 227 delegates in attendance, Maine, Vermont, Georgia, and South Carolina, being the only States not represented. Ephraim Marsh, of New-Jersey, was chosen to preside, and the Convention remained in session till the 25th, and, after disposing of several cases of contested seats, discussed at considerable length, and with great warmth, the question of the power of the National Council to establish a Platform for the Convention, which should be binding force upon that body. Finally, Mr. Killinger, of Pennsylvania, proposed the following:

Resolved, That the National Council has no authority to prescribe a Platform of principles for this Nominating Convention, and that we will nominate for President and Vice-President no man who is not in favor of interdicting the introduction of Slavery into Territory north 36°30′ by congressional action.

A motion to lay this resolution on the table was adopted, 141 to 59. A motion was then made to proceed to the nomination of a candidate for President, which was carried, 151 to 51, the Anti-Slavery delegates, or North Americans, as they were called, voting in the negative, and desiring to postpone the nomination. But being beaten at all points, they (to the number of about 50) either withdrew or refused to take any further part in the proceedings of the Convention, and many of them subsequently supported Col. Fremont for President.

An informal ballot was then taken for President, which resulted as follows:

M. Fillmore of N.Y 71
George Law, N.Y.. 27
Garrett Davis, Ky 13
R. F. Stockton, N.J.. 8
John McLean, Ohio 7
Sam. Houston, Texas 6
John Bell, Tennessee. 5
Kenneth Raynor, N.C. 2
Erastus Brooks, N.Y.. 2
Lewis D. Campbell, Ohio. 1
John M. Clayton, Del.. 1

A formal ballot was then taken, when Mr. Fillmore was nominated as follows:

Fillmore 179
Law 24
Raynor 14
McLean 18
Davis 10
Houston 8

Necessary to a choice, 122.

Millard Fillmore was then declared to be the nominee.

A ballot was then taken for Vice-President, and Andrew Jackson Donelson, of Tennessee, was nominated as follows:

A. J. Donelson, Ten. 181
Percy Walker, Ala.. 8
Henry J. Gardner, Mass.. 8
Kenneth Raynor, N.C. 8

APPENDIX D

Platform of The American Party of Louisiana*

1. We advocate an amendment of the Naturalization Laws, with proper safeguards to preserve the purity of the elective franchise.

2. We advocate the passage of such laws will prevent the immigration of paupers and criminals to this country.

3. We oppose any interference in the vested rights of all persons whether they be of native or foreign birth.

4. We are in favor of non-intervention with slavery by the Federal Government, except for the protection of our constitutional rights.

5. We advocate a high National Policy, such as will afford a stern and unwavering protection to the American name abroad and will follow and guard the American citizen wherever he moves.

6. We believe that America should be governed by Americans, effecting the same through the ballot-box alone, the only legitimate instrument of reform in this country.

7. We believe that the office should seek the man, and not the man the office, and shall oppose the distribution of office among office-seekers or as a reward for partisan services.

8. We will maintain and defend the Constitution of the U.S., the Union as it now exists, and the rights of the States without diminution, insisting upon a faithful performance on the part of the General Government of all the duties enjoined upon it by the Constitution.

9. While we approve of the platform adopted by the late National Council of the American party at Philadelphia, we reject the application of the principles of the eighth article to American Catholics, as unjust, unbounded, and entirely unworthy of our country. We shall forever continue to protest against any abridgement of religious liberty, holding it as a cardinal maximum that religious faith is a question between each individual and his God. We utterly condemn any attempt to make religious belief a test for political office, and can never affiliate with any party which holds sentiments not in accordance with these.

10. We war with no party as such, but shall oppose all who oppose us in the advocacy of these great American principles.

State Policy

- Reform of abuses, and retrenchment in our State expenditures.
- Education of the youth of the country in schools established by the State.

- A constitutional organization of the Swamp Land Commissioners.
- A more efficient administration of the Internal Improvement Department, with a view of improving our inland navigation.

*The American Party adopted the 1855 platform on July 4 at Baton Rouge. It was the only state platform adopted by that party. In future campaigns the American Party would adopt party resolutions. New Orleans *Bee,* September 3, 1855.

NOTES

Abbreviations Used in the Endnotes

HNOC—Historic New Orleans Collection

LSU—Louisiana and Lower Mississippi Valley Collection, Louisiana State University

UT—University of Texas, Center for American History

ICPR—Inter-University Consortium for Political Research, The Institute for Social Research Center for Political Studies, The University of Michigan

Introduction

1. Avery O. Craven, *The Growth of Southern Nationalism: 1848–1862* (Baton Rouge: Louisiana State University Press, 1953), 238; W. Darrell Overdyke, *The Know-Nothing Party in the South* (Baton Rouge: Louisiana State University Press, 1950), 51.

2. Arthur C. Cole, *The Irrepressible Conflict: 1850–1865* (New York: Macmillan Co., 1934), 146; Marc Kruman, *Parties and Politics in North Carolina: 1836–1865* (Baton Rouge: Louisiana State University Press, 1983).

3. Arthur C. Cole, *The Whig Party in the South* (reprinted; Gloucester, MA: Peter Smith, 1962), 309–310.

4. Ray Allen Billington notes that nativism was a significant part of the success of the American Party in the South, including Louisiana. Ray Allen Billington, *The Protestant Crusade: 1800–1860* (New York: Macmillan Co., 1934), 393. W. Darrell Overdyke is of the same opinion. He describes Louisiana as a "veritable hotbed of nativism." Overdyke, *The Know-Nothing Party in the South*, 13.

5. W. Darrell Overdyke, "History of the American Party in Louisiana," *Louisiana Historical Quarterly*, 16 (October 1932), passim, 581–88.

6. Robert C. Reinders, "The Louisiana American Party and the Catholic Church," *Mid-America*, 40 (1958), 218–21.

7. Michael F. Holt, "The Politics of Impatience: The Origins of Know Nothingism," *Journal of American History*, 60 (September 1973), 313, 322; William J. Evitts, *A Matter of Allegiances: Maryland from 1850 to 1861* (Baltimore: Johns Hopkins University Press, 1974), 76–7. Holt and Evitts held to this similar view of voters being "distraught over the moral and social climate they saw around them."

8. Evitts, *A Matter of Allegiances*, 82; Holt, "The Politics of Impatience," 315–19. While Holt has refined his view of the Know Nothings (he no longer identifies its rise with a sudden social and economic upheaval), he agrees with Robert Fogel's *Without Consent or Contract: The Rise and Fall of American Slavery* (New York: W. W. Norton & Co., 1994), 354–80, that the recession of 1854–55 caused Native American laborers to fear increased competition from unemployed immigrants, but Holt now includes political, as well as social sources, for Know Nothings' rise. Michael F. Holt, *Political Parties and American Political Development from the Age of Jackson to the Age of Lincoln* (Baton Rouge: Louisiana State University Press, 1992), 9–10; Frank Towers, *The Urban South and the Coming of the Civil War* (Charlottesville: University of Virginia Press, 2004), 73. However, Towers also says "former Whigs ran the American party, and their wealth and occupations resembled those of the leaders of the old parties."

9. William E. Gienapp, "Nativism and the Creation of a Republican Majority in the North before the Civil War," *Journal of American History*, 72 (December 1985), 529–59; Paul Kleppner, *The Third Electoral System, 1854–1892: Parties, Voters, and Political Cultures* (Chapel Hill: University of North Carolina Press, 1979), 70–72; John Ashworth, *Slavery, Capitalism, and Politics in the Antebellum Republic: Vol. 2: The Coming of the Civil War* (New York: Cambridge University Press, 2007), 345.

10. Kleppner, *The Third Electoral System, 1854–1872*, 70–72. Kleppner sees this anti-party movement wanting to act "beyond the bounds of party."

11. Tyler Anbinder, *Nativism and Slavery: The Northern Know Nothings and the Politics of the 1850s* (New York: Oxford University Press, 1994), xiii.

12. Ibid., xiv.

13. The only statewide study of any detail is W. Darrell Overdyke's published MA thesis, "History of the American Party in Louisiana,"*Louisiana Historical Quarterly*, 15, 16 (October 1932, January, April, July, October 1933) and Marius M. Carriere, "The Know Nothing Movement in Louisiana" PhD diss., LSU, 1977. John David Bladek, "America for Americans: the Southern Know Nothing Party and the Politics of Nativism, 1854–1856," PhD diss., University of Washington, 1998, while about southern Know Nothings, offers very little on Louisiana Know Nothingism. Finally, John Sacher devotes a small part of his recent book on Louisiana politics to Know Nothingism and concludes they are not simply Whigs in disguise. However, he does not go into much detail about the party in the state. John Sacher, *A Perfect War of Politics: Parties, Politicians, and Democracy in Louisiana, 1824–1861* (Baton Rouge: Louisiana State University Press, 2007), 237, 239–40.

14. With the exception of a few well-known Americans (Know Nothings) such as Charles Gayareé, Christian Roselius, George Eustis, and John Edward Bouligny, few personal records remain of Know Nothing leaders' involvement during the short-time the American Party existed in the state.

CHAPTER 1

1. Fred B. Kniffen and Sam Bowers Hilliard, ed., *Louisiana Its Land and People* (Baton Rouge: LSU Press, 1968), rev. ed., 5–10, 34–57.

2. Roger W. Shugg, *Origins of Class Struggle in Louisiana: A Social History of White Farmers and Laborers during Slavery and After* (Baton Rouge: LSU Press, 1939), 8–12.

3. Ibid., 11–13.

4. The exact definition of the word "Creole" continues to perplex historians, sociologists, and contemporaries of the nineteenth century. Some would include all non-Anglo native

Louisianians (including African Americans), while others limit the use of the word to the descendants of the French and Spanish colonials. Joseph Tregle makes a distinction between Latin Creoles and foreign French. He defines Latin Creoles as those whose heritage can be traced to colonial days and he includes the Acadians (descendants of the French Canadians) in this group. The foreign French were those Louisiana residents, according to Tregle, who immigrated to Louisiana during and after the French Revolution. Joseph George Tregle Jr., *Louisiana in the Age of Jackson: A Clash of Cultures and Personalities* (Baton Rouge: Louisiana State University Press, 1999), 37–41, 337–43.

For the purposes of my study, I will use the word "Creole" to refer to those descendants of colonial Louisianians and the French immigrants. Although Tregle correctly noted the differences between the Latin Creoles and the foreign French, the similarities of culture and politics were sufficient to bring them together culturally and politically in opposition to the immigrating Anglo-Americans.

5. There are no census reports extant for the years between 1788 and 1803. In 1803, the United States consul at New Orleans, working with the best documents available, reported that the total population of Louisiana was 49,473. The population figure included residents of areas that did not become part of the state of Louisiana, and when that number is deducted the population of what is known today as Louisiana was 41,803. By 1810 the population had increased to 76,556 and it is estimated the Creoles still outnumbered the Anglo-Americans at this time by at least two-to-one. Francois-Xavier Martin, *The History of Louisiana, from the Earliest Period* (New Orleans: James A. Gresham Publisher, 1882), 300, 347.

It is difficult to estimate the population of Creoles and Anglo-Americans after 1810 since census figures regarding nativities are sketchy at best. One historian estimates that even as late as 1830 the Creoles outnumbered the Americans by a two-to-one ratio. L. W. Newton, "Creoles and Anglo-Americans," *Southwestern Social Science Quarterly*, 14 (1933), 34.

6. Shugg, *Origins of Class Struggle*, 18–19.

7. Bureau of the Census, *Seventh Census of the U.S., 1850: Compendium of the Seventh Census, Louisiana Statistics* (Washington: Robert Armstrong, 1853), 473.

8. Ibid., 482; Shugg, *Origins of Class Struggle*, 62–64.

9. Alcee Fortier, *A History of Louisiana*, 4 vols. (New York, 1904), 3: 217–18; Joseph G. Tregle Jr., "Henry S. Johnson," and "Andre Bienvenu Roman," in *The Louisiana Governors: From Iberville to Edwards*, ed. Joseph G. Dawson III. (Baton Rouge: Louisiana State University Press, 1990), 98–103, 108–113; Judith F. Gentry, "Pierre Auguste Bourguignon Derbigny," 103–108, ibid.

10. Richard P. McCormick, *The Second American Party System: Party Formation in the Jacksonian Era* (Chapel Hill: University of North Carolina Press, 1966), 313.

11. Tregle, *Louisiana in the Age of Jackson*, 466. For a more detailed discussion of Louisiana politics during the 1820s through the mid-1830s, Tregle's *Louisiana in the Age of Jackson* should be consulted.

12. In 1835 the Whig-Creole candidate for governor, Edward Douglas White, defeated the Democrat, John B. Dawson. White received most of his support from south Louisiana and New Orleans, both of which were Creole strongholds. Dawson garnered majorities in heavily Anglo-American north Louisiana and the Florida parishes. In the presidential election of 1836, there was a general lack of enthusiasm for both White and Van Buren. Perry H. Howard, *Political Tendencies in Louisiana*, rev. ed. (Baton Rouge: Louisiana State University Press, 1971), 37–38.

13. McCormick, *The Second American Party System*, 317–18; Judith F. Gentry, "Alexandre Mouton," in *The Louisiana Governors*, 118–22.

14. Shugg, *Origins of Class Struggle*, 123–24.

15. Benjamin Wall Dart, ed., *Constitutions of the State of Louisiana and Selected Federal Laws* (Indianapolis: Bobbs-Merrill Co., 1932), 508; Judith K. Schafer, "Reform or Experiment? The Louisiana Constitution of 1845," in *In Search of Fundamental Law: Louisiana's Constitutions, 1812–1974*, eds. Warren M. Billings and Edward F. Haas (Lafayette: Center for Louisiana Studies, University of Southwestern Louisiana, 1993), 21–36.

16. Benjamin Wall Dart, ed., *Constitutions of the State of Louisiana*, 499–505; Warren M. Billings, "From This Seed: The Constitution of 1812," *In Search of Fundamental Law*, 6–20.

17. Ibid., Schafer, "Reform or Experiment?," *In Search of Fundamental Law*, 21–36; Shugg, *Origins of Class Struggle*, 126–28; Roger W. Shugg, "Suffrage and Representation in Ante-Bellum Louisiana," *Louisiana Historical Quarterly*, 19 (January 1954), 396.

18. Shugg, *Origins of Class Struggle*, 133; Schafer, "Reform or Experiment?," *In Search of Fundamental Law*, 27–30.

19. Ray Allen Billington, *The Protestant Crusade: 1800–1860: A Study of the Origins of American Nativism* (New York: Macmillan Co., 1938), 46, 65–66. Jay P. Dolan, *In Search of an American Catholicism: A History of Religion and Culture in Tension* (Oxford: Oxford University Press, 2001), 56–60.

20. Ibid., 94.

21. Ibid., 127.

22. Ibid., 131–32.

23. *New Orleans Bee*, April 6, 1835. The writer apparently thought that once the United States had "developed," it had "come of age." The *New Orleans Bee* was a Jackson paper in the 1830s, and in the middle part of that decade, it came out against the Louisiana Native American Association. Ironically, in the 1840s it exhibited nativist sentiments (it was now a Whig paper) and in the 1850s the *Bee* sympathized with the nativists of that decade, the Know Nothings.

Hereafter New Orleans will be omitted from all future references to newspapers from that city; place names will be used, however, for all non-New Orleans papers.

24. Ibid., June 7, July 1, 2, 1834.

25. Garnie William McGinty, *A History of Louisiana*, 4th ed. (New York: Exposition Press, 1949), 137; Howard, *Political Tendencies in Louisiana*, 37.

26. Earl F. Niehaus, *The Irish in New Orleans: 1800–1860* (Baton Rouge: LSU Press, 1965), 71, 77.

27. Joseph G. Tregle Jr., "Edward Douglas White, 1835–1839," in *The Louisiana Governors: From Iberville to Edwards*, ed. Joseph G. Dawson III (Baton Rouge: Louisiana State University Press, 1990), 117; *Bee*, April 8, 11, 1835. The use of the term "Native American" refers to those residents of Anglo-American ancestry and not to the current use of the term that refers to those people previously called Indians.

28. Ibid., April 11, 17, 1835.

29. Ibid., April 10, 13, 1835.

30. Ibid., August 1, 1835.

31. Ibid., The ubiquitous Mr. Christy remained a leading figure in Louisiana nativism and became a leading figure in the Know Nothing Party in the 1850s.

32. *Bee*, August 1, 1835.

33. No copies of the *True American* are extant. John Smith Kendall, "Early New Orleans Newspapers," *Louisiana Historical Quarterly*, 10 (July 1927), 397.

34. Niehaus, *The Irish in New Orleans*, 77–78.

35. *Bee*, September 7, 1835.

36. Ibid., March 31, 1832.

37. Ibid., April 17, 1832.

38. Fortier, *History of Louisiana*, 3:225; Henry Righter, ed., *Standard History of New Orleans, Louisiana* (Chicago: Lewis Publishing Co., 1900), 96–97.

39. *Bee*, February 10, 12–13, 1836.

40. Ibid., February 13, 1836. Roselius came to New Orleans in the early nineteenth century from Germany in a virtual state of poverty. In 1827, he was admitted to the bar and appointed attorney general in 1841. Louis Voss, *History of the German Society of New Orleans* (New Orleans: Sendker Printing Service, 1927), 62–64.

41. *Bee*, June 15, 18, 1838; Joseph G. Tregle Jr., "André Bienvenu Roman, Governor, 1831–1835, 1839–1843," *The Louisiana Governors*, 108–113.

42. No copies of the *Anti-Native American* are extant.

43. *Bee*, December 30, 1839. Niehaus, *The Irish in New Orleans*, 79.

44. *Bee*, March 30, 1840, April 1, 3, 1840.

45. John Smith Kendall, *History of New Orleans*, 3 vols. (Chicago: Lewis Publishing Co., 1922), 1:150.

46. *Bee*, April 8, 1840.

47. Ibid., June 13, 15, 1840.

48. Ibid., March 2, 1841.

49. A delegate from the Florida parishes, Thomas Green Davidson, would be haunted during the 1850s for his participation in this nativist movement. As a successful candidate for Congress in the Know Nothing period, he would be charged by Whigs and Know Nothings with his earlier anti-foreign sentiments. He did withdraw from the Native American Association because he favored a regular party organization that would repeal the naturalization laws and the Native American convention voted down his resolution to that effect.

50. *Bee*, March 2, 1841. Naturally, New Orleans had a large delegation but there were delegates from West Feliciana, Livingston, St. Landry, Jefferson, St. Mary, St. Tammany, and Claiborne parishes.

51. Kendall, *History of New Orleans*, 1:156; *Bee*, April 4, 1842.

52. No copies of the *Louisiana American* are extant.

53. *Bee*, April 6, 1842. William Freret soon returned to City Hall. Prieur resigned to accept a more lucrative state post necessitating a special election. Nominated by the Whigs, Freret overwhelmed his Democratic opponent.

54. W. Darrell Overdyke, "History of the American Party in Louisiana," *Louisiana Historical Quarterly*, 15 (October 1932), 584.

55. *Bee*, April 21, 1842.

56. Ibid., April 18, 1842.

57. Ibid., May 4, 1842.

58. *Louisiana Courier*, July 2, 1842.

59. *Bee*, July 4, 1842.

60. Ibid., June 29, 1843, July 3, 1843.

61. Ibid., July 6–7, 9, 1843. The vote in 1840 was 290; in 1842, 270; but in 1843 it was 340.

62. Ibid., August 24, 1843.

63. Ibid., December 20, 22, 1843.

64. Ibid., February 26–28, 1844.

65. Ibid., March 30, 1844; April 2, 5, 1844. The *Bee* noted that in the American section of New Orleans, the Second Municipality, Whig commissioners prevented these illegal voters

from voting. However, in the First and Third Municipalities, areas of large numbers of immigrants, election judges in certain wards permitted them to vote.

Although an Impeachment Court removed Judge Elliott by a 9 to 5 vote, the court ruled its verdict had no bearing on the validity of the disputed naturalization papers. *Bee*, April 8, 1844; Niehaus, *The Irish in New Orleans*, 79–80, Dennis C. Rousey, *Policing the Southern City: New Orleans, 1805–1889* (Baton Rouge: Louisiana State University Press, 1996), 62.

66. *Bee*, July 2–4, 6, 8, 10, 1844; August 5, 1844.

67. Ibid., July 6, 8, 9, 19, 1844; Howard, *Political Tendencies in Louisiana*, 48. "Loco-foco" refers to a more radical group within the Democrats who received their name by using friction matches to light candles at a meeting in New York City in 1835 when conservative Democrats had doused the gas lights in order to break-up the meeting. Arthur Schlesinger Jr., *The Age of Jackson* (New York: Little Brown & Co., 1945) 197.

68. Overdyke, "History of the American Party in Louisiana," 584–85; Pierce Butler, *Judah P. Benjamin* (Philadelphia: G. W. Jacobs and Co., 1907), 87–90; Schafer, "Reform or Experiment?," *In Search of Fundamental Law*, 21–36. Benjamin would later denounce nativism when he joined the Democratic party during the height of Know Nothingism.

69. *Bee*, November 4, 1844.

70. Ibid., November 7, 1844. This newspaper noted that the Democrats secured a 1,200-vote majority in a parish (Plaquemines) that had never previously cast even 400 votes.

71. Ibid.

72. Billington, *The Protestant Crusade*, 206.

73. *Bee*, May 24, 1845; July 25, 1845.

74. Ibid., October 2, 1845; December 6, 1845. One historian has referred to Derbigny in the 1850s as "a late-comer to nativism," but this 1845 run for governor on the Native American Party ticket demonstrates that Derbigny was an early supporter of Native Americanism. Joseph E. Tregle Jr., "Creoles and Americans," in *Creole New Orleans: Race and Americanization*, eds. Arnold R. Hirsch and Joseph Logsdon (Baton Rouge: Louisiana State University Press), 167.

75. Ibid., January 12, 17, 1846.

76. *Daily Picayune*, February 11, 1846. The Democrat Johnson received 12,403 votes and the Whig DeBuys, 10,335. Sidney J. Aucoin, "The Political Career of Isaac Johnson, Governor of Louisiana, 1846–1850," *Louisiana Historical Quarterly*, 28 (July 1945), 941–89.

77. *Bee*, February 13, 1847.

78. Ibid., November 1, 1847.

79. *Plaquemine Southern Sentinel*, September 21, 1848. For a full discussion of the politics of the late 1840s, see William W. Freehling, *The Road to Disunion: Vol. 1: Secessionists at Bay, 1776–1854* (New York: Oxford University Press, 1990), chapter 29.

80. Howard, *Political Traditions in Louisiana*, 57.

81. *Bee*, August 21, 1849.

82. Ibid., October 13, 15–17, 29, 31, 1849; November 1, 1849.

83. Ibid., October 19, 1849.

84. *Louisiana Courier*, October 31, 1849.

85. Ibid., November 2, 1849.

86. *Bee*, October 25, 1849.

87. *Louisiana Courier*, November 19, 1849.

Chapter 2

1. *New Orleans Daily Crescent*, August 10, 1850; November 11, 12, 1850; August 28, 1851; October 29, 1851; December 13, 1852; *Carrollton Star*, May 17, 1851; *New Orleans Commercial Bulletin*, May 17, 1851; October 29, 30, 1852; *West Baton Rouge Capitolian Vis-à-Vis*, November 24, 1852; *Louisiana Courier*, August 10, 1850; September 18, 1850; May 3, 1851; August 18, 1851; September 13, 1851; *New Orleans Daily Delta*, June 11, 1850; August 15, 1850; September 25, 1850; May 6, 1851; August 7, 1852; *New Orleans Daily True Delta*, August 5, 1852. Hereafter New Orleans will be omitted from all future references to newspapers from that city; place names will be used, however, for all non-New Orleans papers.

2. *Daily Picayune*, September 15, 1850; *Daily Crescent*, November 11, 1850.

3. Leslie M. Norton, "A History of the Whig Party in Louisiana" (PhD diss., Louisiana State University, 1940), 332; *Louisiana Courier*, August 10, 1850.

4. *Louisiana Courier*, October 21, 1850.

5. *Daily Crescent*, August 10, 1850.

6. *Plaquemine Southern Sentinel*, November 16, 1850. This newspaper never had kind words for Mr. Soulé. In 1853, it continued its attack on the recently appointed Minister to Spain for his desire to annex Cuba. *Southern Sentinel*, April 16, 1853.

7. *Daily Delta*, August 13, 1850.

8. Ibid., February 7, 1850.

9. *Carrollton Star*, October 11, 1851; *Commercial Bulletin*, October 6, 15, 1851.

10. *Daily True Delta*, May 28, 1851; June 17, 1851; October 25, 1851. John Slidell to James Robb, December 3, 1852, Robb Papers, Historic New Orleans Collection. Hereafter referred to as HNOC. Robb had declined the Whig Party's re-nomination to the senate, and Slidell seemed to be assuring him that Robb's conservative, Whig business views would be protected even if he did not seek the Whig senatorial nomination. Robb and Judah P. Benjamin had been nominated by the Whig convention for Louisiana's two senate seats. G. B. Duncan Jr., R. Toledano, and J. A. Bond (all from New Orleans) to James Robb, October 10, 1851, Robb Papers, HNOC.

11. *Louisiana Courier*, May 27, 1852. Neither Whig nor Democrat favored any distinction between naturalized citizens and native-born Americans in the new constitution. *Daily Crescent*, July 27, 1852; *Daily Delta*, August 7, 1852. Wayne M. Everand, "Louisiana's 'Whig' Constitution Revisited: The Constitution of 1852," in *In Search of Fundamental Law: Louisiana's Constitutions, 1812–1974*, eds. Warren M. Billings and Edward F. Haas (Lafayette: Center for Louisiana Studies, University of Southwestern Louisiana, 1993), 130–34.

12. *DeBow's Review*, 13 (July 1852), 196,

13. Ibid., 3 (January 1847), 351.

14. *Louisiana Courier*, October 30, 1851.

15. *Daily Crescent*, September 26, 1851.

16. Ibid., August 14, 1852; *Commercial Bulletin*, July 26, 1852; July 30, 1852; September 6, 1852; *Daily Delta*, October 26, 1852; Leslie Norton, "A History of the Whig Party in Louisiana," 350–51.

17. *Staats Zeitung*, October 16, 1852. I was assisted in translating some German stories which appeared in scattered German newspapers in New Orleans by George C. Kieser.

18. *Bee*, August 17, 1852; *Commercial Bulletin*, August 17, 1852; *Plaquemine Southern Sentinel*, August 28, 1852.

19. *Bee*, July 8, 1852; *Alexandria Red River Republican*, July 31, 1852; Abner L. Duncan to John Moore, September 2, 1852, Weeks Papers, Department of Archives, Louisiana State University. Hereafter referred to as LSU. The Democrats now claimed that Davidson had recanted his previous philosophy. *Baton Rouge Daily Comet*, September 24, 1852.

20. *Daily True Delta*, March 22, 1852.

21. The Whig Party had succeeded in calling a convention and electing a majority of the delegates to the convention. They supported its passage while the Democrats had several reservations, particularly in regards to representation being based on total population. This clause earned the Constitution of 1852 the epithet of the "nigger-as-good-as white constitution." *Daily Delta*, July 30, 1852; August 7, 1852; *Louisiana Courier*, November 9, 1852; Wayne M. Everand, "Louisiana's 'Whig' Constitution Revisited: The Constitution of 1852," in *In Search of Fundamental Law: Louisiana's Constitutions, 1812–1974*, eds. Warren M. Billings and Edward F. Haas (Lafayette: Center for Louisiana Studies, 1993), 44.

22. *Daily Crescent*, July 27, 1852; August 20, 1852; *Daily Delta*, August 7, 1852. The 1852 constitution removed this discriminatory feature.

23. *Louisiana Courier*, December 15, 1852. Both political parties agreed that the single issue in this state campaign was to control the legislature in order to implement the recently approved constitution. Continuing its decline, the Whig Party completely failed in its objective. *West Baton Rouge Capitolian Vis-à-Vis*, November 24, 1852. Marius M. Carriere Jr., "Paul Octave Hébert, Governor, 1853–1856," in *The Louisiana Governors: From Iberville to Edwards*, ed. Joseph G. Dawson III (Baton Rouge: Louisiana State University Press, 1990), 130–34.

24. *Louisiana Courier*, October 25, 1853.

25. *Daily Crescent*, March 31, 1853; April 5, 7, 1853; *Louisiana Courier*, April 1–3, 1853.

26. Leon Cyprian Soulé, *The Know Nothing Party in New Orleans: A Reappraisal* (Baton Rouge: Louisiana State University Press, 1961), 44.

27. *Commercial Bulletin*, October 19, 1853.

28. *Daily Crescent*, October 18, 20, 21, 1853.

29. Ibid., November 7, 1853.

30. Robert C. Reinders, *End of an Era: New Orleans, 1850–1860* (New Orleans: Pelican Publishing Co., 1964), 18.

31. *Bee*, November 8, 1853. This stronghold in the First District would be the scene of future Election Day violence.

32. The Democrats won a majority of the seats in both houses of the legislature and three of the four congressional seats. *Louisiana Courier*, November 20, 1853.

33. *Address of Charles Gayarré*, to the People of the State on the Late Frauds Perpetrated at the *Elections Held on the 7th November, 1853, In the City of New Orleans* (New Orleans: Sherman and Wharton, 1853), Gayarré Collection, Louisiana and Lower Mississippi Valley Collection, LSU, hereafter referred to as LSU. Gayarré also questioned how the votes could exceed the previous year when the city had experienced the worst yellow fever epidemic in the history of New Orleans. *Plaquemine Southern Sentinel*, December 24, 1853; *Daily Crescent*, December 26, 1853. *Daily Delta*, December 19, 1853; *Baton Rouge Daily Advocate*, January 4, 1854; James Aburton to Charles Gayarré, November 7, 1853, Gayarré Collection, LSU.

34. *Bee*, November 8, 1853; Soulé, *The Know Nothing Party in New Orleans*, 46; Henry Marston to Payne and Harrison, March 21, 1854, Marston Papers, LSU.

35. Billington, *The Protestant Crusade: 1800–1860* (New York: Macmillan Co., 1938), 289–90; *Freeman's Journal*, March 4, 1848, quoted in Billington, *The Protestant Crusade*, 290.

36. Simply stated, the trustee problem resulted over whom should have control over church property, laymen or the church hierarchy. Billington, *The Protestant Crusade*, 289–92. The insistence of the Catholic hierarchy that the clergy should control all church property permitted the nativists to stress the undemocratic features of Catholicism.

37. Ibid., 292, 296–99.

38. Brother Alfonso Comeau, CSC, "A Study of the Trustee Problem in the St. Louis Cathedral Church of New Orleans, Louisiana, 1842–1844," *Louisiana Historical Quarterly*, 31 (October 1948), 897–972.

39. A complete discussion of the trustee problem and division of the public school fund in the United States during the 1850s can be found in Billington, *The Protestant Crusade*, 295–300.

40. Ibid., 302.

41. *Plaquemine Southern Sentinel*, January 21, 1854; *Bee*, January 11, 1854.

42. W. Darrell Overdyke, "History of the American Party in Louisiana," *Louisiana Historical Quarterly*, 16 (October 1932), 87. Gavazzi had become a part of the evangelical church in England and spoke out against priests and Jesuits in Scotland, and North America.

43. *Baton Rouge Weekly Comet*, December 2, 1853.

44. T. H. Harris, *The Story of Public Education in Louisiana* (New Orleans: Delgado Trades School, 1924), 13.

45. *Daily Delta*, February 16, 18, 21, 1851.

46. *Baton Rouge Weekly Comet*, July 28, 1853.

47. *Baton Rouge Daily Comet*, October 27, 1853.

48. *Baton Rouge Weekly Comet*, December 11, 1853; January 5, 1854. The editor reported that a New Orleans paper, the *Southern Journal* (no copies extant), would attempt to persuade the residents of Louisiana of the necessity to divide the public school fund.

49. For a more complete discussion of the failure of the Whig Party in Louisiana and the South, see Arthur Charles Cole's *The Whig Party in the South* (Gloucester, MA: Peter Smith, 1962), chapters VII–IX. For Louisiana, see William H. Adams's *The Whig Party of Louisiana* (Lafayette: University of Southwestern Louisiana History Series, 1973) and John M. Sacher, *A Perfect War of Politics: Parties, Politicians, and Democracy in Louisiana, 1824–1861* (Baton Rouge: Louisiana State University Press, 2007).

50. Overdyke, "History of the American Party in Louisiana," XVI, 256.

51. While his name simply appeared in the newspapers of New Orleans, it is clear that Judson was a supporter of filibustering. Shelley Streeby, *American Sensations: Class, Empire, and the Production of Popular Culture* (Berkeley: University of California Press, 2002), 149–57.

52. *Daily True Delta*, March 15, 1854; *Propaqateur Catholique*, March 27, 1854.

53. Streeby, *American Sensations*, 149–57. Judson apparently brought his Know Nothing views to both St. Louis and New Orleans. He also lived in Nashville where he published a magazine titled *Ned Buntline's Own*.

54. *Daily True Delta*, March 15, 1854.

55. Ibid. Louisiana Know Nothingism and Roman Catholicism are discussed more fully in Chapter III.

56. Ibid.; *The Origin. Principles and Purposes of the American Party* (n.p., n.d.).

57. Soulé, *The Know Nothing Party in New Orleans*, 39; Billington, *The Protestant Crusade*, 384.

58. *Daily True Delta*, March 15, 1854; Billington, *The Protestant Crusade*, 384–85.

59. *Daily True Delta*, March 15, 1854.

60. W. Darrell Overdyke, *The Know-Nothing Party in the South* (reprinted; Gloucester, MA: Peter Smith, 1968), 40–42; Billington, *The Protestant Crusade*, 384–85; *Daily True Delta*, March 15, 1854. Quoted in Tyler Anbinder, *Nativism and Slavery: The Northern Know Nothings & the Politics of the 1850s* (New York: Oxford University Press, 1992), 162–63.

61. *Bee*, March 15, 1854; Soulé, *The Know Nothing Party in New Orleans*, 47–48.

62. *Daily True Delta*, March 17, 19, 1854; *Louisiana Courier*, March 18, 1854. A pro-Reform paper noted that the Independent Reform candidate for mayor and two-thirds of the candidates for alderman and assistant alderman were Democrats. *Bee*, March 18, 1854.

63. *Daily True Delta*, March 9, 1854.

64. Ibid., March 23, 1854; *Louisiana Courier*, March 27, 1854.

65. *Daily True Delta*, March 25, 1854. *Cohen's New Orleans Directory for 1855, Including Jefferson City, Gretna, Carrollton, Algiers, and McDonogh* (New Orleans: Picayune Office, 1855), 306.

66. Ibid., June 30, 1854. The editor of the *True Delta* reported that the railroad directors' "nefarious schemes" had been planned as early as the re-writing of the Louisiana Constitution in 1852. This document permitted the state to subscribe to works of internal improvement.

67. Ibid., April 19, 1854; May 17, 1854. These bonds, secured by a pledge of the property of New Orleans, were to bear interest at 8 percent, 10 percent discounted.

68. Ibid., May 17, 1854. The *True Delta* did mention that a "falling out" among the railroad directors had occurred which may have prompted Campbell to release this letter. For a discussion of railroads and the city of New Orleans for this period, see Merl E. Reed's *New Orleans and the Railroads: The Struggle for Commercial Empire, 1830–1860* (Baton Rouge: Louisiana State University Press, 1966). A more recent history of the political economy of Louisiana and New Orleans can be found in Scott Marler, *The Merchants' Capital: New Orleans and the Political Economy of the Nineteenth-Century South* (Cambridge: Cambridge University Press, 2013).

69. *Daily True Delta*, March 23, 1854.

70. Ibid., June 30, 1854.

71. Ibid., August 17, 27, 1852; September 2, 1852. The *True Delta* also did not report that John Slidell, was very close to the state's railroad interests. Slidell wrote Robb in December 1852 that "popular will is in favor of cooperation on the part of the state in public improvements." Slidell continued that the Democrats "will carry it out in proper spirit." Obviously, party leaders did not always feel bound to party pronouncements. John Slidell to James Robb, December 3, 1852, Robb Papers, HNOC.

72. *Bee*, March 15, 1854; *Daily Crescent*, March 21, 23, 25, 1854.

73. *Commercial Bulletin*, February 26, 1852; *Daily True Delta*, June 25, 1852; *Daily Crescent*, October 31, 1853; November 7, 1853; March 25, 1854; *Baton Rouge Daily Comet*, April 21, 1854.

74. *Daily True Delta*, March 17, 1854; *Louisiana Courier*, March 18, 27, 1854.

75. John M. Sacher, *A Perfect War of Politics: Politics, Politicians, and Democracy in Louisiana, 1824–1861* (Baton Rouge: Louisiana State University Press, 2007), 239–40. Sacher says the Know Nothings were "not just Whiggery in disguise" and "the defection of Democrats into the Know Nothing party and the presence of former Whigs in the Democratic party belie a one-to-one correspondence between Whigs and Know Nothings." Frank Towers, *The Urban South and the Coming of the Civil War* (Charlottesville: University of Virginia Press, 2004), 103. A similar view to Towers can be found in Marius Carriere, "Political Leadership of the Louisiana Know Nothing Party," *Louisiana History*, 21, no. 2 (1985), 186. John Ashworth also offers that "not every Whig had become a Know Nothing, nor had every Know Nothing been a Whig, but there was an unmistakable similarity in personnel as well as in principle." John

Ashworth, *Slavery, Capitalism, and Politics in the Antebellum Republic: Vol. 2: The Coming of the Civil War, 1850–1861* (New York: Cambridge University Press, 2008), 565.

76. *Louisiana Courier*, March 21, 1854.

77. *Daily True Delta*, March 26, 1854. This paper mentioned that the Reform Party had overlooked one-fourth of the population which owned one-third of the assessed property in making up its ticket.

78. Ibid., March 23, 1854. Considering each category there were no naturalized citizens holding a federal office, six of forty-nine state or congressional positions were held by naturalized citizens, only two of twenty parish officials had been born outside of the country, and twenty of sixty-eight naturalized citizens held public office in city government. In Louisiana's state legislature, there were no foreign-born in the house and two foreign-born in the senate. Clearly it was difficult for non-natives to be elected to office in Louisiana. John Kingsbury Elgee to James Robb, June 14, 1855, Robb Papers, HNOC.

79. *Louisiana Courier*, March 19, 1854.

80. *Daily Crescent*, March 17, 22, 1854; *Commercial Bulletin*, March 24, 25, 1854.

81. *Daily True Delta*, March 15, 1854; Soulé, *The Know Nothing Party in New Orleans*, 48, 51–53; Sacher, *A Perfect War of Politics*, 221.

82. *Daily True Delta*, March 29, 30, 1854. The two murdered men and the police chief were all Irishmen.

83. *Daily Crescent*, March 28, 31, 1854; *Bee*, March 29, 1854.

84. *Bee*, April 1, 1854.

85. *Daily True Delta*, March 30, 1854; *Bee*, March 29, 1854. The Democratic Board of Aldermen declared three alderman Reform candidates illegally elected as a result of the destruction of the ballot box. After a new election all three were again successful.

86. Dennis C. Rousey, *Policing the Urban South: New Orleans, 1805–1889* (Baton Rouge: Louisiana State University Press, 1997), 70–73.

87. Democrats believed the Reformers had a peculiar way to reform New Orleans, and if that kind of reform continued no one would risk voting. The Democrats estimated they lost the office of controller, two aldermen, and six assistant alderman positions because of the destruction of the ballot box in the First District. *Baton Rouge Daily Advocate*, March 31, 1854; *Daily True Delta*, March 29–30, 1854.

88. *Thibodaux Minerva*, May 13, 1854; *West Baton Rouge Capitolian Vis-à-vis*, April 5, 1854.

89. *Daily True Delta*, March 15, 1854. However, this paper placed the figure at a more conservative level of five or six hundred members.

90. *Baton Rouge Weekly Comet*, April 21, 1854.

91. Ibid., July 30, 1854; *Plaquemine Southern Sentinel*, May 27, 1854; June 3, 1854.

92. Editorial comment in the *Harrisonburg Independent*, quoted in the *Shreveport South-Western*, October 25, 1854.

93. *Louisiana Courier*, October 15, 1854.

94. *Shreveport South-Western*, October 25, 1854.

95. *Bee*, November 27, 30, 1854; *Plaquemine Southern Sentinel*, December 23, 1854; Soulé, *The Know-Nothing Party in New Orleans*, 58–59.

96. *Thibodaux Minerva*, December 23, 1854.

97. *Plaquemine Southern Sentinel*, July 1, 1854.

98. *Daily Crescent*, June 28, 1854; August 18, 1854; *Plaquemine Southern Sentinel*, May 20, 1854; September 2, 1854; Ashworth, *Slavery, Capitalism, and Politics: Vol. 2*, 578–79.

99. *Daily Crescent*, June 28, 1854.

100. *West Baton Rouge Capitolian Vis-à-Vis,* July 4, 1854.
101. *Plaquemine Southern Sentinel,* September 16, 1854.
102. *Baton Rouge Weekly Comet,* March 31, 1854, *Bee,* May 1, 1854.
103. *Daily True Delta,* March 26, 1854; July 7, 13, 28, 1854.
104. *Bee,* May 1, 1854.
105. Billington, *The Protestant Crusade,* 423. F. A. Lumsden of New Orleans, one of the proprietors of the *Daily Picayune,* represented Louisiana at this National Council meeting. William W. Freehling, *The Road to Disunion: Vol. II: Secessionists Triumphant: 1854–1861* (New York: Oxford University Press, 2007), 86.
106. Sometimes even a Democratic paper in the state admitted that slavery could not permanently exist in the Nebraska territory because of climate and the type agriculture suited to that area. *Louisiana Courier,* March 2, 1854.
107. *Daily Crescent,* June 3, 1854; November 14–15, 1854; *Semi-Weekly Creole,* November 8, 15, 1854.
108. *Louisiana Senate Journal,* March 13, 15, 1854, 107, 127. Louisiana Whigs were no different from most of their southern brethren at this point in the Kansas-Nebraska bill's history since most could "not stand against it within their ranks." Ashworth, *Slavery, Capitalism, and Politics: Vol. 2,* 546.
109. *Daily True Delta,* February 10, 1854; *Baton Rouge Daily Advocate,* February 11, 1854.
110. *Daily Delta,* June 17, 1854.
111. *Louisiana Courier,* May 30, 1854; November 10, 1854. Of course, northern free-soilers and abolitionists leveled the charge of a southern conspiracy against the Know Nothing Party since Know Nothings worked to avoid the slavery issue altogether. Billington, *The Protestant Crusade,* 424. *West Baton Rouge Capitolian Vis-à-Vis,* May 31, 1854; July 5, 1854; *Baton Rouge Weekly Comet,* July 14, 1854.
112. Stephen E. Maizlish, "The Meaning of Nativism and the Crisis of the Union: The Antebellum North," in Stephen E. Maizlish and John J. Kushma, *Essays on American Antebellum Politics: 1840–1860* (College Station: Texas A&M University Press, 1982), 177–78, 187; William Gienapp, *The Origins of the Republican Party, 1852–1856* (New York: Oxford University Press, 1987), 531–58; Michael F. Holt, *The Rise and Fall of the American Whig Party: Jacksonian Politics and the Onset of the Civil War* (New York: Oxford University Press, 1999), 893.
113. *West Baton Rouge Capitolian Vis-à-Vis,* May 31, 1854; July 5, 1854; *Baton Rouge Weekly Comet,* July 14, 1854.
114. *Baton Rouge Daily Comet,* July 14, 1854; *Baton Rouge Weekly Comet,* May 28, 1854; July 16, 1854; November 12, 1854; *Daily Orleanian,* August 11, 1854; *West Baton Rouge Capitolian Vis-à-vis,* September 6, 23, 30, 1854. John Slidell to W. W. Pugh, July 23, 1855, Pugh Family Papers, University of Texas, Center for American History, hereafter referred to as UT.
115. *Daily True Delta,* March 15, 1854.
116. W. Darrell Overdyke, in his "History of the American Party in Louisiana," adheres to this interpretation. Thomas R. Whitney, *A Defence of the American Policy* (New York: Dewitt and Davenport, 1856), 104–105; Gienapp, *The Origins of the Republican Party,* 196.
117. This is the view of Leon Soulé in *The Know-Nothing Party in New Orleans.* Soulé believes that the old Creole-American animus never ceased, and during the 1850s the Creoles consciously used the immigrants to ward off American growth in New Orleans. Soulé disagrees with Overdyke's thesis that the Know Nothing Party in Louisiana did not intend to proscribe Roman Catholics.

118. *Semi-Weekly Creole*, October 18, 1854. A fuller discussion of this seeming contra-diction of Roman Catholics joining an anti-Roman Catholic political party is discussed in Chapter III.

119. Ibid., October 4, 18, 1854. Robert Reinders shares this view; see his "The Louisiana American Party and the Catholic Church," *Mid-America*, XL (1958), 218–28; "Orestes A. Brownson's Visit to New Orleans, 1855," *Louisiana Historical Quarterly*, 38 (July 1955), 1–19; and *End of an Era: New Orleans, 1850–1860* (New Orleans: Pelican Publishing Co., 1964); Ashworth, *Slavery, Capitalism, and Politics: Vol. 2*, 535.

Reinders disagrees with Overdyke that Louisiana was an exception to the anti-Catholi-cism of Know Nothingism. To Reinders, the immigrant waves to Louisiana created a threat to native-born Creoles' control of the Catholic Church since Irish and German Catholics were more likely to obey blindly the Catholic hierarchy. The Creole Catholics had never been good Catholics and many belonged to local Masonic lodges long before Know Nothingism appeared. Then, too, Reinders does not believe, as does Soulé, that the Creole-American con-flict existed in the 1850s. "Through inter-marriage, business and political conservatism, a uni-fied Creole-American upper class existed in New Orleans." Reinders, "Orestes A. Brownson's Visit to New Orleans," 6. For those reasons, argues Reinders, Creole Catholics could and did belong to the Know Nothing Party. The Gallican concept originated in France and was a set of ecclesiastical and political doctrines that viewed papal primacy as limited and that temporal power remained in the hands of civil authority. Antoine Degert, "Gallicanism," *The Catholic Encyclopedia*, Vol. 6 (New York: Robert Appleton Company, 1990).

120. *Baton Rouge Weekly Comet*, August 17, 27, 1854; September 2, 1854; *Thibodaux Minerva*, October 21, 1854.

121. *Propagateur Catholique*, March 17, 25, 1854.

CHAPTER 3

1. There were some Whig newspapers that eschewed the Know Nothing Party in favor of the Democrats, for example, the *Carrollton* (a suburb of New Orleans) *Star*.

2. W. Darrell Overdyke, "History of the American Party in Louisiana," *Louisiana Historical Quarterly*, 16 (October 1932), 272; *Shreveport South-Western*, February 21, 1855.

In the Morehouse Parish election, the Know Nothing candidate had won in November 1854, but the Louisiana House ordered a new election since fraud had been alleged. The American increased his majority in the new election.

3. *Plaquemine Southern Sentinel*, May 12, 1855.

4. Overdyke, "History of the American Party in Louisiana," 272; *Opelousas Patriot*, May 12, 1855; *Baton Rouge Weekly Comet*, June 8, 1855. The town of Clinton is in East Feliciana Parish and both are located in the Florida parishes north of New Orleans, while Plaquemine is in Iberville Parish, a river parish, just south of Baton Rouge. Opelousas is in Southwestern Louisiana in St. Landry Parish.

5. *New Orleans Semi-Weekly Creole*, July 4, 1855; *New Orleans Daily Crescent*, August 14, 1855; *Baton Rouge Weekly Comet*, October 7, 1855; the *Creole* asserted that Merrick's election proved the American strength in the rural parishes of the state.

Hereafter New Orleans will be omitted from all future references to newspapers from that city; place names will be used, however, for all non-New Orleans papers.

6. *Shreveport South-Western*, March 14, 1855; April 4, 1855. Governor Hébert had removed some Democrats from appointive positions and replaced them with what the *South-Western* referred to as "thorough Know Nothings." One biographer of Hébert writes that Whig papers

accused Hébert of being a Know Nothing in order to "cover their own identification and partly destroy the Democratic party." Albert Leonce Dupont, "The Career of Paul Octave Hébert, Governor of Louisiana: 1853–1856," *Louisiana Historical Quarterly,* 31 (April 1948), 523; Marius M. Carriere Jr., "Paul Octave Hébert: Governor, 1853–1856," in *The Louisiana Governors: From Iberville to Edwards,* ed. Joseph G. Dawson III (Baton Rouge: Louisiana State University Press), 130–34.

7. *Bee,* July 25, 1854; *Baton Rouge Weekly Comet,* July 30, 1854; *West Baton Rouge Capitolian Vis-à Vis,* August 30, 1854. Ex-Whigs and Know Nothings decried how even the Whigs in 1852 decided to appeal to Catholics and immigrants and how both parties were now guilty in what one historian has called "the debasement of political life." John Ashworth, *Slavery, Capitalism, and Politics in the Antebellum Republic: Vol. 2: The Coming of the Civil War, 1850–1861* (New York: Cambridge University Press, 2007), 533–34.

8. *West Baton Rouge Capitolian Vis-à-Vis,* September 23, 1854.

9. *Louisiana Courier,* July 24, 1855. To some extent, the Know Nothings' early nativism and reform ideology in Louisiana resembles what the recent scholarship says about Know Nothingism in other areas of the United States. Michael F. Holt, in his *Forging a Majority: The Formation of the Republican Party in Pittsburgh, 1848–1860* (New Haven, Conn.: Yale University Press, 1969) and "The Politics of Impatience: The Origins of Know Nothingism," *Journal of American History,* XIX (September 1973), 309–31, and William J. Evitts in his *A Matter of Allegiances: Maryland from 1850 to 1861* (Baltimore: Johns Hopkins University Press, 1974), discuss the concern of native-born Americans during the 1850s with corruption in politics. In addition to Evitts's statement, above, Holt calls it a "pervasive loss of faith in and an animosity toward politicians." In addition, both authors write of a sense of dislocation caused by rapid social and economic change in those years. Louisiana, however, did not have the same social or economic dislocation during these years, and as a result, the Know Nothing Party in Louisiana was not like that in other parts of the United States, which was "overwhelmingly a movement of the laboring and middle classes." Holt, "The Politics of Impatience," 313, 329.

10. Frank Towers in *The Urban South and the Coming of the Civil War* (Charlottesville: University of Virginia Press, 2004), 73, 102. Baltimore and St. Louis were the two other cities in Tower's book. In a letter to New Orleans businessman James Robb, John K. Elgee felt there was little chance that a naturalized citizen could be elected to any office in the state. James Kingbury Elgee to James Robb, June 14, 1855, HNOC. The only two in the legislature were state senators.

11. *Bee,* March 24, 1855; *Daily True Delta,* March 23, 1855; *Louisiana Courier,* March 26, 1855.

12. *Commercial Bulletin,* June 3, 11, 1855; *Louisiana Courier,* March 28, 1855; June 10, 1855; Leon Cyprian Soulé, *The Know Nothing Party in New Orleans: A Reappraisal* (Baton Rouge: LSU Press, 1961), 64. A police board consisting of the mayor and four recorders (judges) of the city controlled the police of New Orleans. The board had been created in 1853 by the Louisiana legislature which. New Orleans Whigs claimed, intended to remove all power over the police from the recently elected Whig mayor of that city. *Daily Crescent,* November 1, 1853.

13. *Louisiana Courier,* March 18, 1854. One anti-Know Nothing paper did deny that Know Nothingism was a Whig trick. Prior to the state elections of 1855, the *True Delta* doubted that the Whigs of New Orleans "would support such a party." However, rather than a sincere belief, this disclaimer was probably an attempt on the part of the *True Delta* to embarrass the Whigs from joining, what many Democrats thought to be, an anti-Republican party. *True Delta,*

October 21, 1855. Know Nothings in these other southern states had the same problem as Louisiana. For example, Marc Kruman, in his *Parties and Politics in North Carolina, 1836–1865* (Baton Rouge: Louisiana State University Press, 1983), claims that in North Carolina Whig influence dominated the American Party in that state and the Know Nothings were not serious about the national party's ideology. To Kruman, they joined the American Party because it was an alternative to the Democratic Party. Thomas D. Jeffrey, *State Parties and National Politics: North Carolina, 1815–1861* (Athens: University of Georgia Press, 1989), 246–50, and Jonathan M. Atkins, *Parties, Politics, and the Sectional Conflict in Tennessee, 1832–1861* (Knoxville: University of Tennessee Press, 1997), 198–99, agree with Kruman's assessment.

14. *West Baton Rouge Capitolian Vis-à-Vis*, August 23, 1854; *Shreveport South-Western*, August 8, 1855; *Thibodaux Minerva*, August 11, 1855; *Bee*, August 13, 1855; *Clinton American Patriot*, August 18, 1855; *Opelousas Patriot*, September 29, 1855.

15. *Bee*, October 10, 1855; *Louisiana Courier*, July 17, 1855.

16. *Shreveport South-Western*, August 8, 1855; *Clinton American Patriot*, August 18, 1855.

17. *Opelousas Patriot*, September 29, 1855. However, the Americans placed these four former Democrats in the lieutenant governor's slot and three less important offices. The four former Democrats were: lieutenant governor candidate Louis Texada, secretary of state candidate R. G. Beale, auditor candidate Walter Rossman, and superintendent of education candidate O. D. Stillman. *Bee*, July 6, 1855.

18. *Daily Delta*, August 3, 1855; September 24, 1856.

19. *Southern Standard*, July 1, 1855. The *Southern Standard* was a Roman Catholic newspaper printed in New Orleans.

20. *Thibodaux Minerva*, October 13, 1855.

21. *Baton Rouge Weekly Comet*, October 19, 1856. According to the editor of the *Comet*, the president, vice president, secretary, and two speakers at a Democratic political meeting on October 17, 1856, were all old-line Whigs, who now proclaimed Buchanan as "the only man who can save the Union."

22. *Shreveport South-Western*, November 17, 1858.

23. However, in his recent study of Louisiana politics in the 1850s, John M. Sacher, *A Perfect War of Politics: Parties, Politicians, and Democracy in Louisiana* (Baton Rouge: Louisiana State University Press, 2003), 239–40, makes a strong point that the "defection of Democrats into the Know Nothing party and the presence of former Whigs in the Democratic party "belie a one-to-one correspondence between Whigs and Know Nothings." Michael Holt, in his *Political Parties and American Political Development from the Age of Jackson to the Age of Lincoln* (Baton Rouge: Louisiana State University Press, 1992), 148–50, writes that in the South, "old Whigs moved through Know Nothingism into the Democratic party in search for the best way to defend both southern rights and the Union." About Louisiana Whigs, Holt, *The Rise and Fall of the American Whig Party: Jacksonian Politics and the Onset of the Civil War* (New York: Oxford University Press, 1999), 805, 842–910, 934, writes that Louisiana Whigs "chose the new Know Nothing party" with which to work, yet finds that many Creole Catholics Whigs in south Louisiana did not support the Know Nothings in 1855. My data for 1855, however, does demonstrate that many, if not most, did support them, although by the state elections of 1857, Creole Catholic support for the Know Nothings had worn thin. See also on Whigs and Know Nothings, Arthur C. Cole, *The Whig Party in the South* (Washington: American Historical Association, 1914), 308–10; Ray Allen Billington, *The Protestant Crusade: 1800–1860* (New York: Macmillan Co., 1938), 390–91; Perry Howard, *Political Tendencies in Louisiana* (Baton Rouge: Louisiana State University Press, 1971), 75; Roger W. Shugg, *Origins of Class*

Struggle in Louisiana: A Social History of White Farmers and Laborers during Slavery and After,
1840–75 (Baton Rouge: Louisiana State University Press, 1939), 159; Leon Cyprian Soulé, *The*
Know Nothing Party in New Orleans: A Reappraisal (Baton Rouge: Louisiana State University
Press, 1961), 38; W. Darrell Overdyke, "History of the American Party in Louisiana," 16, 258;
John Smith Kendall, *History of New Orleans*, 3 vols. (Chicago: Lewis Publishing Co., 1922), 209;
Arthur Thompson, "Political Nativism in Florida, 1848–1860: A Phase of Anti-Secessionism,"
Journal of Southern History, 15 (February 1949), 39–65; Philip Rice, "The Know-Nothing Party
in Virginia, 1854–1856," *Virginia Magazine of History and Biography*, 55 (1947), no. 1, 61–75, no. 2,
159–67; Arthur C. Cole, "Nativism in the Lower Mississippi Valley," Mississippi Valley Historical
Association *Proceedings*, 6 (1912–13), 258–75; James Broussard, "Some Determinants of Know-
Nothing Electoral Strength in the South, 1856," *Louisiana History*, 7 (Winter 1966), 5–20.

    24. James K. Greer, "Louisiana Politics, 1845–1861," *Louisiana Historical Quarterly*, 13
(January 1930), 81; Kruman, *Parties and Politics in North Carolina*, 160–79; J. Mills Thornton,
Politics and Power in a Slave Society: Alabama, 1800–1860 (Baton Rouge: Louisiana State
University Press, 1978), 325–27. This view is also shared by John Ashworth in his *Slavery,*
Capitalism, and Politics in the Antebellum Republic: Vol. 2, 565. Ashworth notes that in "the
South Americans were ideologically akin to the southern Whigs and even represented similar
regions and constituencies."

    25. Charles E. A. Gayarré, *Address to the People of Louisiana on the State of Parties* (New
Orleans: Sherman, Wharton & Co., 1855), HNOC; Sacher, *A Perfect War of Politics*, 238.

    26. Soulé, *The Know Nothing Party in New Orleans*, 62, 93, 118; Shugg, *Origins of Class*
Struggle in Louisiana, 148; Overdyke, "History of the American Party in Louisiana," *Louisiana*
Historical Quarterly, XVI (April 1933), 268.

    27. Stanley Clisby Arthur, *Old Families of Louisiana*, colla. George Campbell Huchet de
Kernion (New Orleans: Harmanson, 1931), 346.

    28. *Biographical and Historical Memoirs of Louisiana*, 2 vols. (Chicago: Goodspeed
Publishing Co., 1892), vol. 2, 266–68.

    29. John Ashworth, *Slavery, Capitalism, and Politics in the Antebellum Republic: Vol. 2:*
The Coming of the Civil War, 1850–1861 (New York: Cambridge University Press, 2007), 365;
William W. Wall to Thomas C. W. Ellis, March 31, 1856, Ellis Papers, LSU.

    30. Charles Grier Sellers Jr., "Who were the Southern Whigs?" *American Historical*
Review, 59 (April 1954), 343.

    31. W. Darrell Overdyke, Leon Soulé, and Roger Shugg obviously accept the thesis
of Arthur C. Cole and U. B. Phillips that the Whigs were owners of large plantations and
therefore owned large numbers of slaves. In addition, it is apparent that they also accept the
interpretation of Arthur M. Schlesinger and Bray Hammond that the Democrats were incipi-
ent entrepreneurs and men on the make. Arthur Charles Cole, *The Whig Party in the South*
(reprinted; Gloucester, MA: Peter Smith, 1962); Ulrich B. Phillips, "The Southern Whigs, 1834–
1854," in Guy S. Ford, ed., *Essays in American History Dedicated to Frederick Jackson Turner*
(New York: Henry Holt and Co., 1910), 203–30; Arthur M. Schlesinger, *The Age of Jackson*
(Boston: Little, Brown, and Co., 1945); and Bray Hammond, *Banks and Politics in America*
from the Revolution to the Civil War (Princeton: Princeton University Press, 1957).

    32. William L. Barney, *The Secessionist Impulse: Alabama and Mississippi in 1860*
(Princeton: Princeton University Press, 1974), 50–54.

    33. For this study of political leadership, I used the names of Americans and Democrats
who were members of their state, parish, or local central committees. Also, I used the names
of state representatives, senators, local parish and city officials, and political candidates. The

total number of Americans and Democrats used was 137 and 98, respectively. I acquired the information regarding these leaders' age, occupation, real and personal property, place of birth, and number of slaves owned from the *United States Census, 1860, Population and Slave Schedules.* Some additional information came from Joseph Karl Menn, *The Large Slaveholders of Louisiana—1860* (New Orleans: Pelican Publishing Co., 1964).

I also used *Cohen's New Orleans Directory for 1855* (New Orleans: Picayune Printers, 1855); *Myatt and Co.'s Directory, 1857* (New Orleans: L. Pessou and B. Simon, 1857), which includes directory information for Baton Rouge; *Gardner's New Orleans Directory for 1859, 1860* (New Orleans: Bulletin Book and Job Printing Establishment, 1858, 1859); A. Meynier Jr., ed., *Meynier's Louisiana Biographies,* 1882; William Henry Perrin, ed., *Southwest Louisiana: Biographical and Historical* (New Orleans: Gulf Publishing Co., 1891), *Biographical and Historical Memoirs of Louisiana,* 2 vols. (Chicago: Goodspeed Publishing Co., 1892); and Stanley Clisby Arthur, ed. and comp., and George Campell Huchet de Kernion, colla., *Old Families of Louisiana* (New Orleans: Harmanson Publisher, 1931).

It should be noted that the microfilm copy of the 1860 census for several parishes is of poor quality, which accounts for some parishes not being represented. In addition, the size of New Orleans in 1860 made that city most difficult to research.

The efficiency of the census enumerators in several parishes was less than adequate and entries were inconsistent. At times, categories were left blank or one enumerator would not follow what others used for data entry information. For example, several wealthy individuals, whose wealth would suggest the ownership of at least a few slaves, did not have any slaves listed in their possession. The same is true for an individual who had several slaves but no personal or real wealth recorded. However, these omissions should not detract from the conclusions I reached. My universe is sufficiently large enough and it adequately represents the various areas of Louisiana.

34. Barney, *The Secessionist Impulse,* 88.

35. Planters, farmers, lawyers, and town middle class are the four occupational types used. I decided that an individual who owned twenty or more slaves would be classified as a planter; one with fewer than twenty as a farmer.

36. Table 1 (Appendix A). It is impossible to be certain how many Know Nothings may have been lawyers as well as planters. Since the attainment of planter status was great in the antebellum South, probably both Democrats and Know Nothings preferred the title planter rather than lawyer.

37. These individuals will be referred to as "town middle class."

38. Table 1 (Appendix A).

39. Appendix B.

40. Table 2 (Appendix A).

41. Appendix B

42. Shugg, *Origins of Class Struggle,* 153–54. See Joseph G. Tregle Jr., "Another Look at Shugg's Louisiana," *Louisiana History,* 245–81, 17 (Summer 1976), 3. Tregle takes issue with some of Shugg's findings and methodology.

43. Table 1 (Appendix A).

44. The American Party achieved its greatest success in the 1855 gubernatorial election. However, the total number of parishes carried by that party was only sixteen. Therefore, it was necessary to draw my conclusions from the parishes which the Democrats won.

45. Table 3 (Appendix A).

46. Table 4 (Appendix A). It should be noted that there was not sufficient information to make any generalizations regarding those parishes which had little slave ownership.

47. Table 5 (Appendix A).
48. Appendix B.
49. Table 6 (Appendix A).
50. Table 7 (Appendix A).
51. Ibid.
52. Ibid.
53. "Generally speaking, the median is a less efficient measure of central tendency than is the mean. . . ." R. A. Day Jr. and A. L. Underwood, *Quantitative Analysis*, 5th ed. (Englewood Cliffs, NJ: Prentice-Hall, 1986), 19–20.
54. From a high point of 460,474 total arrivals into the country in 1854, the number of arrivals slipped to 224,496 in 1856. Both of these figures include United States citizens returning from abroad; the number in 1856 totaled 24,000 American citizens. Louisiana received 43,028 "passengers from abroad" in 1853, but by 1857 that figure was down to 21,299. As in the United States figures, the Louisiana total also included a small number of American citizens returning from abroad. From 1845 to 1854, 300,000 Europeans came to the United States annually. *DeBow's Review*, 16 (May 1854), 452; XXIV (June 1858), 571; William W. Freehling, *The Road to Disunion: Vol. II* (New York: Oxford University Press, 2007), 86.
55. Charles Gayarré, *History of Louisiana The American Domination*, 4 vols. (New Orleans: F. F. Hansell and Bro., Ltd., 1903), 4:678. However, Avery O. Craven believes the rise of the Know Nothing Party in the South can be attributed to a reluctance of Whigs to join the Democratic Party and opposition to the growing sectional problems, and not to an antipathy to foreigners and Catholics. Avery O. Craven, *The Growth of Southern Nationalism: 1848–1862* (Baton Rouge: Louisiana State University Press, 1953), 238–39.
56. Charles Gayarré, *Address to the People of Louisiana on the State of Parties* (New Orleans: Sherman, Wharton and Co., 1855), 9–13. A copy is in the Charles E. A. Gayarré Papers, Louisiana and Lower Mississippi Valley Collection. Hereafter cited as LSU.
57. *Opelousas Patriot*, April 28, 1855; *Bee*, August 31, 1855.
58. *Opelousas Patriot*, August 18, 1855; *Baton Rouge Weekly Comet*, December 9, 1855.
59. Between 1850 through 1854, the number of foreign-born admitted to New Orleans' Charity Hospital was significant. The following table illustrates this problem of admissions from the foreign-born population (see table 8 in Appendix A). Even a naturalized citizen agreed with the nativist's estimation of the debased condition of the immigrant. In a pamphlet advising the impoverished European to remain in Europe, this author sounded similar to the American nativist when he wrote that the typical immigrant was poor, dirty, and sometimes diseased. *Emigration, Emigrants, and Know-Nothings*, by a Foreigner (Philadelphia: 1854), 5–6, 31.
60. *Daily True Delta*, October 7, 1855.
61. *Opelousas Patriot*, March 24, 1855; *Baton Rouge Weekly Comet*, December 9, 1855.
62. *Bee*, September 5, 1855.
63. *Commercial Bulletin*, October 12, 1855; *Daily Crescent*, October 15, 30, 1855. Know Nothings denied that the First District Court, a criminal court, had jurisdiction in a civil matter such as naturalization. The *Daily Crescent* went so far as to deny any legal standing for any naturalization issued by that court since its inception on April 28, 1853.
64. *Opelousas Patriot*, May 19, 1855; *Plaquemine Southern Sentinel*, May 19, 1855. Plaquemine is located on the Mississippi River, in the southeast Louisiana parish of Iberville, while Grand Coteau and Opelousas are in the south-central parish of St. Landry.
65. *Daily True Delta*, October 7, 1855.
66. Know Nothing warnings in Louisiana about the free-soil proclivity of immigrants began with the debate over the Kansas-Nebraska bill.

67. *Emigration, Emigrants, and Know-Nothings*, 17–24.

68. *Plaquemine Southern Sentinel*, May 12, 1855.

69. Robert T. Clark Jr., "The German Liberals in New Orleans, 1840–1860," *Louisiana Historical Quarterly*, 20 (January 1937), 140.

70. *Thibodaux Minerva*, July 28, 1855; *Daily Delta*, August 16, 1855.

71. Freehling, *The Road to Disunion: Vol. II*, 92–93; Holt, *The Rise and Fall of the Whig Party*, 893, 915–17; Leonard L. Richards, *The Slave Power: The Free North and Southern Domination, 1790–1860* (Baton Rouge: Louisiana State University Press, 2000), 104; Tyler Anbinder, *The Northern Know Nothings and the Politics of the 1850s* (New York: Oxford University Press, 1992), 44–49. Ashworth, *Slavery, Capitalism, and Politics in the Antebellum Republic: Vol. 2*, 565–67. While Holt argues that the antislavery view of northern Know Nothings was more detrimental to southern Know Nothing candidates in 1855 and 1856 than nativism and anti-Catholicism, Louisiana Americans weathered this better than other southern states. Holt, *The Rise and Fall of the Whig Party*, 893. Elizabeth Varon, *Disunion! The Coming of the American Civil War, 1789–1859* (Chapel Hill: University of North Carolina Press, 2008), 261.

72. *Baton Rouge Daily Advocate*, August 16, 1855; September 26, 1855; *Opelousas Patriot*, September 1, 1855.

73. *Louisiana Courier*, September 6, 1855; *Daily True Delta*, September 2, 14, 1855; John Clayton, quoted in *Ashworth, Slavery, Capitalism, and Politics*, 550.

74. *Bee*, September 3, 1855; *Semi-Weekly Creole*, September 26, 1855; November 21, 1855. The *Daily True Delta* noticed that at the time of his vote against the Kansas-Nebraska bill, Hunt said nothing about how it would give foreigners the immediate right to vote in the territories. *Daily True Delta*, October 4, 1855. United States Senator Stephen Adams of Mississippi, in the Thirty-fourth Congress, voiced a similar concern of his Louisiana colleague when he remarked that "the whole education of the foreigners, and their prejudices when they come to this country, are against the institution of slavery; and everything they hear at the North but confirms that prejudice." Richards, *The Slave Power*, 103.

75. *Plaquemine Southern Sentinel*, November 3, 1855.

76. *Daily Delta*, August 16, 1855.

77. John Fredrick Nau, *The German People of New Orleans, 1850–1900* (Leiden, Germany: E. J. Brill, 1958), 18. Nau feels the Know Nothing agitation prompted most Germans to join the Democratic party. Clark, "The German Liberals in New Orleans," 138.

78. *Opelousas Patriot*, August 25, 1855. Just how accurate the editor of the *Patriot* was is open for debate, but he wrote that 99 percent of all foreigners opposed slavery, and that seven-eighths settled in the free states.

79. *Southern Standard*, July 1, 1855; *Daily True Delta*, May 12, 1855; Freehling, *The Road to Disunion: Vol. II*, 92–93; Elizabeth R. Varon, *Disunion: The Coming of the American Civil War: 1789–1859* (Chapel Hill: University of North Carolina Press: 2008), 261–62; James M. McPherson, *Battle Cry of Freedom: The Civil War Era* (New York: Oxford University Press: 1988), 141–44.

80. *Plaquemine Southern Sentinel*, January 20, 1855; *Opelousas Patriot*, March 10, 1855; May 5, 1855. One American, Jeptha McKinney, did resign from the party "because he feared its platform had a secret plank strongly connected with the principles of the northern abolitionists." Sacher, *A Perfect War of Politics*, 246.

81. *Plaquemine Southern Sentinel*, June 16, 1855.

82. Billington, *The Protestant Crusade*, 425–26; Freehling, *The Road to Disunion: Vol. II*, 93–94; Varon, *Disunion*, 261. The 1855 platform was unacceptable to many northerners and a Boston newspaper described it as "moist with the salivary contempt of all honest men." Quoted in Varon, *Disunion*, 261.

83. *Semi-Weekly Creole*, July 28, 1855.

84. Ibid.

85. *Clinton American Patriot*, May 19, 1855.

86. *Bee*, January 25, 1855; *Opelousas Patriot*, March 10, 1855.

87. *Opelousas Patriot*, July 7, 1855.

88. *Bee*, March 8, 1855.

89. Gayarré, *Address to the People of Louisiana*, 18.

90. *Opelousas Patriot*, March 24, 1855; *Daily Delta*, August 16, 1855.

91. *Daily Delta* , August 16, 1855. This goal gave credence to the Democratic charge that the Know Nothing Party wanted to put an end to immigration completely.

92. *Daily Crescent*, September 26, 1855.

93. *The Origin, Principles and Purposes of the American Party* (Philadelphia: 1855), 25.

94. *Daily Picayune*, July 6, 1855.

95. *Daily Delta*, July 12, 1855.

96. *Bee*, September 18, 1855. The increasing of the naturalization period was something on which southern and northern Know Nothings could agree. As Tyler Anbinder notes in his *Nativism and Slavery: The Northern Know Nothings & the Politics of the 1850s* (New York: Oxford University Press, 1992), 136–37, several northern states' legislators pushed for longer probationary periods, as did southerners, in order to Americanize the immigrant to protect republicanism. Of course, northern and southern Americans often had different definitions of what constituted republicanism.

97. *Baton Rouge Weekly Comet*, April 26, 1855; *Clinton American Patriot*, July 14, 1855.

98. *Daily True Delta*, September 4, 10, 1855. The New Orleans Whig delegation at the 1852 constitutional convention was twenty-seven out of twenty-nine permitted seats for the city. The city's delegation primary concern was banking and internal improvement reform and, as Wayne E. Everand writes, "City delegates were especially determined to avoid any argument that could disrupt the debates." The country parishes were politically more evenly divided and, therefore, Whig nativists obviously gave ground on the two year voting requirement in exchange for banks and internal improvements. Wayne E. Everand, "Louisiana 'Whig' Constitution Revisited: The Constitution of 1852," in *In Search of Fundamental Law: Louisiana's Constitutions, 1812–1974* (Lafayette: Center for Louisiana Studies, University of Southwestern Louisiana, 1993), 44–45.

99. *Carrollton Star*, October 30, 1855; November 1, 1855. Democrats also argued that since naturalization was a congressional matter it should be kept out of local affairs. *Daily Delta*, February 1, 1855.

100. Thomas R. Whitney, *A Defence of the American Policy, as Opposed to the Encroachments of Foreign Influence, and Especially to the Interference of the Papacy in the Political Interests and Affairs of the United States* (New York: DeWitt and Davenport, 1856), 155–56.

101. *Plaquemine Southern Sentinel*, June 3, 1854; *Daily Picayune*, February 16, 1855.

102. *Clinton American Patriot*, December 27, 1854.

103. Gayarré, *Address to the People of Louisiana*, 13–15.

104. *Shreveport South-Western*, July 11, 1855.

105. *Plaquemine Southern Sentinel*, June 30, 1855; *Clinton American Patriot*, June 30, 1855.

106. *Daily Crescent*, July 12, 1855.

107. *Daily Picayune*, July 6, 1855. See Appendix D for the American Party state platform. The party adopted only one statewide platform, but they adopted state resolutions for other elections.

108. *Baton Rouge Weekly Comet*, November 25, 1855.

109. *Shreveport South-Western*, September 5, 1855; October 10, 1855; *Daily Crescent*, September 11, 1855; *Thibodaux Minerva*, September 15, 1855; *Bee*, October 4, 1855; *Clinton American Patriot*, October 13, 1855.

110. John Slidell to W. W. Pugh, July 23, 1855, Pugh Family Papers, Center for American History, University of Texas. Hereafter referred to as UT.

111. *Plaquemine Southern Sentinel*, January 27, 1855; *Opelousas Patriot*, March 17, 1855; *Baton Rouge Weekly Comet*, April 26, 1855; *Semi-Weekly Creole*, June 23, 1855.

112. *Baton Rouge Daily Comet*, January 23, 1856.

113. *The Origin, Principles and Purposes of the American Party*, 7–8.

114. *Shreveport South-Western*, September 5, 1855; *Baton Rouge Weekly Comet*, December 9, 1855.

115. *Baton Rouge Weekly Comet*, June 21, 1855; May 3, 1856.

116. Ibid., August 5, 1855; *Baton Rouge Morning Comet*, May 3, 1856.

117. *Baton Rouge Daily Comet*, January 23, 1856; *Clinton American Patriot*, June 30, 1855.

118. *Baton Rouge Daily Comet*, June 21, 1855; *Baton Rouge Morning Comet*, August 14, 1856; November 2, 1856.

119. Gayarré, *History of Louisiana*, IV, 678; Greer, "Louisiana Politics, 1845–1861," 91; Overdyke, "History of the American Party in Louisiana," 261–62; W. Darrell Overdyke, *The Know-Nothing Party in the South* (reprinted; Gloucester, MA: Peter Smith, 1968), 128; *Commercial Bulletin*, June 23, 1855. See Appendix C for the 1855 National American Party platform.

120. *Plaquemine Southern Sentinel*, June 23, 1855; *Baton Rouge Daily Comet*, August 4, 1855; *Baton Rouge Weekly Comet*, August 5, 1855.

121. *Commercial Bulletin*, June 23, 1855; July 2, 1855; *Plaquemine Southern Sentinel*, June 23, 30, 1855; July 14, 1855.

122. Charles Gayarré, "Religious Toleration," *DeBow's Review*, 19 (September 1855), 326–27; *Address to the People of Louisiana*, 33.

123. *Daily Picayune*, July 6, 1855. See Appendix D for the American Party state platform.

124. *Baton Rouge Weekly Comet*, July 11, 1855.

125. *Daily Crescent*, August 4, 1855; *Baton Rouge Weekly Comet*, August 12, 1855; *Opelousas Patriot*, September 29, 1855.

Even on the parish level, Know Nothings noted that they had more Roman Catholic candidates than the Democrats. In St. Landry Parish, which was two-thirds Roman Catholic, the party reported that the Democrats had only one Roman Catholic candidate out of three while the American Party ticket contained all Roman Catholics. *Opelousas Patriot*, September 29, 1855.

126. *Opelousas Patriot*, October 20, 1855.

127. *The Origin, Principles and Purposes of the American Party*, 34–35; Anna Ella Carroll, *The Great American Battle or, The Contest Between Christianity and Political Romanism* (New York: Miller, Orton and Mulligan, 1856), 178, 202. Miss Carroll noted that Louisiana Roman Catholics had stood firm against the papacy's temporal power and applauded them for their resistance. Gallicanism in the 1850s was more accurately neo-Gallicanism since Gallicanism

ended with the French Revolution. The main idea in the eighteenth century was that Gallican Catholics did not recognize any temporal power of the pope. Antoine Dégert, "Gallicanism," (New York: Catholic Encyclopedia, 1909), Vol. 6, 73–78.

128. *Daily Delta*, June 24, 1855; July 10, 1855, 138.

129. *Southern Standard*, July 1, 8, 15, 1855; *Propaqateur Catholique*, July 7, 14, 21, 1855.

130. *Daily True Delta*, September 18, 1855. Charles Gayarré left the American Party in September 1855. He gave as his reason the inability to have the "repose of mind and the independence of action which are incompatible with political life." *Daily True Delta*, September 15, 1855.

131. *Catholic Standard*, October 28, 1955. The *Southern Standard* became the *Catholic Standard* on September 2, 1855.

132. *Propaqateur Catholique*, July 21, 1855.

133. Ibid., July 25, 1855.

134. The *Daily True Delta* asserted that even in New Orleans three American councils had repudiated the denunciation of the religious plank of the National Order by the state council.

135. *Baton Rouge Daily Advocate*, August 1, 1855; *Louisiana Courier*, August 3, 1855.

136. *Daily Crescent*, July 4, 6, 1855.

137. *Louisiana Courier*, August 3, 10, 1855.

138. *Baton Rouge Daily Advocate*, August 1, 1855, September 29, 1855; *Daily True Delta*, October 5, 1855. The specific charities, and the appropriations allocated which Stell assailed, in addition to the Charity Hospital, were the Benevolent Association of the Catholic Ladies of Baton Rouge, $1,000; Les Dames de la Providence (indigent widows), $2,000; and St. Mary's Catholic Boys" Asylum, $3,000.

139. *Daily True Delta*, October 5, 1855.

140. Ibid., September 30, 1855.

141. *Daily Crescent*, October 2, 3, 1855.

142. *Thibodaux Minerva*, October 6, 20, 27, 1855; November 3, 1855; *Bee*, October 8, 1855; *Plaquemine Southern Sentinel*, October 13, 1855; *Daily Crescent*, October 13, 24, 1855; John Moore to Thomas Johnson, August 13, 1855, Weeks Family Papers, LSU.

143. *Bee*, June 30, 1855; *Opelousas Patriot*, August 18, 1855.

144. In the state platform, the American Party listed four planks under the heading "State Policy." One, the second plank, could easily have been interpreted as anti-Catholic and anti-foreign.

1. Reform of abuses, and retrenchment in our State expenditures.
2. Education of the youth of the country in schools established by the State.
3. A constitutional organization of the Swamp Land Commissioners.
4. A more efficient administration of the Internal Improvement Department, with a view of improving our inland navigation.

Baton Rouge Weekly Comet, July 8, 1855.

145. *Opelousas Patriot*, September 15, 1855. This Know Nothing paper reported that at a Democratic rally the only issues discussed were the American's opposition to Catholics, unconstitutionality, inconsistency, bigotry, fanaticism, and tyranny. The hope for a unified Know Nothing Party received a serious blow when many northern delegates walked out of the Philadelphia Convention, led by Massachusetts delegate Henry Wilson because of the "final and inclusive" resolution. Many northerners, like Wilson and Schuler Colfax of Indiana, simply were unwilling to support the American Party if it did not endorse antislavery. Freehling, *The Road to Disunion: Vol. II*, 94.

146. I obtained the election return data from the Inter-University Consortium for Political Research, The Institute for Social Research, Center for Political Studies, The University of Michigan, Ann Arbor, Michigan. Hereafter cited as ICPR. Overdyke, "History of the American Party in Louisiana," 276.

147. Ibid., 277.

148. *Opelousas Patriot*, March 31, 1855.

149. Soulé, *The Know Nothing Party in New Orleans*, 71.

150. ICPR.

151. Howard, Political *Tendencies in Louisiana*, 84.

152. *Thibodaux Minerva*, November 10, 1855; *Daily True Delta*, November 14, 1855; *Opelousas Patriot*, December 1, 1855; *Bee*, October 22, 1855. Another Know Nothing believed that the exclusion of Louisiana's delegation because of Catholic Charles Gayareé's presence had also contributed to an earlier June judicial election defeat. Thomas Ellis to E. P. Ellis, June 28, 1855, Ellis Family Papers, LSU.

153. *Thibodaux Minerva*, November 10, 1855.

154. ICPR; *United States Census, 1850*.

155. Ibid.

156. Ibid. Heavily Catholic St. James and St. Martin parishes increased the majority for the American Party in 1855 over that of the 1852 Whig majority. St. John, St. Mary, and Terrebonne parishes, all with significant Catholic majorities, experienced a slight to moderate decrease in their majorities in 1855 as compared to 1852. Nevertheless, the Know Nothing majorities in these heavily Creole Catholic parishes still suggests that there was a fear of the foreign-born for Native Americans, Catholic or not!

157. *Opelousas Patriot*, December 1, 1855.

158. Howard, *Political Tendencies in Louisiana*, 441–42; *United States Census, 1850*. The presence of foreigners in large numbers suggests that a Native American backlash occurred during the 1855 gubernatorial election.

159. There were 24,938 Irish, 19,675 Germans, and 10,564 French living in New Orleans in 1860. In addition to living in the Third District, some Irish lived in the American or First District and the Fourth District, which was known as the "Irish Channel" and located between Camp Street and the river. Robert C. Reinders, *End of an Era: New Orleans, 1850–1860* (New Orleans: Pelican Publishing Co., 1964), 18–19. Leon C. Soulé, "The Creole-American Struggle in New Orleans Politics, 1850–1862," *Louisiana Historical Quarterly*, 40 (January 1957), 54–55. Joseph G. Tregle Jr., "Creoles and Americans." In *Creole New Orleans: Race and Americanization*, eds. Arnold R. Hirsch and Joseph Logsdon (Baton Rouge: Louisiana State University Press, 1992), 164–66.

160. *Daily Picayune*, March 29, 1854; Soulé, "The Creole-American Struggle in New Orleans Politics," 63.

161. *Louisiana Courier*, November 6, 9, 1855.

162. *Daily Picayune*, November 7, 1855; Marius M. Carriere Jr., "Robert C. Wickliffe, Governor, 1856–1860," in *The Louisiana Governors: From Iberville to Edwards*, ed. Joseph G. Dawson III (Baton Rouge: Louisiana State University Press, 1990), 135.

163. The three parishes which had a slave population of less than 52 percent were the two "urban" parishes of Jefferson and Orleans, and St. Tammany Parish. *United States Census, 1850*; ICPR.

164. *Thibodaux Minerva*, November 10, 1855; Charles Gayareé, *Address on the Religious Test to the Convention of the Assembled in Philadelphia on the 5th of June 1855*, HNOC.

CHAPTER 4

1. The Democratic Party majority was less than 8 percent of the total vote cast. The election return data were obtained from the Institute for Social Research in coded form. However, the official returns are reported in both the *House* and *Senate Journals* of Louisiana for 1855.

2. *Plaquemine Southern Sentinel,* December 1, 1855.

3. Ibid., December 15, 1855.

4. *Thibodaux Minerva,* November 10, 1855; *Baton Rouge Daily Comet,* November 20, 1855; *Louisiana Courier,* November 6, 9, 1855; *Daily Crescent,* November 9, 1855; *Daily True Delta,* November 7, 9, 1855; Leon Cyprian Soulé, *The Know Nothing Party in New Orleans: A Reappraisal* (Baton Rouge: Louisiana State University Press, 1961), 71.

5. *Baton Rouge Daily Comet,* November 27, 1855; *New Orleans Daily True Delta,* December 2, 1855; *Baton Rouge Weekly Comet,* December 2, 1855; January 14, 1856; *New Orleans Daily Crescent,* January 22, 1856; *Louisiana Courier,* February 19, 1856. Hereafter New Orleans will be omitted from all future references to newspapers from that city; place names will be used, however, for all non-New Orleans papers.

6. *Louisiana Courier,* November 6, 9, 1855; *Daily Crescent,* November 6, 9, 1855; *Daily True Delta,* November 7, 9, 1855; Soulé, *The Know Nothing Party in New Orleans,* 71.

7. *Daily True Delta,* November 17, 1855; *Bee,* January 31, 1856; February 14, 25, 1856; March 28, 1856; *Baton Rouge Weekly Comet,* March 23, 1856; W. W. Pugh to Josephine N. Pugh, February 17, 22, 1856, Pugh Family Papers, University of Texas, Center for American History, hereafter cited as UT. The three American senators excluded from their seats were Glendy Burke, Leonce Burthe, and J. J. Michel. The American representatives were A. T. C. Morgan, Thomas Devall, and F.A. Lumsden. The Know Nothing sheriff was Joseph Hufty. All the American candidates were from New Orleans. Pugh also told his wife that the Democratic majority in the legislature planned on amending New Orleans' city charter, presumably, to allow the Democratic legislature to have more control over the city.

In addition, lesser city elected officials were subsequently removed by the Democratic controlled legislature. The Know Nothing *Semi-Weekly Creole* believed that the testimony given in all the contested hearings was "illegal." *Semi-Weekly Creole,* February 2, 1856; *Daily Crescent,* March 27, 1856; W. Darrell Overdyke, "History of the American Party in Louisiana," *Louisiana Historical Quarterly,* 16 (July 1933), 410–12.

The Americans in the legislature filed a minority report which declared all evidence given in behalf of the challengers was unauthorized by law. *Senate Journal,* 1856, 15.

8. *Baton Rouge Weekly Comet,* April 16, 1856; *Baton Rouge Morning Comet,* April 16, 1856; July 10, 1856; *Thibodaux Minerva,* May 10, 1856; *Opelousas Patriot,* May 10, 24, 1856. Thibodaux and Washington are located in Lafourche and St. Landry parishes, respectively, and are in southwest Louisiana. Donaldsonville is in Ascension Parish, a south Louisiana river parish, while Bayou Sara is in West Feliciana Parish (north of New Orleans) in south Louisiana and Minden is in northwest Louisiana.

9. *Baton Rouge Weekly Comet,* April 13, 16, 1856. After the election, the editor noted that the Democratic candidates for the various Baton Rouge municipal positions were Democrats in name only since they had only recently withdrawn from the American Party.

10. *Daily Crescent,* March 18, 1856.

11. *Louisiana Courier,* May 31, 1856.

12. *Daily True Delta,* March 20, 1856; *Bee,* June 2, 1856; *Daily Crescent,* May 10, 22, 1856. In addition, each party accused the other of tyrannical measures. The Know Nothings attacked

the removal of American legislators while the Democrats brought up the "Reform" Council's removal of two Democratic recorders. *Louisiana Courier*, May 29, 1856.

13. *Louisiana Courier*, May 31, 1856.

14. Ibid., June 3, 5, 19, 1856; *Daily Delta*, June 3, 1856.

15. Soulé, *The Know Nothing Party in New Orleans*, 64–65; Dennis C. Rousey, *Policing the Southern City: New Orleans, 1805–1889* (Baton Rouge: Louisiana State University Press, 1997), 70–72.

16. Michael F. Holt, *The Rise and Fall of the American Whig Party: Jacksonian Politics and the Onset of the Civil War* (New York: Oxford University Press, 1999), 893; *Baton Rouge Daily Advocate*, December 7, 1855; John Ashworth, *Slavery, Capitalism, and Politics in the Antebellum Republic: Vol. 2: The Coming of the Civil War, 1850–1861* (New York: Cambridge University Press, 207), 568.

17. *Daily True Delta*, December 30, 1855. *Daily Delta*, February 5, 1856. The Americans, however, blamed the Democrats for the election of the anti-Catholic and abolitionist Banks. *Plaquemine Southern Sentinel*, February 9, 1856.

18. *Daily Delta*, January 8, 1856; *Catholic Standard*, January 20, 1856.

19. *Thibodaux Minerva*, December 22, 1855; *Plaquemine Southern Sentinel*, February 2, 1856. Strong anti-Catholic sentiment did exist in Louisiana, however. The *Louisiana Baptist* of Mount Lebanon, Louisiana, attacked the Know Nothings for their attempt to elect a Catholic chaplain. During the legislative session this paper printed several anti-Catholic articles. *Mount Lebanon Louisiana Baptist*, February 21, 28; April 3, 1856. Only a few issues of this paper are extant.

20. Charles Gayarré, *Address on the Religious Question* (n.p.: 1856), 10, 26. A copy is in the Charles E. A. Gayarré Collection, Louisiana and Lower Mississippi Valley Collections, Louisiana State University. Hereafter cited as LSU.

21. *Semi-Weekly Creole*, March 1, 1856. Representative Eustis addressed the convention and defended the Louisiana Order for admitting Catholics. Eustis assured the convention that his delegation upheld the other principles of Know Nothingism. Another Louisiana delegate from New Orleans likewise defended the policy of admitting Catholics, but he strongly assured the gathering that the order in Louisiana denied the temporal authority of the church.

22. *Baton Rouge Weekly Morning Comet*, October 19, 1856. This paper compared this plank with the oath of allegiance on becoming a citizen, and found no difference. *Baton Rouge Daily Advocate*, March 2, 1856. See Appendix C.

23. *Louisiana Courier*, July 26, 1856; *Catholic Standard*, March 30, 1856; April 27, 1856. The *Catholic Standard* equated the Know Nothings with black Republicanism in that both strove for the political supremacy of the North.

24. *Plaquemine Southern Sentinel*, October 18, 1856; *Baton Rouge Morning Comet*, May 3, 1856; August 14, 1856.

25. *Baton Rouge Weekly Morning Comet*, March 23, 1856; *Baton Rouge Morning Comet*, June 17, 18, 1856.

26. *Baton Rouge Weekly Morning Comet*, October 5, 1856; November 2, 1856; *Baton Rouge Weekly Morning Comet*, June 22, 1856.

27. *Shreveport South-Western*, May 28, 1856.

28. *Fillmore and Donelson Campaign Pamphlet* (n.p., 1856), LSU. *Plaquemine Southern Sentinel*, July 5, 1856; *Baton Rouge Weekly Comet*, October 5, 1856; November 9, 1856; *Daily Creole*, October 17, 1856.

29. Ray Allen Billington, *The Protestant Crusade: 1800–1860* (New York: Macmillan Co., 1938), 428. In *The Road to Disunion: Vol. II*, 86–87, William Freehling writes that when southern Whigs, many of whom would join the Know Nothings, left the Whigs, they hoped their ex-northern brethren would give up their anti-Slave Power rhetoric and they would join together against immigrants. Not only would this allow a North-South alliance on Native American principles, but it would weaken the Democrats, as well as the antislavery issue. Freehling, *The Road to Disunion: Vol. II*, 86–87.

30. Ibid., 427–28; *Plaquemine Southern Sentinel*, March 15, 1856; *Baton Rouge Daily Advocate*, March 2, 1856.

31. *Plaquemine Southern Sentinel*, July 5, 1856; *Opelousas Patriot*, August 30, 1856; *Daily Creole*, September 18, 1856; October 17, 1856; *Baton Rouge Morning Comet*, October 28, 1856. Democrats across the South, as well as in Louisiana, believed that if Fremont was elected in 1856 this would lead the South to a colonial status since the Republican platform clearly indicated they thought the founding fathers had put the nation on the road to antislavery. This was a growing sentiment in the state with which Louisiana Americans had to contend. George Eustis to John Moore, February 5, 1856, Weeks Papers, LSU. Michael Morrison, *Slavery and the American West: The Eclipse of Manifest Destiny and the Coming of the Civil War* (Chapel Hill: University of North Carolina Press, 1997), 179–83.

32. *Bee*, July 21, 28, 1856; *Baton Rouge Morning Comet*, August 12, 1856.

33. *Thibodaux Minerva*, March 15, 1856; *Commercial Bulletin*, July 4, 1856; Alexander Franklin Pugh to (illegible), August 1, 1856, Pugh Family Papers, UT. Franklin—or "Frank," as he signed his letters—believed Fremont would win unless the South united on one man.

34. Elizabeth R. Varon, *Disunion: The Coming of the American Civil War, 1789–1859* (Chapel Hill: University of North Carolina Press, 2008), 274; a miscellaneous campaign pamphlet dated August 17, 1856, in the Ellis Papers, LSU; *Baton Rouge Weekly Comet*, July 20, 1856; September 3, 7, 1856; *Daily Creole*, August 11, 1856; J. J. Slocum to Thomas C. W. Ellis, September 16, 1856, Ellis Papers, LSU. Even though William Freehling believes Fillmore was not popular with most Lower South Whigs, this was not true in Louisiana. Freehling, *The Road to Disunion: Vol. II*, 94–95.

35. William W. Wall to Thomas C. W. Ellis 1856, Ellis Papers, LSU; Henry Marston Diary, Marston Family Papers, LSU.

36. There were other issues that received less attention. For example, the Americans criticized President Pierce's veto of an appropriations bill which included improvement of the Mississippi River. After Buchanan's nomination, Know Nothings noted the inconsistency of a protectionist Buchanan defending a platform which included a free-trade plank and opposed internal improvements. The state Democratic administration also came in for its share of this kind of abuse. Americans opposed the increased extravagance of the administration for what it called the enrichment of partisans, and demanded a Board of Public Works be created in accordance with the 1852 Constitution. The Democrats simply responded that internal improvements by the states have always been a Democratic policy. *Daily Crescent*, May 27, 1856; *Shreveport South-Western*, July 30, 1856; *Daily Creole*, June 20, At; 1856; *Baton Rouge Daily Advocate*, July 10, 1856.

37. Americans noted the Democratic failure to settle the differences between Spain and the United States over Cuba. The conservative Americans feared "another 54°40′ or Fight and the taking of Cuba" if Buchanan was elected and a heightened sectionalism. *Fillmore and Donelson Campaign Pamphlet* (n.p., 1856), LSU; *Shreveport South-Western*, October 17, 1855.

The Democrats generally abided by Pierce's attempts to uphold the United States' neutrality laws while not tolerating any "Old World interference," particularly in Nicaragua. *Catholic Standard*, January 6, 1856; May 11, 1856; *Baton Rouge Daily Advocate*, March 31, 1856.

38. Allan Nevins, *Ordeal of the Union*, 2 vols. (New York: Charles Scribner's Sons, 1947), 2: 494–95. Upon his arrival in New York, Fillmore set the tone for the campaign when he stated that "we have received from our fathers a Union and a Constitution above all price and value, and that man who cannot sacrifice anything for the support of both is unworthy of his country." Nevins, *Ordeal of the Union*, 2: 494.

Billington, *The Protestant Crusade*, 428. Billington writes that Fillmore conducted his campaign on the issue of "preserving the union," and other Know Nothings did not stress nativistic issues.

39. Ibid., 429; Morrison, *Slavery and the American West*, 186. John Bladek, "America for Americans: The Southern Know Nothing Party and the Politics of Nativism, 1854–1856" (PhD diss., University of Washington, 1999), 185. Bladek sees prominent southern Whigs beginning to move into the American Party and moving it away from its nativist origins. Similar to Louisiana, Marc Kruman sees the campaign of 1856 as a time when "the American party became even more exclusively a Whig organization" in North Carolina. Marc Kruman, *Parties and Politics in North Carolina, 1836–1865* (Baton Rouge: Louisiana State University Press, 1983), 171. In Louisiana, the Americans did de-emphasize the ideology of nativism, but the party in Louisiana had been largely controlled by Whigs from the beginning. John Moore to the Shreveport Fillmore Committee, August 27, 1856, Historic New Orleans Collection, hereafter cited as HNOC.

40. Bladek, "America for Americans," 185.

41. *Commercial Bulletin*, October 2, 1856.

42. Ibid., August 9, 1856; *Bee*, August 14, 26, 29, 1856; Elizabeth R. Varon, *Disunion: The Coming of the American Civil War: 1789–1859* (Chapel Hill: University of North Carolina Press: 2008), 274.

43. *Bee*, July 1, 1856; October 2, 1856; *Daily Creole*, September 18, 1856; *Daily Crescent*, September 26, 1856.

44. *Daily Crescent*, September 26, 1856; *Daily Creole*, September 30, 1856; October 22, 1856.

45. *Bee*, October 6, 1856. Governor Wickliffe in his inaugural address, long before the heat of the presidential campaign, stated emphatically that if the North ever became numerically superior over the South in the senate as it had in the House, "the aggressive spirit of the North will direct the legislation of Congress so that the South will be obliged to abandon the Union." *Senate Journal*, 1856, 17–18.

46. *Bee*, October 9, 1856.

47. *Daily Delta*, November 1, 1855.

48. *Baton Rouge Daily Advocate*, July 15, 31, 1856; August 9, 1856; September 6, 1856; *Daily Creole*, October 3, 1856; *Bee*, October 1, 1856. Some northern supporters did claim Fillmore would repeal Kansas Nebraska while southerners denied that he would. Ashworth, *Slavery, Capitalism, and Politics*, 571–72.

49. *Daily Delta*, September 12, 1856; *Louisiana Courier*, August 3, 13, 1856; October 5, 1856. Fillmore had been informed by his former secretary of war, Charles M. Conrad of Louisiana, almost two years before that the Whig's platform was a "declaration of perpetual warfare against the South." Michael Holt, *The Rise and Fall of the Whig Party: Jacksonian Politics and the Onset of the Civil War* (New York: Oxford University Press, 2003), 879.

50. *Daily True Delta*, September 24, 1856; *Congressional Globe,* Thirty-fourth Congress, first session (December 21, 1855). Horace Greeley was the Republican *New York Tribune* editor and William Seward was a Republican United States senator from New York. Ashworth, *Slavery, Capitalism, and Politics*, 574.

51. *Louisiana Courier*, July 26, 1856; *Baton Rouge Morning Comet*, October 25, 1856.

52. *Daily Creole*, August 22, 1856; *Bee*, September 3, 1856; Holt, *The Rise and Fall of the Whig Party*, 931; Ashworth, *Slavery, Capitalism, and Politics*, 576. As Elizabeth Varon and others point out, despite the strong support among Whigs in Louisiana for high tariffs and a merchant community in New Orleans that was also a major part of that Whig base, by the election of 1856, who best supported slavery was the only issue left for southerners. Varon, *Disunion*, 274–75.

53. See Chapter II above. Soulé, *The Know Nothing Party in New Orleans*, 54–115.

54. *Commercial Bulletin*, October 12, 1855; *Daily Crescent*, October 30, 1855; November 1, 1855.

55. *Louisiana Courier*, November 6, 1855.

56. *Daily True Delta*, November 17, 1855.

57. *Louisiana Courier*, November 6, 9, 1855; *Daily True Delta*, November 17, 1855. Following the elections of 1854 and 1855, the Americans reduced the police force's funding and its size, and presumably, to make it more loyal to the Know Nothings. Rousey, *Policing the Southern City*, 66–67.

58. *Senate Journal*, 1856, 18.

59. *Louisiana Courier*, October 21, 1856.

60. Ibid., October 26, 1856; November 12, 1856; *Daily Crescent*, October 31, 1856; November 10, 1856.

61. *Daily Crescent*, November 10, 13, 1856; *Louisiana Courier*, November 12, 1856.

62. *Daily True Delta*, November 6, 1856; James Kimmins Greer, "Louisiana Politics 1845–1861," *Louisiana Historical Quarterly*, 13 (January 1930), 113; Soulé, *The Know Nothing Party in New Orleans*, 82; Rousey, *Policing the Southern City*, 77–78.

63. Election return data were obtained from the Inter-University Consortium for Political Research, The Institute for Social Research, Center for Political Studies, University of Michigan, Ann Arbor, Michigan. Hereafter cited as ICPR. The data was more consistent and accurate than Louisiana data or the state press.

64. Soulé, *The Know Nothing Party in New Orleans*, 81–82; ICPR.

65. Perry H. Howard, *Political Tendencies in Louisiana*, rev. and enl. ed. (Baton Rouge: LSU Press, 1971), 84. The large percentage of Know Nothing votes in New Orleans helped offset the rural Democratic vote.

66. ICPR. Two other Whig parishes in 1852 that voted Democratic in 1856 were St. Landry and Tensas. The Whig majority in St. Landry Parish in 1852 was 61 percent, while in 1856 the Democrats won that parish with a 58 percent majority. In Tensas the Democrats won in 1856 with a 57 percent majority as opposed to their 48 percent effort in 1852.

67. Ibid.

68. Ibid.

69. Ibid.

70. Ibid.

71. Ibid; *United States Census, 1850 and 1860, Louisiana Courier*, August 3, 1856. Senator Judah P. Benjamin, during the campaign, had declared all other issues settled. Pauline A.

Randow, "A Collection of Speeches of Judah Philip Benjamin" (Master's thesis, Louisiana State University, 1970), 149.

72. ICPR.

73. Ibid.; John Moore to Caddo Parish Know Nothing Committee, August 27, 1856, John Moore Papers, Historic New Orleans Collection; *Bee*, September 1, 1856.

74. Howard, *Political Tendencies in Louisiana*, 442, 444.

75. Roger W. Shugg, *Origins of Class Struggle in Louisiana: A Social History of White Farmers and Laborers during Slavery and After. 1840–1875* (Baton Rouge: Louisiana State University Press, 1939), 157; *Bee*, quoted in Scott P. Marler, *The Merchants' Capital: New Orleans and the Political Economy of the Nineteenth Century South* (Cambridge: Cambridge University Press, 2013), 70, 78. Robb had been part of the early New Orleans Reform movement and was also very close to Democrat John Slidell despite of his own Whig background.

76. *Commercial Bulletin*, October 26, 1860. Charles B. Dew, "Who Won the Secession Election in Louisiana," *Journal of Southern History*, 36 (February 1970), 18.

77. Morrison, *Slavery and the American West*, 186; *Commercial Bulletin*, July 4, 1856; *Fillmore and Donelson Campaign Pamphlet*, July 20, 1856, Ellis Family Papers, LSU.

78. *Baton Rouge Weekly Comet*, July 20, 1856; September 7, 1856; *Daily Creole*, August 11, 1856; J. J. Slocum to Thomas C. W. Ellis, September 16, 1856, Ellis Family Papers, LSU.

79. *Commercial Bulletin*, October 2, 1856; Judah P. Benjamin to John Perkins, July 2, 1856, Perkins Papers, Southern Historical Collection, University of North Carolina, hereafter cited as UNC; *Louisiana Courier*, July 19, 1856.

80. *Daily Crescent*, October 7, 1856.

81. Perry H. Howard in his study argues that there is no evidence that slave parishes in Louisiana massively swung over to the Democracy. *Political Tendencies in Louisiana*, 86.

James Broussard, using county election returns in his study on Know Nothing electoral strength in 1856 in the South, concludes that for the South in general there was a massive swing over to the Democracy in those slave counties. In Louisiana, however, the movement was not as great. James Broussard, "Some Determinants of Know-Nothing Electoral Strength in the South, 1856," *Louisiana History*, 7 (Winter 1966), 14.

82. See Tables 9 and 10 (Appendix A) and Appendix B; ICPR; *United States Census, 1850 and 1860*.

83. *United States Census, 1860*. No census data were available for St. Bernard Parish on sugar and cotton production, therefore, the 1850 census data were used.

84. Ibid.

85. Ibid. It is highly improbable that many naturalized citizens voted for the nativist American Party.

86. *United States Census, 1860*; ICPR.

87. Howard, *Political Tendencies in Louisiana*, 85; Broussard, "Some Determinants of Know-Nothing Electoral Strength in the South," 16–17.

88. Charles Gayarré, *Address to the People of Louisiana on the State of Parties* (New Orleans: Sherman, Wharton and Co., 1855), 18, 28, Gayarré Collection, LSU.

89. ICPR; *United States Census 1850 and 1860*. The US Census expresses church membership numbers in church seats, therefore, the percentage is not totally precise.

The four Catholic parishes the Know Nothings failed to win in 1856 that the Whigs had won in 1852 were Lafourche, St. Charles, St. John the Baptist, and St. Landry parishes.

90. ICPR; *United States Census 1850 and 1860*.

91. *United States Census, 1850 and 1860*.

92. *Baton Rouge Weekly Comet*, November 12, 1856; *Shreveport South-Western*, May 13, 1857.

93. *Baton Rouge Weekly Morning Comet*, November 9, 1856.

94. *Daily Crescent*, November 11, 1856; *Bee*, November 8, 1856.

95. *Bee*, November 17, 1856.

96. Ibid.

97. *Baton Rouge Weekly Comet*, November 12, 1856.

98. *Plaquemine Southern Sentinel*, November 15, 1856.

99. Ibid., December 6, 13, 20, 27, 1856.

100. *Bee*, November 21, 1856.

101. Although American newspapers appeared to desert the Know Nothing Party, they remained loyal to basic American Party principles and, at times, various Know Nothing candidates.

102. *Plaquemine Southern Sentinel*, January 24, 1857; *Daily Crescent*, January 28, 1857.

103. *Plaquemine Southern Sentinel*, April 11, 1857; May 16, 1857; June 20, 1857.

104. *Baton Rouge Daily Advocate*, March 3, 1857; May 12, 1857.

105. *Bee*, March 10, 1857; June 12, 1857. Whigs and Know Nothings had always suspected the numerous southern commercial conventions of disunionist sentiments. The commercial convention held in Savannah in 1856 was no different according to the *Baton Rouge Morning Comet*. The editor of the *Morning Comet* warned his readers that he "smells treason in it." *Baton Rouge Morning Comet*, November 27, 1856.

106. Thomas C. W. Ellis to E. J. Ellis, February 10, 1857, Ellis Papers, LSU.

107. *Plaquemine Southern Sentinel*, December 27, 1856.

108. Ibid., May 9, 1857; *Baton Rouge Daily Gazette and Comet*, April 21, 1857. The *Baton Rouge Daily Gazette and Comet* attempted to make something of the successful candidate for mayor, and one selectman, as well as lesser officials-elect of Baton Rouge, had been Know Nothings the year before.

109. *Daily Crescent*, February 26, 28, 1857; *Baton Rouge Daily Gazette and Comet*, February 27, 1857; March 3, 1857; *Daily Creole*, March 17, 1857; John M. Sacher, *A Perfect War of Politics: Parties, Politicians, and Democracy in Louisiana, 1824–1861* (Baton Rouge: Louisiana State University Press, 2007), 264.
The Democrats in the legislature intended to control New Orleans any way they could. In addition to the election bill, the legislature provided for the appointment, by the governor, of all notaries public, constables, justices of the peace, tax collectors, and assessors in the city, while these offices remained elective elsewhere in the state. *Bee*, February 28, 1857; March 14, 17, 1857; *Daily Creole*, March 7, 1857.

110. *Daily Creole*, February 10, 1857; *Bee*, March 11, 1857. However, in the rural parishes where the Democrats had more political strength the Americans opposed partisan judicial elections. *Daily Crescent*, March 28, 1857; *Baton Rouge Weekly Gazette and Comet*, March 29, 1857.
The reasons for not offering any organized opposition in these elections, according to the Democrats, were the lack of any political issues in the judicial election, and the unlikelihood of a fair election in the municipal contest. *Louisiana Courier*, April 5, 1857; June 2, 1857.
The Americans offered another explanation. The tyrannical election law hurt the Democrats, as did a split between Soulé and Slidell Democrats in the city during the municipal campaign. *Daily Crescent*, May 30, 1857.

111. *Bee*, April 7, 1857; *Daily Creole*, April 8, 1857; Soulé, *The Know Nothing Party in New Orleans*, 88.

112. *Louisiana Courier*, May 10, 1857; Soulé, *The Know Nothing Party in New Orleans*, 89.

113. *Shreveport South-Western*, May 13, 1857.

114. Since this was not a gubernatorial election, the only offices contested were those of state auditor, treasurer, and superintendent of education.

115. *Daily Creole*, June 10, 1857; Overdyke, "History of the American Party in Louisiana," 16 (October 1933), 611. The 1857 tariff had reduced the duty on imported sugar, but the Americans' attempt to exploit this came to nothing. *Louisiana Courier*, September 15, 16, October 2, 1857.

116. Even though Democrats were critical of the Know Nothings because of their alleged ties to abolitionism, the American Party was a strong advocate of southern rights, particularly in New Orleans, no matter what the Democrats said. Towers, *The Urban South and the Coming of the Civil War*, 145; Freehling, *The Road to Disunion: Vol. II*, 95. There was simply too much of a political appeal to disfranchise a growing (and foreign-born) northern electorate for southern Americans to ignore.

117. The Democratic *Louisiana Courier* recognized the lack of interest in the nativist issue by the Americans, and asked, "Where is their Platform?" *Louisiana Courier*, July 10, 1857.

118. *Baton Rouge Daily Gazette and Comet*, February 11, 1857; September 7, 1857; *Daily Creole*, March 19, 1857; May 19, 1857; *Opelousas Patriot*, April 25, 1857.

119. *Opelousas Patriot*, February 21, 1857; Freehling, *The Road to Disunion: Vol. II*, 95.

120. *Daily Delta*, June 16, 1857. In the past, this newspaper had usually supported the Democracy, but with increased tensions it became more independent and favored southern rights protected by a southern party.

121. *Shreveport South-Western*, February 11, 1857; Marler, *The Merchants' Capital*, 79.

122. *Daily Creole*, April 4, 1857. Despite their previous support of former President Fillmore's anti-filibustering position in regards to Cuba, Louisiana Know Nothings believed a difference existed between the two situations. In Nicaragua, "no international law was outraged, no usage of civilized government was violated." Therefore, with this logic Americans felt secure in their support of Walker's mission. *Semi-Weekly Creole*, May 3, 1856.

123. *Daily Creole*, June 24, 1857; *Bee*, June 30, 1857. Governor Walker advocated this policy in his Topeka speech of June 1857.

124. *Shreveport South-Western*, July 1, 1857; August 5, 1857; *Daily Crescent*, July 14, 17–18, 22, 1857. In addition, the Americans reported that the Address of the Democratic State Central Committee failed to censure either the president or Governor Walker. *Daily Crescent*, September 10, 1857.

125. Freehling, *The Road to Disunion: Vol. II*, 94.

126. *Congressional Globe*, Thirty-fifth Congress, first session, 1066; *Baton Rouge Daily Advocate*, August 15, 18, 20, 1857; October 5, 1857. For good measure, the *Daily Advocate* attacked the anti-Catholic bias of the American Party.

127. *Bee*, June 11, 1857.

128. *Plaquemine Southern Sentinel*, January 24, 1857; *Daily Crescent*, January 28, 1857; March 12, 1857.

129. *Plaquemine Southern Sentinel*, June 20, 1857; *Baton Rouge Weekly Gazette and Comet*, October 4, 1857; October 27, 1857.

130. *Bee*, October 27, 1857.

131. Overdyke, "History of the American Party in Louisiana," 614; *Baton Rouge Daily Gazette and Comet*, November 3, 1857; *Bee*, November 3, 1857; *Daily Crescent*, November 7, 1857; Soulé, *The Know Nothing Party in New Orleans*, 91.

The American mayor of New Orleans had the courts enjoin the election law. However, the courts lifted the injunction in order to permit the election to proceed without any hindrance. The mayor had suggested this action. *Daily Delta*, October 9, 1857; *Daily Crescent*, October 20, 1857.

132. Plaquemines, St. Bernard, and Algiers, and Districts Two and Three of New Orleans comprised the First Congressional District. The sugar parishes, Jefferson Parish, and Districts One and Four (the American area) made up the Second Congressional District. Incumbent George Eustis had to depend on American supremacy in New Orleans for his victory. Unlike the Second District, the "country" parishes of Plaquemines and St. Bernard could not overcome Know Nothing strength in that part of the city included in the First District. The Democratic majority in Plaquemines and St. Bernard increased from forty-six in 1855 to 160 in 1857. ICPR.

133. The Democrats split between the Slidell faction, who supported the incumbent Thomas G. Davidson, and a state's-right faction. The Know Nothings hoped their candidate Watterson would win as a result of the Democratic discord. *Daily Crescent*, July 17, 1857; Sacher, *A Perfect War of Politics*, 264–65.

134. ICPR. In the Third Congressional District (the Florida parishes and central Louisiana), the Democratic majority increased by over six hundred votes. In the Fourth District (western and northwestern Louisiana), the majority increased by over 1,300 votes.

135. ICPR.

136. Ibid.

137. *United States Census, 1860*. According to the 1860 United States Census, there were no Protestant accommodations in St. James Parish, which the Americans carried by a 168 vote majority out of a total of 488 votes cast. St. Martin, Terrebonne, and West Baton Rouge parishes all had Catholic majorities of well over 60 percent. *United States Census, 1860*.

138. Ibid., ICPR.

139. *United States Census, 1860*.

140. See Tables 9 and 10 (Appendix A) and Appendix B; *United States Census, 1860*; ICPR.

141. *United States Census, 1860*, ICPR.

142. Towers, *The Urban South and the Coming of the Civil War*, 192.

143. Sacher, *A Perfect War of Politics*, 261.

144. *Daily Delta*, February 1, 1855.

145. See Appendix D for the state platform of the American Party.

146. *Report of the Superintendent of Public Education to the Legislature of the State of Louisiana* (New Orleans: John Claiborne, State Printer, 1858), 4; *Acts Passed by the Fourth Legislature of the State of Louisiana* (Baton Rouge: J. M. Taylor, 1858), 93

147. *Louisiana Courier*, February 17, 1856; March 5, 29, 1856.

148. *Senate Reports*, February 19, 1856, 36. Know Nothings cast nine of the twelve negative votes. Democrat Adam Beatty expressed the sentiments of the three Democrats who also voted no when he explained that he "would vote nay because it is a dangerous precedent for the Legislature to remove a man from office under such circumstances." *Senate Reports*, February 19, 1856, 31. The House vote on the removals was numerically recorded. No roll call vote was printed.

149. *Louisiana Courier*, February 19, 1856.

150. *House Reports*, January 24, 1856, 4–5.

151. *Senate Reports*, March 11, 1856, 57; *Senate Journal*, March 11, 1856, 65. The Democratic Registry bill, which finally passed, contained features opposed by the Know Nothings. The

proof of citizenship was not as strict as Americans wanted, and the governor appointed the "register" rather than providing for his election.

152. *Bee*, March 14, 1857.

153. *House Journal*, March 12, 1857, 72; *Senate Reports*, March 12, 1857, 112–20.

154. *House Journal*, February 27, 1857, 61; *Baton Rouge Daily Gazette and Comet*, March 3, 1857. The *Daily Gazette and Comet* reported that three Democrats joined sixteen Know Nothings in opposition to the bill.

155. This subject is more fully discussed above.

156. *Louisiana Courier*, January 6, 1856; Scott Marler's *The Merchants' Capital* offers a thorough treatment of the political economy of New Orleans and the rural parishes in the 1850s, and the expected impact railroads would have on the South's largest city.

157. *Baton Rouge Daily Advocate*, April 4, 1854.

158. *House Journal*, March 11, 1856, 86, 98–99; March 13, 1856, 69; January 19, 1857, 7; February 27, 1857; *Baton Rouge Weekly Gazette and Comet*, March 1, 1857.

159. *Senate Reports*, March 4, 1857, 83–84. The bill had earlier passed the house by a 49 to 26 vote. *House Journal*, February 27, 1857. Since the roll call votes never listed the party affiliation of the members of the House of Representatives, it is at best guesswork as to which party individuals belonged. I knew how many members of the American Party were in the House during various sessions, so I had to base my findings on what party supported various bills and determine party unity as an approximation.

160. *Senate Reports*, March 4, 1856, 46.

161. The parishes represented by the five opponents were: Caddo, Natchitoches, DeSoto, Sabine, Bienville, Claiborne, Winn, Bossier, Morehouse, Union, Ouachita, Jackson, Catahoula, Caldwell, and Franklin, all north Louisiana parishes. *Senate Reports*, March 4, 1857, 83–84.

162. Although senators and representatives from both north and south Louisiana argued over which section of the state received more financial support for internal improvements, there were also indications that opposition to internal improvement projects came from "those whose property lay on the Mississippi River." In addition, one representative from New Orleans protested the resistance of the house to provide aid for New Orleans. A roll call vote is not available to determine the extent of this sectionalism. *House Reports*, February 21, 1856, 34–39; *Senate Reports*, March 18, 1856, 69–70.

163. *Baton Rouge Morning Comet*, February 29, 1856; *Baton Rouge Weekly Comet*, December 21, 1856; *Bee*, March 1, 1858.

164. *Senate Reports*, March 6, 1856, 52–54; *Senate Journal*, March 6, 1856.

165. *Senate Reports*, March 6, 1856, 54; *Senate Journal*, March 15, 1856, 77.

166. *House Reports*, March 18, 1856, 68–70.

167. *Senate Journal*, March 5, 6, 1856, 57–59.

168. Ibid., February 23, 1857, 40; February 10, 1858, 28. No vote was given in the 1858 *Senate Journal*.

169. *Bee*, September 3, 1855.

170. Ibid., October 6, 1855; March 1, 1858; *Shreveport South-Western*, October 24, 1855; *Baton Rouge Morning Comet*, February 29, 1856; *Baton Rouge Weekly Comet*, December 21, 1856; *Baton Rouge Weekly Gazette and Comet*, November 1, 1857; *Daily Creole*, June 10, 1857.

171. *Senate Journal*, March 6, 1856, 59. Five other American senators voted against the chair.

172. *Daily Crescent*, September 14, 1857.

173. *Senate Journal*, March 12, 1858, 108–109. The three Americans were the only opponents to this swamp land bill. The failure of both the *Senate* and *House Journals*—and even

partisan newspapers—to identify consistently the party to which a legislator belonged meant that the labeling politicians by party in Louisiana during the 1850s was difficult and at times impossible. Therefore, some roll call votes by party had to be estimates.

174. *Baton Rouge Morning Comet*, February 29, 1856; *Daily Crescent*, September 28, 1857.

175. *House Journal*, March 4, 1856, 70–72; *House Reports*, March 5, 1856, 45–47. The final vote was thirty-one in favor of the $32,000 appropriation and seventeen opposed. The *Louisiana Courier* reported in its January 26, 1856, edition that the Louisiana House had eighty-eight members, and the Democrats had a seven-member majority. The Know Nothings, therefore, had approximately forty members in the house. *House Reports*, March 19, 1856, 71.

176. *Louisiana Courier*, October 3, 1857.

177. *Daily Creole*, July 18, 1857; *Daily Crescent*, September 28, 1857.

178. *Louisiana Courier*, October 3, 1857.

179. *Senate Journal*, February 19, 1858, 44–50; *House Journal*, February 18, 1858, 43–48.

180. *Senate Journal*, February 19, 1858, 50–51; *House Journal*, February 18, 1858, 48.

181. *Senate Journal*, March 10, 1858, 102.

182. *Senate Reports*, February 23, 1857, 53. In the House of Representatives, no roll call vote was recorded in the *House Journal*. However, George A. Pike, Know Nothing of Baton Rouge, favored the bill which passed that chamber by a 37 to 16 vote. If the American Party opposed leasing the penitentiary, the approximately forty Know Nothings in the House in 1857 took little active interest. *House Journal*, March 8, 1857, 75.

183. Although the Democratic *Baton Rouge Daily Advocate* and *Louisiana Courier* opposed the bill, the majority of senators who voted yes were Democrats, and the Democrats had a majority in the House of Representatives, which did pass the bill. *Baton Rouge Daily Advocate*, March 30, 1858; *Louisiana Courier*, March 4, 5, 14, 17, 1858.

For a more complete discussion of the African apprentice movement in Louisiana, see James Paisley Hendrix's "The Efforts to Reopen the African Slave Trade in Louisiana," *Louisiana History*, 10 (Spring 1969), 97–123.

184. *Senate Journal*, March 12, 13, 15, 1858, 114–15, 117–18; *Commercial Bulletin*, March 18, 1858.

185. *Louisiana Courier*, January 26, 1859.

CHAPTER 5

1. *New Orleans Daily Crescent*, November 7, 1857. Hereafter New Orleans will be omitted from all future references to newspapers from that city; place names will be used, however, for all non-New Orleans papers.

2. E. J. Ellis to John Ellis, November 3, 1857, Ellis Papers, Department of Archives, Louisiana State University Library. Hereafter cited as LSU.

3. John D. Bladek, "America for Americans: The Southern Know Nothing Party and the Politics of Nativism, 1854–1856" (PhD diss., University of Washington, 1998); *Baton Rouge Weekly Gazette and Comet*, October 4, 1857.

4. *Bee*, August 18, 1858.

5. *Plaquemine Gazette and Sentinel*, February 27, 1858; *Bee*, August 18, 1858; *Louisiana Courier*, September 22, 1859.

6. *Plaquemine Gazette and Sentinel*, February 27, 1858; *Baton Rouge Daily Gazette and Comet*, August 7, 1858, January 18, 26, 1859; February 3, 1859.

7. *Plaquemine Gazette and Sentinel*, June 26, 1858.

8. *Baton Rouge Daily Gazette and Comet*, March 16, 1858; April 6, 8, 14, 1858; *Baton Rouge Daily Advocate*, March 22, 1858; April 5, 13, 1858; April 5, 1859.

9. *Daily Crescent*, March 31, 1858; June 2, 1858.

10. *Daily Delta*, May 26, 1858; *Louisiana Courier*, June 6, 1858; *Commercial Bulletin*, June 1, 4, 1858. The *Bee*, which declared itself neutral in this election, admitted party politics had reached a low point in the city. *Bee*, May 15, 1858; *Plaquemine Gazette and Sentinel*, June 5, 1858; David T. Gleeson, *The Irish in the South, 1815–1877* (Chapel Hill: University of North Carolina Press, 2001), 114–15; Leon Soulé, *The Know Nothing Party in New Orleans; A Reappraisal* (Baton Rouge: Louisiana State University Press, 1961), 92–94; Dennis C. Rousey, *Policing the Southern City: New Orleans, 1805–1889* (Baton Rouge: Louisiana State University Press, 1997), 78.

11. *Louisiana Courier*, June 6, 1858; *Bee*, June 7, 1858; *Plaquemine Gazette and Sentinel*, June 5, 1858.

12. Soulé, *The Know Nothing Party in New Orleans*, 95–102; W. Darrell Overdyke, "History of the American Party in Louisiana," *Louisiana Historical Quarterly*, 16 (October 1933), 615–18; John M. Sacher, *A Perfect War of Politics: Parties, Politicians, and Democracy in Louisiana, 1824–1861* (Baton Rouge: Louisiana State University Press, 2003), 267–68; *Louisiana Courier*, June 9, 17, 1858; *Daily Delta*, June 4, 5, 1858; *Commercial Bulletin*, June 4, 1858; *Daily Crescent*, June 4, 8, 1858; *Bee*, June 4, 7, 1858.

13. *Daily Delta*, May 3, 17, 31, 1859; *Daily Crescent*, May 30, 31, 1859; June 8, 1859; May 15, 18, 26, 29, 1860; *Bee*, June 6, 1859, May 1, 26, 1860; *Commercial Bulletin*, June 4, 5, 1860. As in 1858, some Democrats supported the Independent Citizens ticket. However, the *Louisiana Courier* advised Democrats "to give it wide berth." *Louisiana Courier*, May 22, 1859; *Baton Rouge Daily Gazette and Comet*, April 26, 1860.

14. Gleeson, *The Irish in the South*, 114–15; *Commercial Bulletin*, June 4, 1858.

15. *Baton Rouge Weekly Gazette and Comet*, May 23, 1858; *Baton Rouge Daily Gazette and Comet*, August 7, 1858. The *Bee* reported that it would support the Know Nothing Party in New Orleans only for "local objects." *Bee*, May 2, 1859.

16. *Bee*, March 21, 1859; Overdyke, "History of the American Party in Louisiana," 619.

17. *Daily Crescent*, March 21, 1859.

18. Shreveport *South-Western*, April 6, 1859.

19. *Louisiana Courier*, March 22, 1859.

20. *Baton Rouge Daily Gazette and Comet*, October 18, 19, 1859.

21. Ibid., July 1, 1859; October 18, 1859; *Shreveport South-Western*, July 13, 1859; *Alexandria Louisiana Democrat*, August 31, 1859.

22. *Bee*, May 2, 31, 1859; *Baton Rouge Weekly Gazette and Comet*, May 29, 1859.

23. *Shreveport South-Western*, May 4, 1859.

24. *Bee*, May 31, 1859.

25. *Louisiana Courier*, April 6, 1859; *Daily Delta*, April 6, 1859. The conflict resulted from a clash between the Democratic Central State Committee and the parish committee of Orleans Parish over patronage, and who should be the Democratic presidential nominee in 1860. The Central State Committee supported the administration while the Orleans Parish Committee favored Senator Stephen A. Douglas. *Baton Rouge Daily Advocate*, April 26, 1859; *Louisiana Courier*, May 14, 15, 1859; James Kimmins Greer, "Louisiana Politics, 1845–1861," *Louisiana Historical Quarterly*, 13 (July 1930), 448–49; Sacher, *A Perfect War of Politics*, 262–65. None of the accounts of Know Nothingism explains how the name "Rip Sam" originated, but since the

name Uncle Sam had been used as a national personification of the United States since 1812, apparently Know Nothings used "Rip Sam" as an aggressive personification during their heyday.

26. *Daily Delta*, April 26, 1859.

27. *Baton Rouge Daily Advocate*, May 16, 1859. Both Democratic factions held separate primaries to elect delegates to the Democratic state convention.

28. John Slidell to President James Buchanan, May 2, 1859. Slidell Letters, LSU, photocopies of originals in the Buchanan Papers, Historical Society of Pennsylvania.

29. John Claiborne to Alexander Dimitry, June 15, 1859. Dimitry Papers, Tulane University Library Archives.

30. *Bee*, July 7, 1859; Sacher, *A Perfect War of Politics*, 268–74, discusses this Democratic division in some detail.

31. *Commercial Bulletin*, September 9, 1859.

32. In New Orleans, a complicated situation arose. The voters had to contend with four tickets. The regular Democratic ticket of John Slidell and the opposition ticket of Soulé and the Know Nothings vied for state offices, while an Independent American and American Party ticket contested local and legislative offices. New Orleans Know Nothings linked the Independent American ticket with John Slidell. Allegedly, Slidell had agreed to support the Independent Americans in return for their support in his bid for reelection to the United States Senate.

Bee, October 14, 1859; November 2, 1859; *Daily Crescent*, September 26, 1859; October 10, 17, 1859; *Plaquemine Gazette and Sentinel*, October 15, 1859; Soulé, *The Know Nothing Party in New Orleans*, 108–109.

33. *Bee*, September 13, 1859; *Daily Delta*, September 14, 1859.

34. *Baton Rouge Weekly Gazette and Comet*, September 18, 1859; *Baton Rouge Daily Gazette and Comet*, September 15. 1859.

35. *Baton Rouge Weekly Gazette and Comet*, October 16. 1859.

36. Overdyke, "History of the American Party in Louisiana," 622; Thomas Gibbs Morgan to Henry Marston, August 23, 1859, Marston Family Papers, LSU; *West Baton Rouge Sugar Planter*, January 29, 1850, September 17, 1869; Sacher, *A Perfect War of Politics*, 275.

37. *Daily Crescent*, September 17, 23, 1859.

38. Ibid., October 3, 10, 1859.

39. *Louisiana Courier*, April 22, May 20, 1859; *Alexandria Louisiana Democrat*, September 14, 1859.

40. Ibid., September 21, 1859.

41. Overdyke, "History of the American Party in Louisiana," 622.

42. *Daily Crescent*, September 21, 1859.

43. Ibid., October 13, 1859.

44. *Bee*, June 25, 1859; *Louisiana Courier*, October 15, 1859.

45. *Bee*, July 14, 1859.

46. Ibid., June 18, 1859; *Plaquemine Gazette and Sentinel*, April 30, 1859.

47. *Bee*, September 13, 1859.

48. *Daily Delta*, September 6, 1859.

49. Moore received 25,434 votes to 15,587 votes for Thomas J. Wells, the Opposition Party candidate for governor. Bouligny and L. D. Nichols, unsuccessful congressional candidate in the Second District, both ran under the Know Nothing label. Congressman John E. Bouligny would retain his seat in Congress after Louisiana seceded. Soulé, *The Know Nothing Party in New Orleans*, 109–10; *Alexandria Louisiana Democrat*, August 31, 1859; *Bee*, October 14, 1859;

Sacher, *A Perfect War of Politics*, 278; *The Congressional Globe*, Twenty-sixth Congress, first session, 6.

50. *United States Census, 1860*; ICPR.

51. Ibid.

52. Ibid.

53. Ibid.

54. Ibid.

55. Ibid. To understand which factors may have influenced the way voters in a parish may have voted, I used different socioeconomic variables from the *1860 US Census*. I used eight socioeconomic factors: percent slave, percent foreign-born, percent planters, percent Roman Catholic accommodations, farm wealth per acre, per capita wealth invested in manufacturing, sugar production, and cotton production in 1860. These factors helped explain, in part, what kind of voters supported one party or the other.

56. ICPR.

57. *Daily Crescent*, September 21, 1859.

58. ICPR.

59. *Shreveport South-Western*, December 8, 1858.

60. *Baton Rouge Daily Gazette and Comet*, February 27, 1858; March 5, 1858; Ibid., July 18, 1859.

61. *Bee*, October 30, 1858; August 6, 1859.

62. Ibid., July 18, 1859.

63. *Baton Rouge Daily Gazette and Comet*, March 12, 1859.

64. *Louisiana Courier*, March 17, 1858; September 8, 1858.

65. *Plaquemine Gazette and Sentinel*, March 13, 1858.

66. *Daily Crescent*, February 4, 1858; March 30, 1858; July 10, 1858.

67. Ibid., March 19, 1858.

68. *Bee*, April 24, 1858.

69. *Opelousas Patriot*, July 31, 1858; April 16, 1859.

70. *Bee*, December 12, 1857; *Daily Crescent*, December 16, 1857; *Louisiana Courier*, December 16, 1857; January 3, 1858. Yet the *Louisiana Courier* regretted to see the southern press condemn Buchanan. And Buchanan's failure to denounce British interference in the Paulding intervention in Nicaragua provoked the Democratic *Daily Delta* to demand that the Louisiana legislature speak out against Buchanan. *Daily Delta*, January 9, 15, 1858.

71. *Bee*, December 15, 1857; *Daily Crescent*, December 16, 1857. The Democratic *Daily Delta* also criticized Buchanan for sustaining Governor Walker's meddling in Kansas. *Daily Delta*, December 2, 1857.

72. *Bee*, November 8, 1858.

73. *Daily Crescent*, May 5, 1858; August 13, 31, 1858; September 11, 1858; October 14, 1858; *Bee*, October 1, 19, 1858.

The Buchanan administration supported the pro-slavery Lecompton constitution approved by the voters of Kansas. However, the free-state party in Kansas held a referendum and voted overwhelmingly against Lecompton. In order to admit Kansas under Lecompton, the administration offered the voters of Kansas a compromise, the English Compromise. This compromise offered admission to the Union for Kansas if she voted for a normal grant of land. In effect, Lecompton would be resubmitted. For a fuller discussion of Lecompton, the English Compromise, and Douglas's opposition, see Michael F. Holt, *The Crisis of the 1850s* (New York: Wiley, 1978), 203–10, David M. Potter, *The Impending Crisis: America Before the*

Civil War, 1848–1861 (New York: Harper Collins, 1976), 197–327, and Michael A. Morrison, *Slavery and the American West: The Eclipse of Manifest Destiny and the Coming of the Civil War* (Chapel Hill: University of North Carolina Press, 1997), 198–207. *Baton Rouge Daily Advocate*, September 14, 1858; *Opelousas Patriot*, October 23, 1858.

74. *Bee*, November 8, 1858.

75. Ibid., April 13, 1859.

76. *Daily Crescent*, February 7, 1860.

77. *Bee*, January 31, 1860; *Baton Rouge Daily Gazette and Comet*, February 21, 1860.

78. *Daily Crescent*, March 1, 1860.

79. *Bee*, November 8, 1858.

80. Ibid., February 3, 1860. The *Bee*, however, soon despaired of any likelihood of a union movement. Less than a month after this article appeared, an article in the *Bee* reported a union movement could not succeed. *Bee*, February 28, 1860.

81. Ibid., May 15, 25, 1860.

82. Ibid., May 15, 1860.

83. *Daily Crescent*, March 21, 1860; May 12, 1860; *Baton Rouge Daily Gazette and Comet*, May 26, 1860.

84. Mary Lilla McLure, "The Elections of 1860 in Louisiana," *Louisiana Historical Quarterly*, IX (October 1926), 661.

85. *Daily Crescent*, July 16, 21, 1860. This newspaper refused to back Douglas as Pierre Soulé had urged and asked why the South should unite behind John C. Breckinridge instead of Bell.

86. *Louisiana Courier*, February 15, 17, 21, 1860; May 23, 1860; June 5, 9, 1860; July 26, 1860; Judah P. Benjamin, *Congressional Globe,* Thirty-sixth Congress, first session, 1060.

87. Ibid., August 7, 1860.

88. *Daily Delta*, July 21, 1860.

89. *Baton Rouge Weekly Gazette and Comet*, December 27, 1857; *Baton Rouge Daily Gazette and Comet*, January 29, 1858; May 21, 1858; June 10, 24, 1858.

90. *Baton Rouge Daily Gazette and Comet*, April 4, 1860; June 20, 1860.

91. *Daily Crescent*, April 10, 1860; *Louisiana Courier*, February 10, 1859; April 3, 1860.

92. Ibid., August 29, 1860; *Baton Rouge Daily Advocate*, September 14, 1860; *Plaquemine Gazette and Sentinel*, October 6, 1860; The *Plaquemine Gazette and Sentinel* of September 29, 1860, reported that the *Catholic Standard* of New Orleans supported the Southern Democratic nominee Breckinridge.

93. *Baton Rouge Daily Advocate*, November 1, 1860. This speech followed the pre-election riots in Louisville and other American cities between natives and foreigners.

94. *Louisiana Courier*, July 21, 22, 1860. The Democratic *Louisiana Courier* was not blatantly anti-foreign, but the paper's position must have seemed ironic to Native Americans in the state.

95. *Shreveport South-Western*, March 30, 1859. *DeBow's Review*, vol. 16, 452, May 1857; vol. 23, 505, November 1857; vol. 24, 571, June 1858.

The *Shreveport South-Western* reported that Germany and Ireland already sent their surplus population and the US could now expect a continued decrease in immigration.

96. The Democrats did confront Bell and his supporters with that candidate's alleged nativism. As discussed earlier, that issue received little attention in 1860.

97. *Bee*, May 4, 1860.

98. *Baton Rouge Daily Gazette and Comet*, May 11, 1860; *Daily Picayune*, August 2, 1860.

99. *Bee,* December 10, 1859; January 20, 1860.

100. *Baton Rouge Weekly Gazette and Comet,* May 13, 1860; *Commercial Bulletin,* October 26, 1860; Sacher, *A Perfect War of Politics,* 285–86; *Plaquemine Gazette and Sentinel,* July 7, August 11, 1860.

101. Greer, "*Louisiana Politics,*" 475; McLure, "The Elections of 1860 in Louisiana," 663. There are no extant copies of the *Louisiana Signal. Daily Crescent,* October 9, 1860; *Baton Rouge Daily Gazette and Comet,* August 28, 1860.

102. James Robb "to a friend," August 9, 1860, HNOC; James Robb to Alonzo Church, November 20, 1860, HNOC. Apparently, there was a division in the Robb family since James also wrote his sister in March 1861 offering "conciliatory words to smooth the differences of opinion about the secession crisis." James Robb to "My Dear Sister," March 22, 1861, HNOC. *Baton Rouge Weekly Gazette and Comet,* June 24, 1860.

103. *Louisiana Courier,* August 22, September 13, 1860.

104. Ibid., July 25, August 4, 1860; *Daily Delta,* October 26, 1860.

105. *Louisiana Courier,* September 11, 1860.

106. Breckinridge's vote was 22,681, followed by Bell with 20,204, and then Douglas with 7,625.

107. *Louisiana Courier,* May 17, 23, 1860; *Daily Delta,* August 22, 1860.

108. *United States Census, 1860;* ICPR.

Roger Shugg in his book, *Origins of Class Struggle in Louisiana,* 161, states that the large slaveholders were "fervent sectional patriots." Shugg could have easily continued and added they were also among the most fervent Unionists.

109. *United States Census, 1860;* ICPR. Bell and Douglas did carry fewer "poor" parishes than did Breckinridge, but "wealthy" parishes could be found in both the Breckinridge and his opponents' columns.

110. William L. Barney, *The Secessionist Impulse; Alabama and Mississippi in 1860* (Princeton: Princeton University Press, 1974), 150–52. Barney discusses this relationship in detail in Chapter 3.

111. See Tables 9 and 10 (Appendix A); *United States Census, 1850, 1860;* ICPR.

112. Ibid. Perry H. Howard, *Political Tendencies in Louisiana* (Baton Rouge: Louisiana State University Press, 1971), 91, 93. Howard points out that 45 percent of Douglas's vote and 31 percent of Bell's vote came from urban Orleans and Jefferson parishes. Breckinridge received only 12 percent of his vote in this area.

113. See Table 9 (Appendix A); *United States Census, 1860;* ICPR. Howard in his study does not find the unifying support cotton planters were supposed to give Breckinridge. Yet this group did give the Southern Democratic candidate significant support in Louisiana. Howard, *Political Tendencies in Louisiana,* 94.

114. See Table 9 (Appendix A); *United States Census, 1860;* ICPR; Shugg, *Origins of Class Struggle in Louisiana,* 161; Howard, *Political Tendencies in Louisiana,* 94.

Although there is no apparent relationship between cotton or sugar production and the vote for any of the candidates, in the parishes which gave majorities to Breckinridge (twenty-nine), only six produced a significant number of hogsheads of sugar. Only three produced an insignificant number of bales of cotton.

115. See Table 10 (Appendix A); *United States Census, 1850, 1860;* ICPR.

116. Ibid.

117. Ibid.

118. Ibid.

119. ICPR.

120. Barney, *The Secessionist Impulse,* 151–52.

While variables extracted from the census show no significant relationship, parishes with a more vigorous growth in agriculture, slaves, and whites tended to support Breckinridge more than Bell and Douglas. See Tables 8 and 9 (Appendix A).

121. McLure, "The Elections of 1860 in Louisiana," 667.

122. Joseph G. Tregle, "George Eustis, Jr., Non-Mythic Southerner," *Louisiana History,* 16 (Fall 1975), 383–90; Andrew R. Dodge and Betty K. Koed, eds., *Biographical Directory of the United States Congress, 1774–2005* (Washington, DC: United States Government Printing Office, 2005), 684, 1026. Robert E. May, *The Southern Dream of a Caribbean Empire, 1854-1861,* (Baton Rouge: Louisiana State University Press, 1973), 115-16.

EPILOGUE

1. Marc W. Kruman, *Parties and Politics in North Carolina, 1836–1865* (Baton Rouge: Louisiana State University Press, 1983); Jonathan M. Atkins, *Parties, Politics and the Sectional Conflict in Tennessee, 1832–1861* (Knoxville: University of Tennessee Press); and John Ashworth, *Slavery, Capitalism, and Politics in the Antebellum Republic: Vol. 2: The Coming of the Civil War* (New York: Cambridge University Press, 2007), 540, all agree that "most southern Know Nothing leaders had been Whigs."

2. William J. Cooper, *The Politics of Slavery* (Baton Rouge: Louisiana State University Press, 1980). William Cooper covers almost three decades of Southern politics and emphasizes the unity which existed among white southerners in the political forum. He, along with John V. Mering, "The Slave-State Constitutional Unionists and the Politics of Consensus," *Journal of Southern History,* 43 (August 1977), attribute the unity to the dominate role played by the slavery issue. All southern politicians argued, these historians claim, their respective parties were equally able to protect the honor of the South by being strong on slavery.

BIBLIOGRAPHY

Note on Sources: While I have used manuscripts from archives that I visited, I have also used photocopies, microfilm, and electronic formats. I have not made any distinctions in my citations and I have always cited the location of the original document.

MANUSCRIPT COLLECTIONS

Louisiana and Lower Mississippi Valley Collections, Louisiana State University

Butler Family Papers
Thomas Butler Papers
Ellis Family Papers
Thomas C. Ellis Papers
Benjamin Flanders Papers
Charles E. A. Gayarré Collection
Hennen-Jennings Papers
Liddell Family Papers
Robert M. Lusher Papers
Marston Family Papers
McGrath Scrapbook
Jeptha McKinney Papers
Samuel Peters Papers
Samuel Peters Jr. Diary
A. Franklin Pugh Papers
William W. Pugh Family Papers
Snyder Family Papers
Pierre Soulé Papers
Weeks Family Papers

Tulane University Library Archives

Alexander Dimitry Papers
Slidell Letter Book

Mississippi Department of Archives and History

John F. H. Claiborne Collection

University of Tennessee Library

Pugh Family Papers

Williams Research Center, Historic New Orleans Collection

Butler Family Papers
Lemuel P. Conner Papers
James D. B. Debow Letter
Charles E. A. Gayarré Collection
John J. Moore Papers
James Muggah and Muggah Family Papers
James Robb Papers
John Slidell Letter

Loyola University of Louisiana (New Orleans)

Charles E. A. Gayarré Novel

The University of Texas-Austin, Center for American History

W. W. Pugh Family Papers

Southern Historical Collection, University of North Carolina-Chapel Hill

Andrew McCollam, Andrew Papers

John Perkins Papers

CONTEMPORARY ACCOUNTS:
PRINTED LETTERS, PAMPHLETS, AND SPEECHES

Busey, Samuel. *Immigration: Its Evils and Consequences* (New York, n.p., 1856).
Carroll, Anna Ella. *The Great American Battle or, the Contest Between Christianity and Political Romanism* (New York: Miller, Orton, and Mulligan, 1856).
Emigration, Emigrants, and Know-Nothings, by a Foreigner (Philadelphia: n.p., 1854).
Fillmore and Donelson Campaign Pamphlet (n.p., 1856).
Gayarré, Charles E. A. *Address of Charles Gayarreé* to the People of the State on the Late Frauds *Perpetrated at the Election Held on the 7th November, 1853 in the City of New Orleans* (New Orleans: Sherman, Wharton & Co., 1853).

———. *Address to the People of Louisiana on the State of Parties* (New Orleans: Sherman, Wharton & Co., 1855).

———. *Address on the Religious Test to the Convention of the American Party Assembled in Philadelphia on the 5th of June 1855.*

———. *The School for Politics: A Dramatic Novel* (New York: 1854).

The Know Nothing Almanac and True American's Manual for 1855 (New York, n.p., 1855).

Mercier, Alfred. *Biographic de Pierre Soulé, Senateur á Washington* (Paris: Dentu, 1848).

The Origins, Principles and Purposes of the American Party (n.p., n.d.).

Printed letter of John Perkins Jr. to Dr. Delony and others to the Democratic Meeting at Clinton, Louisiana October 18, 1856 (Clinton, Louisiana).

Speech of Colonel Thomas G. Hunt at the Houma Barbecue of Terrebonne on the 15th of September (New Orleans, 1855).

Tisdale, W. S., ed. *The Know Nothing Almanac and True American's Manuel for 1856* (New York, n.p., 1856).

Whitney, Thomas R. *A Defence of the American Policy, as Opposed to the Encroachments of the Foreign Indulence, and Especially to the Interference of the Papacy in the Political Interests and Affairs of the United States* (New York: Dewitt and Davenport, 1856).

BIOGRAPHICAL DIRECTORIES

Arthur, Stanley Clisby, ed. and comp., and George Campbell Huchet de Kernion, colla. *Old Families of Louisiana* (New Orleans: Harmanson, 1931).

Biographical and Historical memoirs of Louisiana, 2 vols. (Chicago: Godspeed Publishing Co., 1892).

Cohen's New Orleans Directory for 1855 (New Orleans: Picayune Printers, 1855).

Dunn, Captain C. T. *Historical and Geographical Description of Morehouse Parish, its Natural Resources, Etc.* (New Orleans: J. S. Rivers, 1885).

Gardner's New Orleans Directory for 1859, 1860 (New Orleans: Book and Job Printing Establishment, 1858, 1859).

Meyniere, A., Jr., ed. *Meynier's Louisiana Biographies* (n.p., 1882)

Mygatt and Co.'s Directory, 1857 (New Orleans: L. Poseur and B. Simon, 1857).

Perrin, William Henry, ed., *Southwest Louisiana: Biographical and Historical* (New Orleans: Gulf Publishing Company, 1891).

PUBLICATIONS OF THE LOUISIANA STATE GOVERNMENT

Acts Passed by the Legislature of the State of Louisiana, 1853– 60.

Board of Administrators of the Charity Hospital, Annual Reports, 1850–54.

Cotton, J. B. *Report of the Superintendent of Elections to the Legislature of the State of Louisiana* (New Orleans, 1858).

Journal of the House of Representatives, 1853–60.

Journal of the Senate, 1853–60.

Louisiana House Reports, 1853–60.

Louisiana Senate Reports, 1853–60.

Official Report of Debates in the Louisiana Convention, 1844 (New Orleans, 1845).

Report of the Superintendent of Public Education to the Legislature of the State of Louisiana, 1857–1858 (New Orleans: John Claiborne, State Printer, 1858).

Publications of the United States Government

Dodge, Andrew, and Betty K. Koed, eds. *Biographical Directory of the United States Congress, 1774–2005* (Washington, DC: United States Government Printing Office, 2005)
Historical Census Browser, University of Virginia. United States Census data retrieved from the University of Virginia Geospatial and Statistical Data Center: *http://mapserver.lib. virginia.edu/collections/* (no longer live).
Seventh Census of the United States, 1850: Compendium of the Seventh Census, Louisiana Statistics.
Statistics of Agriculture (Washington, Government Printing Office, 1864).
United States Census, 1860, Population and Slave Schedules.
United States Congress. *Congressional Globe* (Washington, 1854–1857).

Newspapers

New Orleans Newspapers

Bee (*L'Abeille de la Nouvelle-Orleans*) (1831–61, bilingual)
Carrollton Star (1851–56)
Catholic Standard (1855–56)
Commercial Bulletin (1851–61)
Daily Creole (1856–60)
Daily Crescent (1850–62)
Daily Delta (1850–61)
Daily Picayune (1846–60)
Daily True Delta (1850–61)
Le Propagateur Catholique (1851–56)
Louisiana Courier (*Courier de la Louisiane*) (1830–61, bilingual)
Louisiana Stats Zeitung (1852, scattered)
Semi-Weekly Creole (1854–56)
Southern Standard (1855–56)

Baton Rouge and West Baton Rouge Newspapers

Baton Rouge Daily Advocate (1854–59)
Baton Rouge Daily Comet (1852–56)
Baton Rouge Daily Gazette and Comet (1856–60)
Baton Rouge Morning Comet (February 5, 1856–December 27, 1856)
Baton Rouge Weekly Advocate (1845–55, 1856–59)
Baton Rouge Weekly Comet (1853–56)
Baton Rouge Weekly Gazette and Comet (1856–62)
Baton Rouge Weekly Morning Comet (1853–56)
Plaquemine Gazette (scattered)
Plaquemine Gazette and Sentinel (1858–61)
Plaquemine Southern Sentinel (1848–58)
West Baton Rouge Capitolian Vis-à-Vis (1852–54)
West Baton Rouge Sugar Planter (scattered)

Country Newspapers

Alexandria Louisiana Democrat (1859–60)
Alexandria Red River Republican (1847–48; 1850–53)
Clinton American Patriot (1854–56)
Mount Lebanon Louisiana Baptist (1856, scattered)
Opelousas Patriot (1855–61, bilingual)
Shreveport South-Western (1850–August 12, 1857; September 9, 1858–September 18, 1860)
Thibodaux Minerva (1853–56)

Statistical Information

Much of my source material was acquired in coded form from the Inter-University for Political Research, Institute for Social Research, Center for Political Studies, the University of Michigan, Ann Arbor, Michigan. The following material I received in coded form: United States Census, 1850 and 1860, Louisiana; Farm Real Estate Values, 1850–59, Louisiana: Louisiana Election Returns, 1850–62; Louisiana Candidate Name List, 1850–62; and Louisiana Partisan Divisions, 1834–78.

Secondary Sources General Histories

Adams, William H. *The Whig Party of Louisiana.* The USL History Series, No. 6, eds. Glenn R. Conrad, Allen Begnaud, and Mathé Allain (Lafayette: University of Southwestern Louisiana Press, 1973).
Altschuler, Glenn C., and Stuart M. Blum. *Rude Republic: Americans and Their Politics in the Nineteenth Century* (Princeton: Princeton University Press, 2000).
Ashworth, John, Slavery. *Capitalism, and Politics in the Antebellum Republic: Vol. 2: The Coming of the Civil War, 1850–1861* (New York: Cambridge University Press, 2007).
———. *The Republic in Crisis, 1848–1861*(New York: Cambridge University Press, 2012).
Atkins, Jonathan M. *Parties, Politics, and the Sectional Conflict in Tennessee, 1832–1861* (Knoxville: University of Tennessee Press, 1997).
Burnham, Walter Dean. *Presidential Ballots, 1836–1892* (Baltimore: Johns Hopkins University Press, 1955).
Carey, Anthony G. *Parties, Slavery, and the Union in Antebellum Georgia* (Athens: University of Georgia Press, 1997).
Cole, Arthur C. *The Irrepressible Conflict: 1850–1865,* Vol. VII of *A History of American Life,* eds. Arthur M. Schlesinger and Dean Ryan Fox (New York: Charles Scribner's Sons, 1934).
———. *The Whig Party in the South.* (Washington, DC: American Historical Association, 1913).
Cooper, William J., Jr. *The South and the Politics of Slavery, 1828–1856* (Baton Rouge: Louisiana State University Press, 1978).
Craven, Avery O. *The Coming of the Civil War* (Chicago: University of Chicago Press, 1942).
———. *The Growth of Southern Nationalism: 1848–1862,* Vol. VI of *A History of the South,* eds. Wendell Holmes Stephenson and E. Merton Coulter (Baton Rouge: Louisiana State University Press, 1953).
Crofts, Daniel W. *Reluctant Confederates: Upper South Unionists in the Secession Crisis* (Chapel Hill: University of North Carolina Press, 1989).
Diket, A. L. *Senator John Slidell and the Community He Represented in Washington, 1853–1861* (Washington, DC: University Press of America, 1982).

Doherty, Herbert, *The Whigs of Florida, 1845–1854* (Gainesville: University of Florida Press, 1959).

Evans, Eli N. *Judah P. Benjamin, the Jewish Confederate* (New York: Free Press, 1988).

Fehrenbacher, Don E. *Constitutions and Constitutionalism in the Slaveholding South* (Athens: University of Georgia Press, 1989).

Fogel, Robert. *Without Consent or Contract: The Rise and Fall of American Slavery* (New York: W. W. Norton & Co., 1989).

Freehling, William W. *The Road to Disunion: Vol. I: Secessionists at Bay, 1776–1854* (New York: Oxford University Press, 1991).

———. *The Road to Disunion: Vol. II: Secessionists Triumphant, 1854–1861* (New York: Oxford University Press, 2007).

Gienapp, William E. *The Origins of the Republican Party, 1852–1856* (New York: Oxford University Press, 1987).

Gleeson, David T. *The Irish in the South, 1815–1877* (Chapel Hill: University of North Carolina Press, 2001).

Green, George D. *Finance and Economic Development in the Old South: Louisiana Banking, 1804–1861* (Stanford: Stanford University Press, 1972).

Hammond, Bray, *Bank and Politics in America from the Revolution to the Civil War* (Princeton: Princeton University Press, 1957).

Holt, Michael F. *The Political Crisis of the 1850s* (New York: W. W. Norton, 1978).

———. *Political Parties and American Political Development from the Age of Jackson to the Age of Lincoln* (Baton Rouge: Louisiana State University Press, 1991).

———. *The Rise and Fall of the American Whig Party: Jacksonian Politics and the Onset of the Civil War* (New York: Oxford University Press, 1999).

Hyde, Sarah L. *Schooling in the Antebellum South: The Rise of Public Education in Louisiana, Mississippi, and Alabama* (Baton Rouge: Louisiana State University Press, 2016).

Kleppner, Paul. *The Third Electoral System: 1853–1892* (Chapel Hill: University of North Carolina Press, 1979).

Kruman, Marc W. *Parties and Politics in North Carolina, 1836–1865* (Baton Rouge: Louisiana State University Press, 1983).

Link, Arthur S., and Robert W. Patrick, eds. *Writing Southern History: Essays in Historiography in Honor of Fletcher M. Green*, chapters 4–9 (Baton Rouge: Louisiana State University Press, 1965).

May, Robert E. *The Southern Dream of a Caribbean Empire, 1854–1861*, (Baton Rouge: Louisiana State University Press, 1973).

McCormick, Richard P. *The Second American Party System: Party Formation in the Jacksonian Era* (Chapel Hill: University of North Carolina Press, 1966).

McCrary, Peyton. *Abraham Lincoln and Reconstruction: The Louisiana Experiment* (Princeton: Princeton University Press, 1978).

Miller, Kerby A. *Emigrants and Exiles: Ireland and the Irish Exodus to North America* (New York: Oxford University Press, 1985).

Morrison, Michael A. *Slavery and the American West: The Eclipse of Manifest Destiny and the Coming of the Civil War* (Chapel Hill: University of North Carolina Press, 1997).

Nevins, Allan, *Ordeal of the Union: A House Dividing, 1852–1857* (New York: Charles Scribner's Sons, 1947).

Nichols, Roy Franklin. *The Disruption of American Democracy* (New York: Macmillan Co., 1948).

Potter, David M. *The Impending Crisis, 1848–1851* (New York: Harper & Row, 1976).

Richards, Leonard L. *The Slave Power: The Free North and Southern Domination, 1790–1860* (Baton Rouge: Louisiana State University Press, 2000).

Schlesinger, Arthur M., Jr., ed. *History of American Presidential Elections*, 4 vols. (New York: Chelsea House, 1971).

———, ed. *History of United States Political Parties*, 4 vols. (New York: Chelsea House, 1973).

Sears, Louis M. *John Slidell* (Durham, NC: Duke University Press, 1925).

Silbey, Joel. *The Partisan Imperative: The Dynamics of American Politics Before the Civil War* (New York: Oxford University Press, 1985).

Stampp, Kenneth M. *America in 1857: A Nation of the Brink* (New York: Oxford University Press, 1990).

Thornton, J. Mills. *Politics and Power in a Slave Society: Alabama, 1800–1860* (Baton Rouge: Louisiana State University Press, 1978).

Towers, Frank. *The Urban South and the Coming of the Civil War* (Charlottesville: University of Virginia Press, 2004).

Tregle, Joseph G., Jr. *Louisiana in the Age of Jackson: A Clash of Cultures and Personalities* (Baton Rouge: Louisiana State University Press, 1999).

Varon, Elizabeth R. *Disunion: The Coming of the American Civil War, 1789–1859* (Chapel Hill: University of North Carolina Press, 2008).

Walther, Eric H. *The Shattering of the Union: America in the 1850s* (Lanham, MD: Rowman and Littlefield, 2003).

Wooster, Ralph A. *The People in Power: Courthouse and Statehouse in the Lower South, 1850–1860* (Knoxville: University of Tennessee Press, 1969).

LOUISIANA AND NEW ORLEANS: BOOKS

Baudier, Roger. *The Catholic Church in Louisiana* (New Orleans: n.p., 1939).

Billings, Warren M., and Edward F. Haas, eds. *In Search of Fundamental Law: Louisiana's Constitutions, 1812–1974* (Lafayette: Center for Louisiana Studies, University of Southwestern Louisiana, 1993).

Butler, Pierce. *Judah P. Benjamin, American Crisis Biographies*, ed. E. P. Oberholtzer (Philadelphia: G. W. Jacobs and Co., 1907).

Dawson, Joseph G., III, ed. *The Louisiana Governors: From Iberville to Edwards* (Baton Rouge: Louisiana State University Press, 1990).

Diket, A. L. *Senator John Slidell and the Community He Represented in Washington, 1853–1861* (Washington, DC: University Press of America, 1982).

Fortier, Alceé. *A History of Louisiana*, Vol. III (New York: Manzi, Joyant and Co., 1904).

Gayarré, Charles E. A. *History of Louisiana: The American Domination*, Vol. IV (New Orleans: F. F. Hansell and Brother, Ltd., 1903).

Harris, T. H. *The Story of Public Education in Louisiana* (New Orleans: Delgado Trades School, 1924).

Howard, Perry H. *Political Tendencies in Louisiana*, rev. ed. (Baton Rouge: Louisiana State University Press, 1971).

Hyde, Samuel C., Jr. *Pistols and Politics: The Dilemma of Democracy in Louisiana's Florida Parishes, 1810–1899* (Baton Rouge: Louisiana State University Press, 1998).

Kendell, John Smith. *History of New Orleans*, 3 vols. (Chicago: Lewis Publishing Co., 1922).

Kniffen, Fred B., and Sam Bowers Hilliard. *Louisiana Its Land and People*, rev. ed. (Baton Rouge: Louisiana State University Press, 1988).

Marler, Scott P. *The Merchants' Capital: New Orleans and the Political Economy of the Nineteenth Century South* (Cambridge: Cambridge University Press, 2013).

Martin, Francois-Xavier. *The History of Louisiana, from the Earliest Period* (New Orleans: James A. Gresham, 1882).

McGinty, Garnie W. *A History of Louisiana*, 4th ed. (New York: Exposition Press, 1949).

Menn, Joseph Karl. *The Large Slaveholders of Louisiana-1860* (New Orleans: Pelican Publishing Co., 1964).

Nau, John Frederick. *The German People of New Orleans, 1850–1900* (Leiden, Germany: E. J. Brill, 1958).

Niehaus, Earl F. *The Irish in New Orleans: 1800–1860* (Baton Rouge: Louisiana State University Press, 1965).

Reed, Merl E. *New Orleans and the Railroads: The Struggle for Commercial Empire, 1830–1860* (Baton Rouge: Louisiana State University Press, 1966).

Reinders, Robert C. *End of an Era: New Orleans, 1850–1860* (New Orleans: Pelican Publishing Co., 1964).

Rightor, Henry, ed. *Standard History of New Orleans, Louisiana* (Chicago: Lewis Publishing Co., 1900).

Rousey, Dennis C. *Policing the Southern City: New Orleans, 1805–1889* (Baton Rouge: Louisiana State University Press, 1997).

Sacher, John M. *A Perfect War of Politics: Parties, Politicians, and Democracy in Louisiana, 1824–1861* (Baton Rouge: Louisiana State University Press, 2007).

Sears, Louis Martin. *John Slidell* (Durham: Duke University Press, 1925).

Shugg, Roger W. *Origins of Class Struggle in Louisiana: A Social History of White Farmers and Laborers during Slavery and After, 1840–75* (Baton Rouge: Louisiana State University Press, 1939).

Voss, Lewis. *History of the German Society of New Orleans* (New Orleans: Sendker Printing Service, Inc. 1927).

Wall, Bennett H., ed. *Louisiana: A History* (Wheeling, IL: Harlan Davidson, 1997).

NATIVISM AND KNOW NOTHINGS: BOOKS

Anbinder, Tyler, *Nativism and Slavery: The Northern Know-Nothings and the Politics of the 1850s* (New York: Oxford University Press, 1992).

Billington, Ray Allen. *The Protestant Crusade: 1800–1860, A Study of the Origins of American Nativism* (New York: Macmillan Co., 1938).

Overdyke, W. Darrell. *The Know-Nothing Party in the South* (Baton Rouge: Louisiana State University Press, 1950).

Schmeckebier, Laurence F. *History of the Know-Nothing Party in Maryland*, Vol. XVII of *The Johns Hopkins University Studies in History and Political Science* (Baltimore: Johns Hopkins University Press, 1999).

Soulé, Leon Cyprian. *The Know Nothing Party in New Orleans: A Reappraisal* (Baton Rouge: Louisiana State University Press, 1961).

GENERAL HISTORIES: ARTICLES

Alexander, Thomas B., et al. "The Basis of Alabama's Two-Party System." *Alabama Review*, 19 (October 1966), 243–76.

———. "Who Were the Alabama Whigs?" *Alabama Review*, 16 (January 1963), 5–19.

McWhiney, Grady. "Were the Whigs a Class Party in Alabama." *Journal of Southern History*, 23 (November 1957), 510–22.

Mering, John V. "The Slave-State Constitutional Unionists and the Politics of Consensus." *Journal of Southern History*, 43 (August 1977).

Sellers, Charles G. "Who Were the Southern Whigs?" *American Historical Review*, 59 (January 1954), 335–46.

Phillips, Ulrich B. "The Southern Whigs, 1834–1854." In Guy Ford, ed. *Essays in American History Dedicated to Frederick Jackson Turner* (New York: Henry Holt and Co., 1910), 203–10.

LOUISIANA AND NEW ORLEANS: ARTICLES

Aucoin, Sidney J. "The Political Career of Isaac Johnson, Governor of Louisiana, 1846–1850." *Louisiana Historical Quarterly*, 28 (July 1945), 941–89.

Carey, Rita K. "Samuel Jarvis Peters." *Louisiana Historical Quarterly*," 23 (April 1947), 439–80.

Clark, Robert T., Jr. "The German Liberals in New Orleans, 1840–1860." *Louisiana Historical Quarterly*, 20 (January 1937), 137–51.

Comeau, Brother Alfonso, CSC. "A Study of the Trustee Problem in the St. Louis Cathedral Church of New Orleans, Louisiana, 1842–1844." *Louisiana Historical Quarterly*, 31 (October 1948), 897–972.

Dart, Henry P., ed. "Autobiography of Charles Gayarré." *Louisiana Historical Quarterly*, 12 (January 1929).

Dew, Charles B. "The Long Lost Returns: The Candidates and Their Totals in Louisiana's Secession Election." *Louisiana History*, 10 (Fall 1969), 353–69.

———. "Who Won the Secession Elections in Louisiana." *Journal of Southern History*, 36 (February 1970), 18–32.

Dupont, Albert L. "The Career of Paul Octave Hébert, Governor of Louisiana, 1853–1856." *Louisiana Historical Quarterly*, 31 (April 1948), 491–552.

Evans, Harry H. "James Robb, Banker and Pioneer Railroad Builder of Antebellum Louisiana." *Louisiana Historical Quarterly*, 23 (January 1940), 170–258.

Freeman, Arthur. "The Early Career of Pierre Soulé." *Louisiana Historical Quarterly*, 25 (October 1940), 971–1127.

Grass, Louis. "J. P. Benjamin." *Louisiana Historical Quarterly*, 19 (October 1936), 964–1068.

Greer, James Kimmins. "Louisiana Politics, 1845–1860." *Louisiana Historical Quarterly*, 12 and 13 (July and October 1929), 381–425; 555–610; (January, April, July, October 1930), 67–116, 257–303, 444–83, 617–54.

Hendrix, James Paisley, Jr. "The Efforts to Reopen the African Slave Trade in Louisiana." *Louisiana History*, 10 (Spring 1969), 97–123.

Kendell, John Smith. "Early New Orleans Newspapers." *Louisiana Historical Quarterly*, 10 (July 1927), 383–401.

———. "The Municipal Elections of 1858." *Louisiana Historical Quarterly*, V (July 1922), 357–76.

Landry, Thomas. "The Political Career of Robert C. Wickliffe, Governor of Louisiana." *Louisiana Historical Quarterly*, 25 (July 1942), 345–401.

McClure, Mary Lilla. "The Elections of 1860 in Louisiana." *Louisiana Historical Quarterly*, 9 (October 1926), 235–59.
Newton, L. W. "Creoles and Anglo-Americans." *Southwestern Social Science Quarterly*, 15 (1933), 132–46.
Reinders, Robert C. "Orestes A. Bronson's Visit to New Orleans, 1855." *Louisiana Historical Quarterly*, 38 (July 1955), 1–19.
Roland, Charles P. "Louisiana and Secession." *Louisiana History*, 19 (Fall 1978), 389–99.
Sacher, John M. "The Sudden Collapse of the Louisiana Whig Party." *Journal of Southern History*, 65 (May 1999), 221–48.
Shugg, Roger. "Suffrage and Representation in Ante-Bellum Louisiana." *Louisiana Historical Quarterly*, 19 (January 1954), 390–406.
Soulé, Leon Cyprian. "The Creole-American Struggle in New Orleans Politics, 1850–1862." *Louisiana Historical Quarterly*, 60 (January 1957), 54–83.
Tregle, Joseph G., Jr. "Another Look at Shugg's Louisiana." *Louisiana History*, 17 (Summer 1976), 245–81.
———. "George Eustis, Jr., Non-Mythic Southerner." *Louisiana History*, 16 (Fall 1975), 383–90.
Wooster, Ralph A. "The Louisiana Secession Convention." *Louisiana Historical Quarterly*, 34 (April 1951), 103–133.
———. "The Structure of Government in Late Antebellum Louisiana." *Louisiana Studies*, 14 (Winter 1975), 361–78.

NATIVISM AND KNOW NOTHINGS: ARTICLES

Broussard, James. "Some Determinants of Know-Nothing Electoral Strength in the South, 1856." *Louisiana History*, 7 (Winter 1966), 5–20.
Carman, Harry J., and Reinhard Luthin. "Some Aspects of the Know Nothing Movement Reconsidered." *South Atlantic Quarterly*, 39 (April 1940), 213–34.
Carriere, Marius. "Anti-Catholicism, Nativism, and Louisiana Politics in the 1850s." *Louisiana History*, 34 (Fall 1994), 455–74.
———. "Slavery, Consensus, and the Louisiana Know-Nothing Party." *Mid-America*, 67 (April–July 1984), 51–63.
———. "Political Leadership of the Louisiana Know-Nothing Party." *Louisiana History*, 21 (Spring 1980), 183–95.
Cole, Arthur C. "Nativism in the Lower Mississippi Valley." Mississippi Valley Historical Association *Proceedings*, 6 (1912–13), 258–75.
Holt, Michael F. "The Politics of Impatience: The Origins of Know Nothings." *Journal of American History*, 60 (September 1973), 309–331.
Jeanfreau, Vance Lynn S. "Louisiana Know Nothings and the Elections of 1855–1856." *Louisiana Studies*, 4 (Fall 1965), 222–64.
Maizlish, Stephen E. "The Meaning of Nativism and the Crisis of the Union: the Know Nothing Movement in the Antebellum North." In Stephen E. Maizlish and John J. Kushma, eds., *Essays on American Antebellum Politics: 1840–1860* (College Station: Texas A&M University Press, 1982).
Overdyke, W. Darrell. "History of the American Party in Louisiana." *Louisiana Historical Quarterly*, 15 (October 1932), 581–88.
Reinders, Robert C. "The Louisiana America Party and the Catholic Church." *Mid-America*, 40 (1958), 218–28.

Rice, Philip. "The Know-Nothing Party in Virginia, 1854–1856." *Virginia Magazine of History and Biography*, 55 (January, April 1947), 61–75; 159–67.

Stephenson, George M. "Nativism in the Forties and Fifties with Special Reference to the Mississippi Valley." *Mississippi Valley Historical Review*, 9 (December 1922), 185–202.

Thompson, Arthur. "Political Nativism in Florida, 1848–1860: A Phase of Anti-Secessionism." *Journal of Southern History*, 15 (February 1949), 39–65.

Wooster, Ralph. "An Analysis of the Texas Know Nothings." *Southwestern Historical Quarterly*, 70 (January 1967), 414–23.

THESES AND DISSERTATIONS

Bladek, John David. "America for Americans: The Southern Know Nothing Party and the Politics of Nativism, 1854–1856." PhD diss., University of Washington, 1998.

Diket, A. L. "John Slidell and the Community He Represented in the Senate, 1853–1861." PhD diss., Louisiana State University, 1958.

Duchein, Mary Scott. "Research on Charles E.A. Gayarré." Master's thesis, Louisiana State University, 1934.

Follett, Edith Chalin. "The History of the Know Nothing Party in Louisiana." Master's thesis, Tulane University, 1910.

Freeman, Arthur. "Early Career of Pierre Soulé." Master's thesis, Louisiana State University, 1936.

Gordy, Ruby N. "The Irish in New Orleans: 1845–1855." Master's thesis, Louisiana State University, 1960.

Greer, James K. "Louisiana Politics, 1845–1861." PhD diss., University of Texas, 1937.

Kinabrew, Letitia. "The Whig Party in Louisiana." Master's thesis, Tulane University, 1922.

McCleish, Dolph W. "Louisiana and the Kansas Question, 1854–1861." Master's thesis, Louisiana State University, 1939.

Norton, Leslie M. "A History of the Whig Party in Louisiana." PhD diss., Louisiana State University, 1940.

Randow, Pauline A. "A Collection of Speeches of Judah Philip Benjamin." Master's thesis, Louisiana State University, 1970.

Sanders, Gary E. "The Election to the Secession Convention in Louisiana." Master's thesis, Louisiana State University, 1968.

Socola, Edward M. "Charles E. A. Gayarré, A Biography." PhD diss., University of Pennsylvania, 1954.

Tregle, Joseph G., Jr. "Louisiana in the Age of Jackson: A Study in Ego-Politics." PhD diss., University of Pennsylvania, 1954.

INDEX

Democratic Party press, 38, 69
Democrats, 7, 12, 40–41, 69, 71, 72, 78, 81, 85,
  86, 94, 112–13, 116, 117, 121, 122, 189n31,
  198nn25–26
Derbigny, Charles, 23, 51, 68; and nativism,
  169n74
Derbigny, Pierre, 11
Deshields, L., 23
Dew, Charles, 89–90
Douglas, Stephen A., 120
DuBuys, William, 24
Dupre, Jacques, 17
Duralde, J. V., 68

elections: Catholic vote, 72–73; debated in
  state legislature, 76; 1844 presidential
  election, 23; 1854 elections, 41; 1854
  violence in New Orleans, 41–42; 1855
  election, 68, 72, 116–17; 1856 election,
  86; 1857 election, 94; 1860 election,
  117; 1860 presidential election, 127,
  202n106; Election Day fraud, 32; Know
  Nothing Party success, 47–48; New
  Orleans municipal, 49; state elections,
  199n32
Elliott, Benjamin, 22
England, John, 13
ethnic rivalry, 12
Eustis, George, 79, 81, 98, 127
Evitts, William, 5–6

Faubourg Marigny, 17
Faubourg St. Mary, 17
filibustering, 83, 96
Fillmore, Millard, 82; and repeal of Kansas-
  Nebraska Act, 190n48; on the Union,
  190n38
Florida parishes, 9, 10
foreign-born residents, 60–61, 73, 81–82, 94,
  181n59; 1860 population in New Orleans,
  186n159; membership in political parties, 53; opposition to slavery, 58–59;
  residency requirements, 24
fraud: in 1856 New Orleans election, 86–87;
  in Morehouse Parish, 176n2; and partisan election law, 101–2; and registry law
  in New Orleans, 76

Freehling, William, 97; on anti-foreign
  strategy, 189n29
free soil, 44
French people: Catholics, 10; descendants,
  10–11
Freret, James, 30–31
Freret, William, 18, 20

Gallican Catholics, 8, 46, 68, 130, 184n127
Gavazzi, Alessandro, 34
Gayarré, Charles, 32–33, 50, 51, 62, 64, 67–68,
  69, 75, 79, 91, 171n33, 185n130; on foreign
  influence, 57–58
Gazette and Sentinel, 109
Genois, Charles, 18
Gibson, John, 16
Gienapp, William, 6, 45
Greater New Orleans area: high support for
  Fillmore in 1856, 91; large Catholic and
  foreign-born population, 6
Guion, George, 19

Hardy, Charles W., 71
Hébert, Paul O., 31, 48, 176n6
Herrick, E. T., 42
Holland, J. H., 17
Holt, Michael, 5, 50, 165n8; on antislavery
  and northern Americans, 45; on south-
  ern Know Nothings, 45
Hunt, Randall, 59, 107
Hunt, T. G., 60, 63; on Kansas-Nebraska Act,
  59–60

illegal voters, 168n65
immigration, 14, 43, 162, 181n54; affects
  elections, 129; ethnic differences, 10;
  foreign immigrants, 15; Germans and
  antislavery, 60; influx of immigrants, 10;
  from Ireland and Germany, 9, 13, 32; and
  nativism, 29–30; New Orleans population 42 percent immigrant, 10
Independent Citizens ticket, 110

Jackson, Andrew, 11
Jacksonian politics, 12, 16
Jesuits, 35, 45. See also Society of Jesus
Johnson, Henry, 11, 20

Printed in the United States
By Bookmasters